THE FUTURE
IS NOT FIXED

THE FUTURE IS NOT FIXED

Short Plays Envisioning a Global Green New Deal

Compiled by Chantal Bilodeau

APPLAUSE
THEATRE & CINEMA BOOKS
Essex, Connecticut

APPLAUSE
THEATRE & CINEMA BOOKS

An imprint of Globe Pequot, the trade division of
The Rowman & Littlefield Publishing Group, Inc.
4501 Forbes Blvd., Ste. 200
Lanham, MD 20706
www.rowman.com

Distributed by NATIONAL BOOK NETWORK

Library of Congress Cataloging-in-Publication Data
ISBN 978-1-4930-6465-6 (pbk. : alk. paper)
ISBN 978-1-4930-6466-3 (electronic)

♾™ The paper used in this publication meets the minimum requirements of American National Standard for Information Sciences—Permanence of Paper for Printed Library Materials, ANSI/NISO Z39.48-1992.

Contents

Acknowledgments

With the world seemingly in a perpetual state of crisis, it is good to remember that there are many people to be grateful for, including everyone involved in the creation and publication of this book: playwrights, organizers, designers, editors, researchers, and publishers, among others.

My deepest gratitude goes to the fifty playwrights featured in this anthology, whose plays made Climate Change Theatre Action 2021 (CCTA) possible. Their responses to the theme "Envisioning a Global Green New Deal" give us a glimpse of what our future might look like if we dare to imagine and shape it. They remind us that we often have more power than we think, especially when we come together as a community. In the fall of 2021, despite the many ups and downs of the COVID pandemic, these plays reached 10,000 people around the world. Through the publication of this anthology, they will no doubt reach many more and hopefully provide inspiration for more plays and more climate action.

A very special thank you goes to my friend and partner Ian Garrett at the Centre for the Sustainable Practice in the Arts. I am grateful for his creative thinking and unwavering support in organizing this project year after year. Many heartfelt thanks also to my close collaborators Julia Levine and Thomas Peterson. Their help and enthusiasm in bringing CCTA to life and assembling the plays into this anthology was invaluable. Ciara Cornelius was also pivotal in coordinating and communicating with our organizers.

I want to thank researchers Tarah Wright, professor in the Department of Earth and Environmental Sciences at Dalhousie University, and Bethany McMorine, undergraduate student in environmental studies and dance at York University. Their research about whether the CCTA 2021 plays can help close the societal hope gap around climate change is intriguing and plants the seed for more studies of the presence and impact of hope on audiences.

CCTA 2021 was enriched by the work of Tanja Beer, Ian Garrett, and Tessa Rixon who co-taught a class between York University, Griffith University, and Queensland University of Technology to develop ecoscenographic response to the plays. This course worked in parallel with the Global EcoDesign Charette organized by Triga Creative to develop design concepts for all fifty plays as a means of exploring the practice of sustainable design. The designs will be on display as part of World Stage Design 2022 in Calgary in August 2022. I offer them a warm thank you for sharing the results of this exploration with us.

I am also grateful to Nassim Balestrini, Shana Bestock, and Joan Lipkin for their thoughts on organizing CCTA events in various contexts.

I cannot overstate the importance of the more than 1,000 CCTA organizers and artists who participated in the 125 events that made up this project. Their dedication and resilience in the middle of a pandemic was remarkable, and their events showed a scope and ambition that far exceeded what we have seen in previous years. They proved once again that plays can do wonderful things: educate and empower students and artists, build communities, inspire climate action, and offer reasons to hope.

Last but not least, I am grateful for the patience and attentive support of Chris Chappell, Senior Editor, and all the staff at Applause Books who helped make this book a reality.

Introduction

Chantal Bilodeau

The event caused my students to study climate change issues far more deeply than they would have on their own, and it caused them to see how the arts can be an impactful way of starting a conversation about climate change and environmental justice.
—Paula Cizmar, Associate Professor of Theatre Practice in Dramatic Writing, Los Angeles, University of Southern California

Moving through the pandemic, this special event encouraged us to look at climate justice from new angles and has strengthened our bond to each other and our reciprocal relationship with food.
—Francine Dulong, Co-Founder and Artistic Director, Blooming Ludus, Halifax, Nova Scotia, Canada

What struck me so poignantly about the project was not just how it impacted an audience on the final day, but witnessing how the seven youth evolved from day one to that moment. I saw them experience firsthand how their passion for the arts can also tangibly engage with an urgent global crisis.
—Kristina Watt Villegas, Artistic Leader, 100 Watt Productions, Ottawa, Ontario, Canada

How do we make theatre during a pandemic, when the very act of gathering has become life-threatening? How do we talk about the climate crisis when millions of people are suffering from isolation, risking their lives to keep their communities safe, healthy, and fed, and fighting for their next breath? Is it fair to bring attention to a slow-moving crisis when we are in the middle of a fast-moving one? Do we run the risk of overwhelming people and contributing to numbness and despair?

These were the questions swirling in my head when, in March 2021, the fifty playwrights represented in these pages were sending me the plays they had been commissioned to write for the series of readings and performances comprising

Climate Change Theatre Action 2021 (CCTA). The COVID-19 vaccine had only just become available in the United States, Broadway was still closed, and most of us were Zoomed out from conducting all personal and professional business online. Was theatre a luxury we couldn't afford, a distraction from the main task at hand: surviving a deadly virus?

At the same time, the lockdowns had inadvertently revealed how much of an impact human activity has on the environment and, when that activity is curtailed, how quickly the Earth can recover. With the reduction in particle pollution, stars suddenly lit the New York sky, vistas of the Himalayas appeared out of the fog, and since we were no longer everywhere, animals started reclaiming cities. For a brief moment, we got a glimpse of what the world could look like if our footprint were lighter.

And perhaps most importantly, the protests following the murder of George Floyd in the summer of 2020 had brought deep wounds to the surface and made abundantly clear how everything is connected. Racism, colonialism, economic inequality, environmental discrimination, not to mention habitat loss and pandemics—in today's world, it is impossible to isolate one issue from the others. Our social, economic, and political systems are so intertwined and determine so much of how we live our lives that to make change in one area, we need to make change everywhere.

And so I decided to forge ahead.

I was not the only one. Through 2020 and 2021, productions moved outdoors or online, plays were written for audiences of one, and audio pieces were recorded to accompany walks in cemeteries and parks. Out of necessity, theatre became more experimental and experiential, merging storytelling with environmental awareness, often unintentionally. In big cities in particular, the need to escape the four walls of our apartments were met with invitations to go outside and rediscover our urban green spaces.

This is not entirely surprising given our species' innate need for connection and our propensity for storytelling. Survival, it turns out, requires more than just staying six feet apart. More than once in 2020 and 2021, I found myself moved to tears by artistic works that captured the moment and connected me to a community and a sense of hope: a dance piece in a parking lot, lit by the headlights of cars parked in a circle around the performers; a song reminding us that "we are built for joy"; a commercial for a gum brand that humorously and poignantly portrayed our longing for each other.

The pandemic also coincided with the rise of the youth climate movement led by Swedish activist Greta Thunberg, and with major climate events such as the heat wave of 2021, in which the Pacific Northwest saw temperatures climb above 120 degrees Fahrenheit and wildfires decimated huge tracts of land. One of the consequences of these events has been a marked shift in how people think about climate change, and whether they think about it at all. This is encouraging.

In the theatre, I have noticed a significant increase in efforts to engage with the climate crisis from both artists and institutions. In Canada, the field has taken huge strides, thanks in great part to the support of the Canada Council for the Arts, with the creation of projects like Creative Green Tools, Climate Art Web, and organizations like SCALE. In the United States, Theatre Communications Group held a Climate Action and Environmental Justice Summit for the first time in 2021 and has recently implemented Climate Action Monthly Meetings. In the United Kingdom, Julie's Bicycle continues to lead the way in greening the cultural sector.

In 2021, I helped run the application process for the Earth Matters on Stage Ecodrama Playwrights Festival, founded by Larry Fried and Theresa May. The call was for plays that engaged with environmental justice and/or environmental disruption. To my great surprise, we received over 300 applications. Even just a few years ago, that number would have been unthinkable; there weren't that many playwrights writing ecologically themed plays. But things are changing. I have faith especially in the young generation—those who have never known a world without climate change. They know their future is at stake and they are determined to pick up where their parents and grandparents left off. This too is encouraging.

There is still a long way to go and many obstacles to overcome in order to avoid the worst impacts of the climate crisis. But these new developments give me hope that our field is finally recognizing its responsibility in reducing carbon emissions, and the leadership role it can play in telling stories that help us imagine a just and thriving future. I offer the plays included in this anthology as our contribution to these efforts.

What Is Climate Change Theatre Action?

Inaugurated in 2015 and hosted biennially, CCTA is a worldwide series of readings and performances of short plays about climate change, presented to coincide with the United Nations Conference of the Parties—the annual meetings where world leaders gather to discuss strategies to reduce global carbon emissions. It is spearheaded by the Arts & Climate Initiative (formerly The Arctic Cycle), in partnership with the Centre for Sustainable Practice in the Arts, and aims to bring communities together and inspire them to take action on climate.

Early in the year, we commission fifty playwrights, representing every inhabited continent, to write a five-minute play about an aspect of the climate crisis based on a prompt. We then make this collection of plays available to anyone interested in presenting an event in their community during a three-month window in the fall. Events can range from readings to fully produced performances, from podcasts to film adaptations. Organizers are encouraged to design their event to reflect their own aesthetic and the needs of their community, and to include additional material by local artists.

To emphasize the "Action" part of Climate Change Theatre Action, we also invite organizers to think about an action—educational, social, or political—that can be incorporated into their event. These actions may involve the scientific community, local environmental organizations, and political or direct action. In the past, organizers have hosted panel conversations with scientists, pledged to reduce consumption or adopt plant-based diets, raised money for hurricane relief and tree-planting efforts, and written letters to legislators to demand policy change.

The five-minute format of the CCTA plays is not accidental. We want the plays to be as user-friendly as possible so they can be presented in a variety of contexts and accommodate a wide range of budgets, including productions with no budget at all. The short format means that the plays require few resources to perform, and they can be presented individually as part of larger events—such as conferences or festivals—or grouped together in any number to create an evening of theatre. They can also be studied in classes, shared at family gatherings, performed on podcasts, read at marches—the possibilities are endless.

Envisioning a Global Green New Deal

CCTA 2021 took place from September 19 to December 18, 2021. Once we had selected our fifty playwrights, we offered the following prompt:

> We are asking you to write an original one- to five-minute play under the theme "Envisioning a Global Green New Deal." The Green New Deal is a US policy platform that has been adopted by climate advocates worldwide. Its goal is to reduce greenhouse gas emissions while also addressing problems like economic inequality and racial injustice. It includes recommendations such as investing in renewable energy; rethinking industrial agriculture; guaranteeing living wages, sick leave, and retirement security; ensuring that clean air, clean water, and healthy food are basic human rights; honoring the rights of Indigenous people; and promoting justice and equity for frontline and vulnerable communities. Please use this as a starting point to write your play; you certainly don't have to be literal about it. However, we encourage you to be as bold and forward thinking as you can, and show us what *your* dream future looks like—and how we might get there.

Coming on the heels of the disastrous Trump presidency, this was a political theme by design. Our aim was to build on the efforts of the Sunrise Movement and the work of Representative Alexandria Ocasio-Cortez to push climate policies through the United States Congress. And since the Green New Deal has equivalents in several countries, we thought the theme provided an opportunity to highlight the work being done everywhere.

The theme was also an effort to steer playwrights toward positive stories in order to counter the overwhelmingly negative narratives being fed to us by mainstream media and popular entertainment. After years of a steady diet of policy failures and climate disasters, post-apocalyptic films and dystopian novels, our collective imagination has latched on to worst-case scenarios and lost the ability to even consider the possibility of success (whatever success may mean at this point). But positive stories highlighting pro-environmental values can help change this perception and lead to greater engagement. A recent study published in *Scientific Reports* (2022) states:

> Our findings show that narratives can be crucial tools to motivate policy support and begin the process of behavior change. [. . .] Advocates, including members of the public, artists, writers, and policymakers, can utilize storytelling to not only narrate climate actions, but also convey the mental states and values that drive it. Based on our findings, we expect those advocates—both real and fictional—whose actions are accompanied by cues of their pro-environmental intentions may be more effective in motivating climate policy support and actions intentions, compared to those whose actions appear to be driven by a desire to gain social approval, or another unrelated cause.*

Finally, the playwrights were asked to make their plays as flexible as possible so they could be adapted to different mediums to accommodate constantly changing COVID restrictions. Many are one-person plays. Some are meant to be recorded and presented as vlogs. Others are written specifically to be performed online.

How to Use This Book

The goal of this anthology is to make these fifty plays available to as many people as possible. While the official CCTA 2021 season is over, there are no restrictions on using the plays in private or in classroom settings. However, if the plays are presented in a public space in front of an audience, we ask that permission from the playwrights be secured first. Most playwrights are easily contacted online, but if you need help reaching anyone, you can email info@artsandclimate.org and we will assist you.

For ideas on how to use the plays and to see what organizers have done in the past, visit the "Events" page on the Climate Change Theatre Action website (www.climatechangetheatreaction.com/events/). In 2021, because of the pandemic, many events were held online. But throughout our four-season history, venues have ranged from city streets to national forests, from private backyards to farms, and from schools and universities to theatres, libraries, and churches. Some events are fully produced and presented on theatre stages; others are intimate readings for family and friends. What they all have in common, however, is a desire to bring people together around an important issue, and to facilitate inclusive and supportive conversations.

In addition to the plays, the first section of this book includes four essays by members of our greater CCTA family, providing insights on various aspects of the project. Shana Bestock, Producing Artistic Director for Penguin Productions,

---

* Sabherwal, A., Shreedhar, G. Stories of intentional action mobilise climate policy support and action intentions. *Scientific Reports* 12, 1179 (2022). https://doi.org/10.1038/s41598-021-04392-4

and Nassim Balestrini, Professor of American Studies and Intermediality at the University of Graz, write about their collaboration engaging students in a series of events in Austria. Joan Lipkin, Founding Artistic Director of That Uppity Theatre Company, shares her experience producing CCTA events since 2017 and taking the most recent one to a historic street in St. Louis, Missouri. The academic trio of Tanja Beer, Senior Lecturer in Design at Griffith University (Australia), Ian Garrett, Associate Professor of Ecological Design for Performance at York University (Canada), and Tessa Rixon, Lecturer at Queensland University of Technology (Australia), describe their semester-long exploration of ecoscenography with their students, which led to the creation of seed designs for all fifty plays. And last but not least, Bethany McMorine, undergraduate student in Environmental Studies and Dance at York University, and Tarah Wright, Professor in the Department of Earth and Environmental Sciences at Dalhousie University, identify the major themes present in the plays in a study looking at the plays' potential to bridge the climate change "hope gap."

The Way Forward

As I write this, another wave of COVID-19 is threatening to wash over the US Northeast. The latest IPCC report suggests that though it is *theoretically* possible to stay below 1.5 degrees Celsius of warming—what is considered a "safe" amount of warming to avoid the worst impacts of climate change—it is *unlikely* we will. And Russia's invasion of Ukraine is challenging our long-held ideas about the state of democracy in the West. Like it or not, both our fast-moving and slow-moving crises are here to stay. And we now have a third crisis—the invasion of a sovereign country leading to the killing of thousands of civilians and displacement of millions more.

It would be easy, and even reasonable, to give in to despair. But despair is the easy way out. Despair is accepting a future that we think is fixed. It is letting those in power shape what's ahead of us without our consent. If Ukrainians can risk their lives to defend their country, the rest of us owe it to them to defend our Earth so their fight, and the fight of all those who believe in democratic values, is not in vain. So I get up every day and choose to believe that all of us alive in this moment are here for a reason. I choose to believe that we are being presented with the unique opportunity to help humankind take an evolutionary leap. I choose to believe that we have been tasked with becoming better versions of ourselves for the survival of the species.

So please, use the plays in this anthology to connect and share stories. Use them to build strength and courage and resilience. Share them with your friends and your neighbors, with your coworkers and people walking down the street. Let's together build the steps that will get us through this evolutionary bottleneck. Because if we succeed, what's waiting for us on the other side will truly be ours.

Part I

THOUGHTS ON CLIMATE CHANGE THEATRE ACTION

Climate Change Theatre Action in Graz: Power and Possibility

Nassim Balestrini and Shana Bestock

We're Nassim Balestrini, professor of American studies and intermediality at the University of Graz, Austria, and Shana Bestock, producing artistic director for Penguin Productions in Seattle, Washington. We met through Chantal Bilodeau, artistic director of the Arts & Climate Initiative, and developed this project. We brought different perspectives, life experiences, and professional expertise to it. Working together, we learned a lot, were able to support students from multiple directions, and created a complex event and experience for all. Here's our project in both of our voices.

• • •

Nassim: Climate Change Theatre Action (CCTA) has brought thousands of people from a growing number of countries and backgrounds into face-to-face and virtual conversations. Thanks to an email that Chantal wrote in the summer of 2020, Shana and I began to get acquainted with each other's work. Chantal's hunch that a theatre artist and educator like Shana and a literary studies professor like me would be excited about collaborating on matters related to dramatic performance and climate change proved true. With the support of a Fulbright grant and funding from the Division for Arts and Humanities at the University of Graz, Shana spent six adventurous weeks in Austria.

The focus of our project was to integrate arts education into the literary studies classroom through preparing and carrying out CCTA events. Students in two seminars in our American Studies program—one on planetarity theories and/in American Studies, the other one on ecocritical approaches to climate change drama and poetry—selected a set of three plays each. In less than a month, Shana guided them to develop two "Deal Me a New Green" events subtitled "Performing Planetarity" and "Rethinking Climate and Performance." After the presentations, the students shared with audiences of students, professors, and members of the university community how they developed the performances and how they approached the dramatic texts, first from specific theoretical vantage points and subsequently from the perspective of performance.

For students who usually focus on applying theoretical concepts to critical analyses of printed literary texts, the experience of voicing dramatic lines, listening to performed words, embodying dramatic characters, and designing spaces and movements opened up unexpected ideas and feelings about theatre as a vehicle for climate change discourse. Two particularly memorable observations connect both performances in my mind. First, during both panel discussions, students emphasized that they were struck by how their group melted into an unexpected ensemble that created something in unison. Second, audience comments on the emotional impact of the performances elucidated the power of climate change theatre in inspiring feelings of doom or feelings of hope for the future.

Throughout the learning process, during the events, and in written reflections submitted after the events, students emphasized that they not only enjoyed the successful dialoguing between artistic concepts/practices and literary/cultural studies concerns but that they also felt empowered by the multiplicity of perspectives with which they approached the plays. This empowerment impacted the way they look at their scholarly projects and, for those who are in the teacher-training program, the way they envision teaching their own students.

The universally positive response to the experience from students and faculty members, as well as from others outside the immediate university/classroom context, has encouraged me to assume that this project can and will lead to changes in how I teach drama and theatre from now on, and how I continue to promote the role of theatre in communicating climate change. During the intensive weeks of collaboration, Shana and I met frequently to talk about the next step in the students' process of developing the shows, and the ways in which the discourses of theatre practice and arts education can engage with those of literary and cultural studies.

In this context, it was striking to read the students' accounts of how theatre practice allowed them to perceive and contribute to theoretical concepts in practice. Recent conceptualizations of planetarity seek alternatives to economics-focused understandings of globalization and encourage new ways of thinking about relationality (among humans, but also within the Earth as an ecosystem). One of the students argued that performing the CCTA plays made her realize "what relationality can mean on a small scale"; the coherence experienced in the group then facilitated envisioning "how relationality could function on a bigger scale." Similarly, a student in the same group found that developing the performances and discussing this process in different constellations allowed them "to actively work with the knowledge we had acquired to discuss problems and their possible solutions." Several students also emphasized that practical theatre work and learning about climate change are ways in which humanities scholarship and the arts can foster climate change awareness, and teachers can convey climate-related issues in the ESL classroom and in collaboration with teachers in other fields. In one instance, a future teacher of English and biology rejoiced in the fact that she can now envision how creative classroom activities can bridge the perceived gap between science and language instruction.

The intensive efforts that the students invested in this project under our guidance led one student to write that her group moved "from 'messy' to 'magic'" within a mind-bogglingly short time and that this has changed the way she approaches texts for performance. And, beyond the impact felt on an individual level, numerous students were inspired and hopeful because they saw themselves as multiplying the effects that—because of pandemic-related restrictions—they achieved with only a fraction of the audience we would have attracted otherwise: "even when we only did this on a small scale, we will carry this experience out and we will carry it on. We will talk about it to our friends, we will share and remember it with our colleagues. And maybe we will inspire others who, in turn, will share it." This vision of effort and impact fueled Shana's visit and our shared work on our small contribution to CCTA.

· · ·

(Quotes in italics are student reflections, published with their permission.)

Shana: My partnership with Nassim illuminated the brilliance of the CCTA vision: working on a very large scale (climate change, international cooperation and understanding, the role of arts in social justice movements) through a very small scale (short plays, finite windows of time, small rooms, small groups). We were able to connect on a deeply human level, fundamentally shift our sense of power and possibility, and produce concrete, bite-sized, easily measurable, high-impact outcomes.

The plays in this collection directly and indirectly explore the tools we need to confront the greatest existential threat we will experience in our lifetime. But working on these plays with people twice-removed in perspective— academics and educators versus practitioners, Austrians versus Americans—I saw theatre with new eyes, and understood why it is a tool that climate justice needs: it provides a space for multiple kinds of sensibilities (actors, directors, designers, makers, thinkers, etc.) to move a narrative forward, and a biofeedback system designed to increase our capacity for empathy, understanding, resilience, and wonder.

The performance and everything leading up to it opened my eyes to new ways of formulating and communicating meaning.

Working in a cross-cultural and interdisciplinary capacity, outside of typical theatre spaces, I was invited to articulate and encourage others to appreciate the tremendous gifts of this craft, the most important one being: we get to have so much fun! Every moment of this project was rich in discovery, and working with such brilliant academic researchers was like directing a team of dramaturgs, each one with fascinating insight, eager to collaborate in a spirit of inquiry and critical thinking.

The different perspectives of my group members made me see things I had not seen and feel emotions I had not felt when reading the plays by myself.

One of my favorite moments in the process was during casting, when Nassim seemed impressed by my ability to strategically set ourselves up for various scenarios in case some students were not available for rehearsals or performances. Flexible casting and alternate rehearsal plans are the air that theatre practitioners breathe. I had never thought of it as a curriculum plan, or even really a skill. Working with Nassim, I learned not only about her areas of expertise, including her deep knowledge of theatre history and aesthetics, but also about my own. Ours was an international partnership that felt like a gift exchange.

I feel like I really understand theatre for the very first time in my studies.

During our process, I saw sparks of understanding when participants realized how arts integration can support all sectors and all styles of learning. Educators, students, and activists of all ages got excited about integrating play and performance into their work in order to more fully explore, articulate, and embody scientific and academic concepts. Shy individuals gave full-throated performances, and highly theoretical thinkers found that passion, humor, and empathy helped them understand their thoughts more clearly. Students left the experience better equipped for the performative aspects of teaching, and more confident in their own authentic voice.

Theatre-making was a brilliant choice to teach us about the concept of planetarity and relationality. Embracing the interconnectedness of the group on a microlevel made us understand how relationality could function on a bigger scale.

Our CCTA project was a bridge between academia and practice, and between mind and body. We began by sifting through the fifty plays from the CCTA 2021 collection and together chose three representative pieces—an empowering exercise that built interpersonal, intellectual, and emotional strength. There were tons of surprises as students lobbied for unexpected plays, opening up rich dialogues and new perspectives. One of my favorite aspects of our collaboration were these discussions around which plays we should perform and why. These young academics approached the selection process with thoughtful, passionate, and rigorous inquiry and revealed themselves to be terrific dramaturgs. I've kept some of their written work as examples of how dramaturgy can be enriched by academic perspectives, and how as artists we may never know what sparks our work might ignite across great spans of time and space.

We began by pushing desks aside and getting on our feet with basic collaborative storytelling exercises, exploring shared narratives, improvisation, and the tools of a theatre practitioner—body, voice, imagination, and spatial relationship. We also used basic text analysis tools, such as objectives, tactics, given circumstances, and pursuing actions. We rehearsed our plays moving in and out of practical and theoretical discussions, supporting students in crafting a post-play discussion that could engage and include the audience in this dynamic inquiry.

For my future research, I have a greater understanding of what the terms "connection" and "interrelatedness" mean as I have experienced them through different senses.

Putting up a CCTA event doesn't require an elaborate theatre or years of drama school. We performed in an echoey room with uneven lighting, wearing FFP2 masks and basic blacks. Our props were mostly cardboard and tape, miscellaneous household items, industrial desks, and chairs. Actors held scripts. There were directorial notes I swallowed, potential we could glimpse but didn't have time to realize. Does any of that matter as much as what did happen?

I laughed, I cried. I felt the raw power of the simplest of theatrical tropes—a group of actors breaks free of the proscenium stage and puts the audience in the round to hear a chorus of voices; an actor pounds on a desk, startling us with unexpected violence; two actors look radiantly at a flashlight, endowing it with the warmth of the sun. I felt my whole being respond both to the stories and to the people telling them. We all stretched to meet each other in the place of risk and connection.

Enriching experience is an understatement. It was a journey on which I was able to get different perspectives on climate change and artistic practice, viewing them as a scholar, a spectator, and eventually as a performer myself.

Every moment of our time in Graz connected us to a global conversation. Being part of the CCTA festival fostered trust in ourselves, our art form, our collaborators, and our community. And that, in turn, released us to make powerful art. Our work in Graz was a powerful reminder to focus on the transformations that are possible—the transformations that are happening everyday—so we can continue the work, find the light, and activate joy in our lives. The future is here, now. There is no time for perfection.

The planetary focuses on the relationality of everything, even the nonhuman. Being aware of the fact that everything is interconnected urges humanity to think and act responsibly, as each action has a consequence. The theatre experience brought this theory to life.

In conversations with students, faculty, colleagues, and community members, I came to feel keenly that our project's power lay in counteracting anxiety and grief over planetary damage through the cultivation of resilience and joy. CCTA expands our collective capacity by fostering creative, collaborative problem-solving—both head-on in the face of the climate crisis but also around it. We felt replenished after our performance, ready to take on the world's next challenge.

• • •

We are so grateful for all the people who made this project happen, and for the opportunity to forge a collective vision of effort, impact, and hope. We look forward to building on our collaboration, using our discoveries as fuel for new connections. We appreciate the time, energy, and care it takes to listen to one another, and to invite diverse lived experiences to the table.

Our CCTA project helped us experience how theatre integrates story, experience, knowledge, science, and aesthetics in ways that create unique opportunities to move individuals, groups, and humanity toward imagining and building a more thriving future.

A student said it best: "*In order to become proactive, we should make hope our main fuel.*"

• • •

Nassim Balestrini is full professor of American studies and intermediality at the University of Graz, Austria, and director of the Centre for Intermediality Studies there. She researches and teaches US-American and Canadian literatures and cultures from the eighteenth century to the present. Her publications address adaptation and intermediality, life writing, hip-hop culture (most recently on Indigenous and Alaskan artists), contemporary poetry, ecocriticism, and climate change theatre. She favors comparative and interdisciplinary approaches in her research, which frequently cuts across literary genres, media, ethnicities, and cultures. CCTA has been part of her efforts to foster productive conversations among academics, artists, and off-campus communities.

Shana Bestock is a multidisciplinary artist, educator, and nonprofit leader born and raised in Seattle, Washington. She has directed over 200 productions with youth ensembles, overseen over 120 professional productions, and worked with a wide variety of regional theatres, schools, and community organizations. For seventeen years Shana served as Seattle Public Theater's artistic and education director. Five years ago, she founded Penguin Productions, facilitating creative adventures in community arts to fuel the future with a focus on youth development and leadership, gender equity, and social justice. Through her artistic and engagement work, Shana strives to increase our capacity to connect, reflect, and activate in order to make a more curious, compassionate, and creative world.

Taking It to the Streets:
From Obstacles to Opportunities

Joan Lipkin

We have to find a new art and a new psychology to penetrate the apathy and the denial that are preventing us making the changes that are inevitable if our world is to survive.

—Ben Okri

Early on in life, I was already aware of environmental issues. I knew about them because of the colds and sore throats and bouts of pneumonia I endured growing up on the southside of Chicago. I even did a rudimentary project about air pollution for the sixth grade science fair. Running cotton balls over the sooty window ledges of our apartment building to gather evidence, my efforts were more anecdotal than scientific, but they fueled my youthful instincts. Our building and others in the neighborhood burned bituminous coal and it was making people sick.

Unfortunately, my project was something of a singularity. There was little in the news or our educational system about pollution and environmental issues. Our biology classes in high school, purportedly one of the best in the city, were about how different forms of life developed on Planet Earth, but never about what might threaten them or what is needed to protect them and us.

My years in the theatre as a writer, director, producer, and activist have been more focused on other social justice movements, including LGBTQ+ rights, reproductive choice, disability and racial equity, gun sense, and immigration reform, all of which are still topical and carry their own sense of urgency to this day. But when I came upon Climate Change Theatre Action (CCTA), I perceived a pathway to bringing the issue of climate change to a wider public through the compelling medium of theatre. As we theatre-makers and -goers know, story has a way of speaking to people where facts, even indisputable facts, do not.

The arts world is catching up and realizing the relevance of climate change as a focus, but much of the philanthropic world still lags behind. In St. Louis in 2017, when I first proposed doing a traveling program of CCTA-commissioned plays to one of our primary funders, we were not supported for the first time in many years because the review panel deemed the proposal uninteresting and irrelevant. I appealed the decision and lost, which just reinforced how much this kind of programming is needed.

Hopefully, the last several years have awakened more people in the United States to the realities of catastrophic climate change and mass planetary extinction. But we were not there yet when I first engaged with this subject in St. Louis, and the denial of much of the population there and elsewhere continues to require ongoing creativity and strategies to attract attention and action.

Turned down by funders our first time producing the event, it was clear that we would need to find other sources of revenue to put on the work as well as to identify a central performing space. Although disappointed, I chose to reframe obstacles as opportunities, in order to promote creativity and necessary thinking outside the proverbial box. To put it baldly: business as usual was not cutting it, so outside the box we went.

The Ethical Society of St. Louis was willing to rent us space, but we had no designated income stream to pay for even that, much less for actors, staff time, printing, or promotion. And the traditional "earned income" from ticket sales was not an option, since it was important to us that the event be free of charge. I felt this was vital to encourage a diversity of attendance, and to ensure that economics would not be a barrier for anyone.

We decided to look for organizations that would want to partner with us, would see the value of a program like this, and could benefit from making their work more visible through a resource fair after the performance. We asked each group to donate on a sliding scale to help cover our costs, but made it clear that no one would be turned away. The model of shared costs is not a new one, but it is very effective and will be increasingly needed going forward, as we consider issues of equity, diversity, accessibility, and inclusion in the theatre and other areas that are so vital for our culture.

The resource fair also made it possible for these groups to meet each other and find points of synchronicity and collaboration. All told, we had twenty-two groups including the Missouri Coalition for the Environment, NAACP, and Litzsinger Road Ecology Center. And the excitement after the performance was palpable. The power of this informal coalition, along with our trenchant theme and the uniqueness of our medium, attracted media coverage. When I was asked for an interview on KWMU, St. Louis Public Radio, I requested to also bring someone from the local chapter of the Sierra Club. The club's director later thanked me and said he could never have gotten on the air, despite months of trying, without my help. I responded that the arts are both a way to tell a story as well as a story in and of themselves.

Our event was successful by virtually any measure. We had a full house, and closed with a standing ovation. People networked and connected with different organizations. Our actors learned more about climate change and became committed to the issue. We received coverage not only from the local public radio and community radio stations but we were also the subject of a video story by the Higher Education Channel. The Ethical Society so appreciated what we did that they invited us back to do an abbreviated program for their Sunday morning platform—and this time, they declared, they would pay us.

Since then, I have presented many iterations of Climate Change Theatre Action, each with its own challenges and opportunities. I produced an event in 2019 in conjunction with Saint Louis University to see how CCTA's commissioned pieces, which were not always penned with a proscenium in mind, might play in a formal performing space. We engaged a multicultural group of percussionists to entice people into the University's Mark Wilson Studio Theatre with their drumming, and offered homemade cookies to further welcome them. I directed half of the pieces and a professor in the theatre department directed the others. I also collaborated with a graduate student to stage Greta Thunberg's historic "How Dare You?" address to the United Nations for several voices and set it to cello. Following the performance, we asked an environmental expert to speak about action steps we all might take.

As an educator who has worked on multiple college campuses throughout the United States, I believe schools are optimal places to stage the CCTA plays, thereby engaging the next generation of activists. But climate change is a global crisis that demands awareness and action on multiple fronts. After the 2019 event, I continued to wonder how we might reach other constituencies, including voters who can exert influence on the policymakers.

When the next UN Conference of the Parties (COP) meetings came around in the fall of 2021, I was determined to collaborate with CCTA again and to expand our potential audience base and exposure. This time, there was an even bigger problem than funding. The pandemic raised serious safety issues and understandably discouraged potential attendees. At that time, few people—including myself—were going to the theatre in St. Louis. And the specter of a disintegrating planet was hardly a box office draw. Yet I remained convinced that performance was key to invigorating a dazed and overwhelmed public reeling from an enormity of factors.

I decided that we should put on a festive outdoor event in the business district on one of the historic streets in St. Louis. There would be greeters and music and even a traveling organic bubble blower. In keeping with the core values of my company on visibly promoting racial and gender equity and confronting ageism, we assembled a large and diverse cast, ranging from children to the elderly, with several female directors. Since voter registration is part of our regular outreach (an engaged electorate being crucial to any effective movement toward environmental sustainability and justice), our voter registration table was the first thing people saw when they checked in for the event.

We deliberately but not exclusively chose humorous pieces from the CCTA collections, feeling they might be best suited for drop-in audiences. I frequently utilize humor in my work, especially when it comes to difficult subject matter. Laughter increases receptivity to messaging, promotes community, and decreases anxiety. It is also subversive as heck when done well.

Then it was time to connect more closely with the neighborhood to ensure not only cooperation but enthusiasm. I talked with the manager of Jeni's

Splendid Ice Creams, who provided coupons for discounts. With my creative team, we met with every business within a several-block radius, asking permission to put resource tables for organizations in front of some of their stores and suggesting that the increased traffic would be good for everyone. One of the primary developers in the area provided free parking for all of our volunteers and performers—a hefty donation to be sure—and thanked me for bringing people to the area when business had been down.

We arranged with four art galleries along the boulevard to host simultaneous performances. Each gallery agreed to host two plays in rotation, making it possible for people to see all eight pieces we presented within a few hours.

For safety, attendance at galleries was limited to around twenty people—all of whom were required to wear masks—and we kept the doors propped open. To create visual continuity, we made T-shirts for our volunteers that said "Climate Change Is Real." These volunteers acted as hosts in the galleries and on the street, answering questions.

We were blessed with beautiful weather that day, and our event included two dance companies that performed their climate change pieces outdoors multiple times. We designed an intense promotional campaign that highlighted each gallery, which we shared on multiple social media platforms. We also met several times with the gallery directors to ensure their enthusiasm and to ask them to promote our event to their constituencies as well, resulting in thousands of contacts, many of whom were new to us.

Our goal was to reach beyond our own familiar circles, to cross-pollinate with other art forms, to provide an engaging and informative event, and, of course, to inspire hope and action, even in a pandemic.

The resource tables helped us connect the theatrical worlds we were presenting with concrete realities. A newer group in town, 360 STL, which is taking on the fossil fuel industry, attracted many volunteers for a protest and rally outside the St. Louis Federal Reserve Bank the following week. We wound up participating, helping to design their event so it would be more theatrical, including leading chants, organizing attendees to show signage to passing cars, and even performing our Greta Thunberg piece with the college performers who had been at our event the week before.

Having produced CCTA events in many settings, each with their own pluses and minuses, I have to say that our outdoor event was my favorite, even if it was the most challenging logistically. Many of the people who came had gotten a notice from one of the art galleries, or perhaps read the story in *St. Louis Magazine,* or heard my interview on KMOX radio. We also had access to outdoor foot traffic—people who happened to be out on a beautiful Saturday afternoon. Many of them detoured to check us out, and the model we constructed, of brief plays rotating in the galleries with outdoor dance, accommodated them.

I have come a long way from trying to go it alone as a middle schooler sounding the environmental alarm. No longer am I a lone voice. I'm greatly encouraged by the power of our growing community to share the message, and by the role the arts can play in helping people receive it. My involvement with this work has deepened my connection to the urgency of climate change, and my belief in both the gifts and responsibilities theatre artists have to use our unique skills as storytellers.

The last few years have been a time of great reckoning about racism, economic inequity, climate change, and public health. If this pandemic has shown us anything, it is that there is no business as usual right now or for the foreseeable future. But we have ourselves and each other, and many things are possible when we ignite our sleeping imaginations and use the arts to engage. Theatre and social change can happen anywhere. There's a good argument to be made for taking it to the streets.

• • •

An internationally recognized playwright, director, producer, educator, facilitator, and social activist, **Joan Lipkin** is the founding artistic director of That Uppity Theatre Company, DisAbility Project, Dance the Vote, and Playback NOW! St. Louis. She has worked on environmental justice for years, most recently creating curriculum for teaching climate change and storytelling online. A recipient of many awards including Woman of Achievement; Visionary; Bravely; Arts Innovator; and the Ethical Humanist of the Year. Her work has been widely produced and anthologized in *Best American Short Plays*, *Scenes from a Diverse World*, and *Amazon All Stars*, and featured in the rapid-response theatre projects Climate Change Theatre Action, Every 28 Hours, and After Orlando.

Global Network Learning EcoDesign Charrette

Ian Garrett, Tanja Beer, and Tessa Rixon

Historian Yuval Noah Harari refers to civilization as a fiction we agree to. Conversely, we can look at "fiction," "narrative," or even "performance" as an effort to (re)create and redesign civilization. In *Performance and Ecology: What can Theatre Do?*, Carl Lavery highlights the ecological potential in the work of Karen Christopher and Sophie Grodin, which requires artists to be open to each other and more-than-human materials. The 2021 Climate Change Theatre Action (CCTA) EcoDesign Charrette was part of a Global Networked Learning initiative between York University (Canada), Griffith University (Australia), and Queensland University of Technology (Australia), and aimed to train emerging designers to explore the potential of sustainable design across vast distances, and coordinate with professional colleagues the world over.

Over twelve weeks, between October 2021 and February 2022, students across the three universities came together to explore ecoscenography through a series of provocations, which included digital approaches to scenography, First Nations perspectives on land-based practice, and sustainable costume design. A parallel professional EcoDesign Charrette, organized by Triga Creative in Toronto, joined many of these meetings, in addition to reading through and discussing all of the CCTA 2021 plays.

A central focus of this project was to consider new modes of theatre-making that have an increased awareness of ecologies and global issues. Unlike typical theatre productions where the performance season is precedent and dictates the design schedule, ecoscenography is comprised of three stages—the three Cs—that are considered equally fundamental to the aesthetic consideration of the work: co-creation (pre-production), celebration (production), and circulation (post-production). Students and participants were encouraged to take a place-based approach to reconsidering theatre's dominant "create-to-dispose" mentality through the three Cs of ecoscenography, where temporary designs were explored through a longer and more interconnected time frame.

The students' responses were incredibly varied in style and demonstrated a full spectrum of scenographic approaches to performance designs. Many took a site-specific approach, choosing to explore design outside of conventional theatre spaces. For example, Gabi Harris's response to *The Pageant* by Paula Cizmar was to create a multisensory walking experience at dusk along a trail in the pristine landscape of Springbrook National Park, in the Gold Coast Hinterland of

Australia, with the actors performing the play in segments along the path. In the play, three committee members plan the program for the Pageant, an annual event celebrating the huge journey undertaken by humans to make changes to protect the planet. Using environmentally friendly lighting combined with natural materials, Gabi's design aimed to celebrate the beauty of Australia's untouched landscape and remind us of our role in keeping this utopia thriving. In the design, the audience was provided with lanterns made from upcycled milk bottles to attract insects for the glow worm cave along the walk and to assist with performance lighting.

Urban space became the inspiration for Samantha Foley, who set her design for *Mizhakwad* (*The Sky Is Clear*) by Dylan Thomas Elwood, a play about the destructive power of capitalism, in a local shopping center parking lot. Samantha created the barren "forest" landscape described in the play by sourcing abandoned cars from local scrap yards, and costumes were created from the waste of the retail outlets inside the shopping center. The play's hopeful ending was depicted through the transformation of the old cars into a permanent community garden of native trees, plants, and vegetables after the performance, providing a much-needed green space at the shopping center. The vision of the garden included programming which encouraged waste recycling and composting from the retail stores.

For many students, the specific needs or challenges facing their communities inspired a uniquely local response to the text. Michelle Hair's concept for *Book of G* by Nelson Diaz-Marcano grew from the desire to help regional Australian communities unlock the potential of upcycling building materials and soft plastics. Michelle's design is intended to tour throughout regional areas, evolving and

Design by Gabi Harris (Griffith University, Australia) for *The Pageant* by Paula Cizmar. The aim was to create a multisensory walking experience lit by glow worms and homemade lanterns at dusk along a trail in Springbrook National Park, Gold Coast, Australia.

Design by Samantha Foley (Griffith University, Australia) for *Mizhakwad* (*The Sky Is Clear*) by Dylan Thomas Elwood. Her concept proposed converting a carpark into a performance space and community garden.

Example design by Michelle Hair (Queensland University of Technology, Australia) for *Book of G* by Nelson Diaz-Marcano). Each community interaction would produce a unique physical structure, utilizing recycled materials from the community. This example design echoes the Australian bus stop, an important community space within regional towns.

being added to by "Gen Z" groups in each location. With the support of a small team of touring facilitators, each community would create a unique stage that remains as a legacy to making change for the future. Michelle's costume design utilizes fabric scraps overlaid with the performer's own clothing to echo the recycled nature of the physical design.

Kelsey Booth's design for *Molong* by Damon Chua similarly sought to engage regional Australian communities through a tourable design concept. Kelsey's response repurposes common Australian waste materials—Corflute and discarded rubber tires—into a physical structure that highlights the barren void that will remain in a future where the natural world has collapsed. By embracing flat, modularized components, the design cleverly considers the logistical and environmental challenges of touring works across Australia's vast geography.

As ecoscenographers, we are deeply committed to reducing the environmental harm of our field, both in academic and professional settings, including through the creation of infrastructure that leverages the benefits of international cooperation without the significant impacts of travel. This is true both as a means to provide opportunities for students, and as an example for the global performance field when considering distance collaboration, particularly as it connects to touring and arts-related travel. There were significant considerations in these projects regarding ecological impacts, costs, and accessibility. There were also the more immediate considerations of the COVID-19 pandemic: Canada's borders were limited to essential travel, while Australia was not allowing travel in or out of the country, even though day-to-day life had returned to an

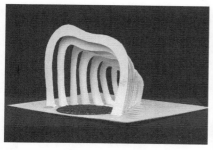
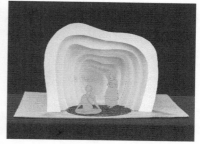

Kelsey Booth's (Queensland University of Technology, Australia) seed concept for *Molong* by Damon Chua. Kelsey's circular design process sees the Corflute repurposed into tree guards for local revegetation projects in the communities visited throughout the tour, and the rubber pieces donated to local playgrounds.

Mattea Kennedy's (York University) seed concept for *Lifeday* by Jessica Huang. Mattea states: "I thought of the Reverend Billy Graham—although I am somewhat more of a fan of the Reverend Billy and the Church of Stop Shopping. Inasmuch as this play is set squarely in the future, for me there was something of a 1960s hopefulness in the text, for me. I created a series of slides that are abstractions of familiar objects, taken directly from the text. I envisaged them accompanying the performance in real time. For example, as the performer says, 'natural gas', we would see the slide depicting the reconfigured gasworks. I manipulated these everyday objects in a program that created a kaleidoscope image."

almost pre-pandemic mode of social interaction. The course was an attempt to overcome these challenges to share our climate of attention, first with one another and then with the global design community.

• • •

Ian Garrett is a designer, producer, educator, and researcher in the field of sustainability in arts and culture. He is associate professor of ecological design for performance at York University, the director of the Centre for Sustainable Practice in the Arts, and producer for Toasterlab, a mixed-reality performance collective.

Dr. Tanja Beer is an ecological designer, community artist, and senior lecturer in design at the Queensland College of Art, Griffith University, Australia. With more than twenty years of professional experience, Tanja has created over seventy designs for a variety of theatre companies, events, exhibitions, and festivals, in Australia and overseas.

Tessa Rixon (née Smallhorn) is an academic and freelance designer for live performance with a focus in vision systems and content design. In her professional practice, she has worked across a range of dance, drama, music, and festival projects as a lighting designer, vision and systems designer, technical coordinator, and stage manager.

Reducing the Hope Gap? An Examination of Climate Change Theatre Action 2021 Plays

Bethany McMorine and Tarah Wright

While much of the global population is aware of climate change, very few feel able to combat it. Scientific and media messaging often provokes fears that not only fail to engage audiences but serve to dishearten, demoralize, and desensitize them, and can lead to climate change fatigue. Fear messaging may seem like a good way to get people's attention, but it can also act as a tool to distance individuals from personal engagement. Fear messaging can cause counterintuitive reactions, and scholars are beginning to recognize a societal "hope gap" where individuals who are presented with discouraging and often ominous communications about climate change, without being given any tools to create change, are made to feel helpless and often become paralyzed.

There is much work to do within the scientific and media realms to improve the messaging around climate change, but there is also a unique role that the arts can play in changing societal norms and working toward a sustainable future. Solving climate change requires significant and fundamental cultural shifts where society is asked to reconsider its relationship with the planet and feel empowered to create change. Artists and the wider cultural community have a unique and critical role to play in changing culture, reimagining how to live on the planet, and, potentially, offering hope. The arts in their many forms can aid in developing pro-environmental societal norms by awakening emotional responses in an audience in a way that traditional science and education media cannot (Doll and Wright 2019), and by encouraging sensitivity to the environment (Eernstman and Wals 2013). The arts can also provide a freeing and exploratory communication structure that is not restricted by scientific boundaries, allowing for a process of free inquiry. Through open dialogue, the arts can offer insights and give voice to differing views and opinions, portraying contemporary culture while also showcasing preferred ideals (i.e., a healthy and just planet) in appropriate and appealing ways without being an agent of propaganda. As Currin (2019) states, the arts can offer audiences a way to sort through the climate emergency.

In 2021, Climate Change Theatre Action (CCTA) asked fifty playwrights from around the world to write an original one- to five-minute play under the theme "Envisioning a Global Green New Deal." The playwrights were prompted to examine various climate change solutions presented by the Green New Deal (e.g., investing in renewable energy, rethinking industrial agriculture, guaranteeing living wages, honoring the rights of Indigenous people, etc.), and to dream what a future could look like and how we might get there. In essence, CCTA put the playwrights in a unique position to help offer climate hope.

As environmental scholars (Bethany, an undergraduate student in environmental studies and dance, and Tarah, a professor of environmental science) and as artists ourselves (Bethany is a dancer, and Tarah worked as a singer and in musical theatre for a decade before beginning her career in academia), with a true desire for finding ways in which our two passions can intersect, we wanted to examine the text, dialogue, and stage directions for the fifty play scripts from the CCTA 2021 season and showcase the major themes that emerge, with a specific focus on examining the plays for their potential to bridge the climate change "hope gap."

What We Found

After reading through all of the plays, we came up with a list of twenty-four relevant emerging themes. The following section discusses some of the themes that we found most interesting and provides examples of how they manifested in the plays.

Responsibility. The theme of responsibility showed up in the scripts in three different ways: (1) responsibility lies with the individual; (2) responsibility lies with the group; and (3) responsibility lies with institutions. The question of who is responsible for climate change and its solutions is an important theme to consider when contemplating the hope gap. In North America, the rhetoric of the

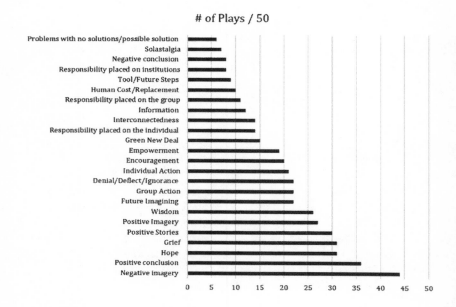

media and institutions often blames the climate crisis on individuals, instead of holding large emitters and contributors accountable. When the fault is solely placed on individuals, it can make them feel overwhelmed and hopeless, which in turn contributes to the hope gap. In our interpretation, the plays reinforce this idea (i.e., fourteen plays talking about individual responsibility vs. eight plays talking about institutional responsibility). An example of responsibility being placed on the individual is seen in the script *The Eternity of Diapers* by Carla Zúñiga Morales, where a daughter brings her boyfriend home to meet her parents. The new "boyfriend" is a personified dirty diaper that the daughter's parents threw out twenty-nine years prior and that has been floating in the Mapocho River. The diaper explains that it does not break down over time and blames the parents for their choice to use disposable diapers rather than point to the societal norms of the time, the economics around diaper purchasing, or the responsibility of companies to create a biodegradable disposable diaper.

An illustration of responsibility being placed on the group is seen in Haeweon Yi's play *So This Is the Last Apple Pie*. The play involves a conversation between Sia and her mother, Hana. Hana serves Sia a piece of the last apple pie as Sia's grandma, Nana, is forced to let go of her orchard for economic and climatic reasons:

HANA: Which bird are you waiting for?

SIA: Skylark.

HANA: That one used to fly over Nana's orchard a lot when I was young.

SIA: Really?

HANA: But I don't see them anymore.

SIA: Why?

HANA: Pesticides. Probably, pesticides.

SIA: But Nana doesn't use them, does she?

HANA: No, but many of her neighbors do. They don't seem to have a choice now.

This part of their conversation identifies Nana's neighbors as pesticide users, which is the most likely cause of the decline of the Skylark bird. Responsibility placed on a group can have some of the same effects as responsibility placed on the individual.

Responsibility placed on institutions was present in only eight of the fifty scripts. Research has shown that governments, large corporations, and other institutions are the primary contributors to fossil fuels and the climate crisis (Gustafson et al. 2020). Not acknowledging this contribution or holding these institutions accountable is directly related to the hope gap. When the responsibility of larger organizations is acknowledged, it changes the typical narrative of "individuals at fault" to responsibility being put on institutions, holding them accountable. *At What Cost* written by Kiki Rivera is a story set in Hawai'i in the not-so-distant future. Tūtū Poni is telling young Namaka and Ana a story from fifty years prior when Tūtū Alice and the people came together to defend their land. They were protesting the building of a wind farm that made people sick, would displace Indigenous communities, and endanger native birds and bats. As they face the police, Tūtū Poni says:

> You're late, Fake State! Your leadership has failed! Your dependence on tourism and protection of foreign investments and the price of progress has accelerated us into our demise! (*Dancing.*) Climate change is here! Climate change is here! Bring in the deal, abolish the system, climate change is here!

Tūtū Alice is confronting institutions for not protecting her people and their environment. It is this type of rhetoric, which puts the onus on major emitters, that can help to reduce the hope gap. While this type of messaging was present in some of the plays, we were surprised to find that more responsibility was not put on larger organizations and emitters.

Encouragement. Encouragement is the act of offering support, hope, or confidence. It can help oppose the feelings of helplessness that come with climate fatigue and the hope gap. In the plays we reviewed, encouragement is offered by a single oyster in Miranda Rose Hall's *The Oysters*. An oyster colony in the Chesapeake Bay becomes discouraged while performing a ritual meant to comfort an oyster who has lost hope. They tell the story of their survival, but the story slowly morphs into a tale of being overharvested, seeing their water polluted, and experiencing the loss of life around them. The Single Oyster encourages the colony by reminding them of their position in the web of life and she tell them this:

> I am an Eastern Oyster,
> an ancient bivalve mollusk,
> and though I don't know what the hour will bring,
> what the day will bring,
> what the future will bring,
> I go on for love of all oysters!
> We must go on for love of each other!
> We go on for love of the water!
> We shall band together and filter the bay,
> how else could we possibly fill the day?
> We do what we can! What else can we do?
> Oysters! Hey Oysters, I'm talking to you!

The Single Oyster encourages the colony to continue to filter the bay despite the ecological disaster. The script finishes with the Oysters renewed and filled with hope to continue on.

Individual Action. Stories or examples of individuals taking action are important in relation to the hope gap as continual fear messaging can make people feel helpless and powerless. Many of the playwrights tackle this issue by showing audiences examples of people making a difference. The play *Small But Mighty* by Mwendie Mbugua is the perfect example of this particular theme. The narrator, Tamu, dressed as a bee, tells a story to a group of children. The story involves a farmer who encroaches on an area where a bee colony is living and sprays the flowers and plants with pesticides, causing the bees to die. After a while, Asali, a small bee, decides to do something about it. She comes up with a plan, which she shares with her hive:

> "Friends!" she said. "Bwana Farmer has been poisoning us for some time now and we have lost many because of it. Before he came, the garden was alive and home to many of us. We need to return to our peaceful days. This is what we shall do . . ." All the bees gathered round to listen. "Tomorrow," she shared, "we don't go to work!"

She convinces her hive to go on strike and in the end, her plan works. She discovers that though she is small, she is mighty and has the ability to make a difference. Although it is a children's story, the message of individual action is still visible.

Future Imagining. Future imagining is the ability to conceptualize a possible reality for the future. In order to have this present, there must be enough hope that a future will exist. In the introduction of the script *Love Out of the Ruins*, Zoë Svendsen states:

> The act of imagining alternative futures might usher into reality possibilities that previously had been excluded. . . . imagining otherwise can offer a refuge from the ruins of the present—bearing witness to the fact it doesn't have to be like this.

Imagining is critical as it is the first step to taking action. Once a goal or future state is imagined, a roadmap can start to be built to envision how to get there.

An example of future imagining is in *DreamSong* by Heidi Kraay. In the play, preteen friends Az and Berry are having their last evening together before being evacuated due to the California wildfires. Berry is moving away after losing her house. During their interaction, Az encourages Berry to imagine her desired future:

> AZ: [. . .] What's the future you want? Come on, imagine. See it!

BERRY: This is such a—. Alright, Dad and I get our house back. Like you said.

AZ: Good. And?

BERRY: And? My aunt in Flint . . . can trust her water again. Everyone gets clean water.

AZ: Keep going, what else?

BERRY: And I dunno . . . the fires stop raging so we can stay here. Everyone has a job . . . and we take care of the ones who can't work. Grown up leaders and rich people stop playing games with our planet, and us. Nobody's hungry. Nobody has to leave their home, but when they do, they're welcome where they wanna go. We get the global temperatures down, like Mrs. Thatcher said, so the polar bears stop drowning. And nobody's sick, the air's clean . . .

The occurrence of future imagining being present in just under half of the CCTA 2021 scripts suggests that this subject is an important consideration for playwrights wishing to provide hope for their audiences. It also suggests that the playwrights themselves may not have spent much time imagining what a hopeful future might look like and may not be in a position to convey this vision to their audience. It tells spectators that they can dream and imagine a better future, and that there is indeed a future to dream of.

Positive Stories and Imagery. Positivity is a way to give people hope, close the hope gap, and provide motivation to continue working. Pat To Yan's *The Last Bee Is Flying Over the Sky* concludes with positive imagery. It begins with the last bee not knowing that it is the last bee. The bee discovers a large mountain of dead bees and panics. It becomes very hungry but cannot find any flowers with pollen. It sees people who are walking in and out of caves and are throwing fireballs at each other. The last bee flies higher and higher to escape the smoke but it misses flowers. It decides to go back down to search for them and discovers the forest is returning to the color green:

The last bee sees a flower. A beautiful bee is resting on the flower. For the first time, the last bee is feeling shy. The last bee keeps its distance from the beautiful bee for a while, wondering how to fly toward the beautiful bee—beautifully.

Even through destruction and death, the last bee does not give up hope but perseveres and finds beauty in the world around it.

Hope. Hope is an attitude of optimism, expectation, and trust in the preferred outcome of an event or circumstance. It has been established that opportunities to see, experience, and feel hope are required to close the "hope gap" that many feel when encountering climate issues. One demonstration of hope can be found in the final sentence of *The Persistence of Possibility* by Karen Elias, where the playwright tells a story of two children who had to evacuate during the 2018 California fires. The story ends with the narrator saying that as images of the fires spread on TV, youth activists demanded that the Democratic Party support the Green New Deal. It was signed three months later, which the narrator says is a beginning. The play finishes with "Go. Hurry. It's not too late." This particularly poignant line encourages the audience to continue their climate work, emphasizes that it is not yet too late, and that their actions will still make a difference.

The script *Consultation,* written by Dylan Van Den Berg, is about a meeting between a First Nations person (indicated as person B in the script) and a white person wearing a suit (indicated as person A in the script). This meeting is a "consultation," where person A is meeting with the Original Peoples before making "the deal" (the details of which are not specified in the script). When person B is asked what they would like to see happen, they explain the truths of colonization and the effects of the climate crisis on their people. They want to share this truth and the knowledge of how to care for the land. Throughout the consultation, the one particularly hopeful line is: "We keep tryin'—clingin' on to somethin' we can't see—a hope or a spool of a dream which might lead us way back to how things used to be." Despite all of the challenges and neglect their people have suffered, person B states that they still hold on to a hope that might lead them back to how things used to be.

Negative Imagery. Negative imagery is present in almost every script. This is not a surprise; climate change is an inherently negative topic. Further, it is important to note that negativity can be utilized in theatre to create drama, tension, and propel the plot forward. This said, the constant use of negativity can drive audiences toward negative thoughts, which has the potential to increase the hope gap. Negative imagery is present in *Confessions of the Little Match Girl to the Star* by Kamil Haque. The text is delivered by the Little Match Girl. Although not explicitly stated, it is assumed that the girl is houseless and out in the cold at night time. After striking one match at the beginning of the play, she only has two left. While she is confessing to the stars, she says:

> All I see is a world already burning. A world of people suffering. People dying. Entire ecosystems collapsing. A world where the only fairy tale is the gospel according to money. When I go, who will even notice but the stars? Look, the clock is inching closer to doomsday. I don't want to believe that the world is evil. I don't want to be angry. I don't want to fight anymore. I'm so tired. My body aches. I feel drained. My arms hurt.

The little girl is recounting how she feels exhausted from only seeing negative things around her, such as suffering, greed, and her own negative and painful experiences. The play concludes with the girl striking her last match and being unable to breathe.

Positive and Negative Conclusions. The conclusion of a script is what the audience is left with. It is what sticks in their minds and what is enduring. Thirty-six of the plays conclude positively while only eight conclude negatively, which may have an impact when it comes to the hope gap. It should be noted that a few of the scripts have endings that are both positive and negative or utilize dark humor. An example of this is *The Penguin* by Nicolas Billon. The story is delivered by an actor dressed in a penguin costume, who promises his story has a happy ending. The story is of a penguin and an albatross in Antarctica. The albatross tries to warn the penguin that there is a polar bear ahead. The smart penguin realizes that it must not be possible because there are no polar bears in Antarctica. The albatross continues to try to warn the penguin by saying that may have been true in the past, but she has a better vantage point than the penguin and can see the polar bear. The penguin disregards the albatross and decides the white mass seen up ahead must be a large scoop of ice cream, and continues to venture forward. This is how the script concludes:

> And to his shock and surprise, it is *not* a giant scoop of vanilla ice cream. It's a polar bear. This makes the penguin frown, because he really doesn't want to admit that the albatross was right. His worry is short-lived, however, because the polar bear grabs the penguin like it's a stray piece of popcorn chicken and chomps down on him. Nom nom nom. (*Raises their index finger.*) And this is our happy ending. Because now, the penguin is spared the indignity of realizing how irrational it is to deny the existence of a polar bear in Antarctica while simultaneously accepting the presence of a giant scoop of vanilla ice cream on a glacier.

Although the script literally ends negatively with the penguin meeting his demise in the form of a polar bear, the author utilizes humor to create an amusing and lighthearted conclusion while also revealing some of the ridiculousness of society's denial of science and climate issues.

Our Conclusions

There are many themes in the CCTA 2021 plays related to hope. Further, in our reading of the plays, there were many instances where we found themes that could potentially help audiences bridge the hope gap. However, some themes were uncovered that might unintentionally widen the hope gap. For example, we found that many of the scripts put an emphasis on individual action and responsibility. As previously mentioned, this is a common rhetoric in North American media and institutional messaging. In many ways, this line of thinking places unnecessary blame on individuals while large corporations and institutions who are the major contributors to the climate crisis are not targeted. As Murray Bookchin states: "It is inaccurate and unfair to coerce people into believing that they are personally responsible for present-day ecological disasters because they consume too much or proliferate too readily." (Bookchin, quoted in Doyle et al. 2016). This messaging is reinforced in the scripts. Messaging where the fault is put on individuals can evoke feelings of helplessness and hopelessness, which can contribute to the hope gap. While we agree that individual actions are important in the climate movement, we suggest that playwrights in the future consider where to place the burden of action, and to what extent placing the onus on the individual may increase the hope gap.

It should also be noted that negative imagery is used in almost every single script. While this may help to present the "truth" about the science, and the cultural and political consequences of climate change, we argue that the consistent use of negativity has the potential to perpetuate and increase negative thoughts for audience members, which could actually widen the hope gap. We would never want to "prescribe" what images playwrights bring into their work, but this use of negative imagery should be contemplated and considered by playwrights who wish to effect change and reduce the hope gap among their audience members.

This study was able to identify the major themes related to hope and the hope gap found in these plays, and to provide some analysis of the text used in the scripts. However, there are many opportunities to continue this research and address some of the issues that were beyond the scope of this particular study. For example, this research only examined the words of the scripts; audience response to the live work was not examined. Future studies could ask audience members to fill out a survey before and after watching the plays to track the extent to which their thoughts about hope and the hope gap concerning the climate crisis were altered. Further, demographic information could be collected during these surveys to determine if there are any patterns in the data related to the gender, geographic location, age, and/or spiritual beliefs of the audience members. Finally, we recommend that the CCTA scripts be analyzed each season to document the themes that arise and to determine how climate change and the hope gap are approached.

In conclusion, it is our sincere hope that this study can be used by playwrights and arts practitioners to understand the importance of their role in relation to climate change, what the hope gap is, and their potential impact on the hope gap through their artistic efforts. Further, we hope that other researchers can use this work as a case study to continue to understand what the hope gap is and how it manifests in the arts. Finally, we hope that our study helps to elucidate the hope gap in the arts and that it demonstrates the importance and role that theatre and the arts can play when intersecting with the environmental movement.

• • •

Bethany McMorine is a dance artist who began her career in Ottawa, Ontario. She has studied multiple dance forms and trained in singing, acting, and voice work. She graduated with a double major in dance and environmental studies at York University, and completed the Cultural and Artistic Practice Certificate.

The program allowed Bethany to fuse together her interests in the arts and the environment. This is where her passion for researching the intersection of the arts and the environment began, which led her to working with Dr. Tarah Wright and Climate Change Theatre Action.

Tarah Wright is a professor and the director of the Education for Sustainability Research Group at Dalhousie University. Her research is focused on the field of education for sustainable development, with specific emphasis on bioaffinity and nature exposure, sustainability in higher education, and the role of the arts in influencing cultural norms, encouraging pro-environmental behavior, and providing drivers for the creation of a sustainable future. Tarah and her family make their home in the city of Halifax, the ancestral and unceded territory of the Mi'kmaq People, in the Acadian Forest Bioregion, at the edge of the Atlantic Ocean.

Works Cited

Currin, G. H. (2019, December 5). "Music for Our Emergency." NPR. Retrieved June 6, 2021. https://www.npr.org/2019/12/05/784818349/songs-our-emergency-how-music approaching-climate-change-crisis

Doll, S., and Wright, T. (2019). "Climate Change Art: Examining How the Artistic Community Expresses the Climate Crisis." *International Journal of Social, Political and Community Agendas in the Arts*, 14 (2): 13–29. https://doi:10.18848/2326-9960/CGP/v14i02/13-29

Doyle, T., McEachern, D., and MacGregor, S. (2016). *Environment and Politics*, 4th ed. London: Routledge, Taylor & Francis.

Eernstman, N., and Wals, A. (2013). "Locative Meaning-Making: An Arts-Based Approach to Learning for Sustainable Development." *Sustainability*, 5, 1645–60.

Gustafson, A., Marlon, J. R., Goldberg, M. H., Wang, X., Ballew, M. T., Rosenthal, S. A., and Leiserowitz, A. (2020). "Blame Where Blame Is Due: Many Americans Support Suing Fossil Fuel Companies for Global Warming Damages." *Environment: Science and Policy for Sustainable Development*, 62 (2): 30–35. https://doi:10.1080/00139157.2020.1708649

Hall, M. R. *The Oysters*. (2021, July/August). Climate Change Theatre Action.

Haque, K. (2021, July/August). *Confessions of the Little Match Girl to the Star*. Climate Change Theatre Action.

Kraay, H. (2021, July/August). *DreamSong*. Climate Change Theatre Action.

Svendsen, Z. (2021, August). *Love Out of the Ruins*. Climate Change Theatre Action.

Van Den Berg, D. (2021, July/August). *Consultation*. Climate Change Theatre Action.

Yan, P. T. (2021, July/August). *The Last Bee Is Flying Over the Sky*. Live performance in Climate Change Theatre Action.

Yi, H. (2021, July/August). *So This Is the Last Apple Pie*. Climate Change Theatre Action.

Zúñiga Morales, C. (2021, July/August). *The Eternity of Diapers*. Climate Change Theatre Action.

Part II

THE PLAYS

WHISTLER

Giancarlo Abrahan

Giancarlo Abrahan is from the island of Bohol in the Philippines and is based in Metro Manila, where he works as a writer, translator, director, and producer. He is currently a lecturer at the University of the Philippines Film Institute; managing director of Dulaang Sibol, a theater group in Ateneo de Manila; and workshop director of Linangan sa Imahen, Retorika, at Anyo (LIRA), an organization of poets writing in the Filipino language.

Playwright's Statement

Replacement is at the heart of our hopeful reimagination of a sustainable and equitable future. Our dream is greener because we have seen the numbers, the disturbing environmental cost. However, replacement inevitably means displacement, which comes with a lot of misunderstanding and a very human cost.

• • •

On a rooftop, at the edge of a city; on its edge, three chairs are whistling—three in a row, in different pitches, almost mechanical. They summon a cool wind . . . Unless otherwise stated, the chairs keep whistling mechanically, followed by the sound of a cool wind.

A BOY enters. Sits on one of the chairs, closes his eyes, whistles too. His own song.

The wind sings back whenever the BOY whistles his song.

This first time, the wind carries with it TWO MEN who take a seat on the other chairs. They join the BOY and the chairs in whistling.

Suddenly, we are on a mountain. The BOY takes a step toward the audience.

BOY: On our island, all men were brothers of a sister of one of my mother's friends. We were all related. (*Whistles.*) If not family, at least familiar.

(*Whistles.*) I learned from them this secret song that summons the winds to our island.

(*The MEN demonstrate how to whistle—purse lips, wiggle out tongue, press tip against teeth, and then blow air out.*)

BOY: Now, machines are able to do what even the restless tongues of island men couldn't do: Call the wind without taking a breath.

(*The MEN and the BOY stop whistling, and narrate their history around the stage. Their CHAIRS keep whistling.*)

BOY: The real trade, though, was squeezing milk out of our mountains. Like they were breasts. Calcium was very important then. It might still be today, depending on which doctors you ask. Except the world developed lactose intolerance. So we had to look for calcium elsewhere, and forget certain flowers. Heads had to learn to wear new hats, arms had to acclimatize to sleeves.

(*The mechanical whistling finally stops. The cool wind stops blowing. A siren wails. In new positions on the stage, the MEN and the BOY sit on their chairs.*)

BOY: Anyway, our mountains had been flat-chested for a while. And so we were given . . .

(*A WOMAN enters and gives envelopes to the MEN and the BOY.*)

WOMAN: A green new deal.

(*The MEN and the BOY open the envelopes. On sheets of paper, transcriptions of their misinterpretations.*)

MAN 1: A gray nude eel.

MAN 2: Agreein' you'd hell.

BOY: Agri, no deal!

WOMAN: No, no, no . . . Green.

MEN: Green.

WOMAN: New.

MEN: New.

WOMAN: Deal.

MEN: Deal.

WOMAN: Green. New. Deal.

MEN: Green. New. Deal.

BOY: Green New Deal?

WOMAN: Yes, Green New Deal! We're running out of time . . .

(The siren wails faster and louder. Again, transcriptions of the MEN's misinterpretations.)

MAN 2: Ah—grain you'd heal . . .   MAN 1: Grin you deal . . .
Agreein' you'd hell . . .   Granule dill . . .
Uh . . . angry no deal!   Gray nude eel.

(Both MEN shake the hands of the WOMAN. The WOMAN exits.)

WOMAN: You're welcome!

MAN 1: Yes, thank you. Good morning!

MAN 2: Well, hello there! Good morning.

(The mechanical whistling returns. So does the cool wind. The MEN put their chairs in the original position, and then exit.)

BOY: I'm not so sure how much they understood. We were just doing the right thing. I'm not very good at leaving, you see. I never get to say goodbye. When I heard of the emergency, I just knew I had to move. But I'm not very good at dance, you know. And so I let my song and chance take me. When these men—who were brothers of a sister of one of my mother's friends—when they took the deal, they just took off. Their direction: away from the island. And so it was for me.

(The BOY stands up, and starts whistling on the edge of the stage. The wind starts singing again. Suddenly, we are back on a rooftop, at the edge of a city. The WOMAN enters again, stares at the view. The BOY notices.)

BOY: (*Whistles.*) Good morning!

WOMAN: Oh yeah . . . Morning!

(The wind sings back. The WOMAN takes a deep breath, smells something sweet.)

WOMAN: You smell that? Oh, fresh air!

BOY: (*Whistles.*) You mean, sweat air?

WOMAN: I did mean fresh.

BOY: But the sweat air, that's me. (*Whistles.*) Not just fresh. That's me!

WOMAN: Well . . . (*Sniffs.*) You neither look sweaty nor smell sour to me.

BOY: No, no, no . . . I meant *sweet* air. (*Whistles.*) That's me.

WOMAN: Sweet and fresh, I didn't know there was a difference.

(The BOY stops whistling. The mechanical whistling carries on . . . The BOY watches the cool wind as it passes by.)

BOY: (*Breathes deeply.*) There . . . That's plain fresh air. We worked so hard for that!

WOMAN: (*Breathes deeply.*) I see . . . Well, not really see. But I can feel it in my lungs.

BOY: But sweat—you can actually hear it, too . . . (*Whistles.*) Listen.

(The wind sings back. The WOMAN hears. The BOY gestures for the WOMAN to breathe. The BOY and the WOMAN breathe deeply. The BOY licks his lips, the WOMAN hers.)

WOMAN: Ah . . . Sweet air!

BOY: And if you're lucky, the wind sometimes brings not only a song but also rain.

WOMAN: And does rain taste any different?

BOY: Like sweat mangoes.

WOMAN: Oh, salty?

BOY: If it's rain called by my song, it's gonna be the sweatest.

WOMAN: Well, I've tried dried mangoes and really loved them.

BOY: (*Stops whistling, annoyed even.*) But dried mangoes aren't mangoes.

WOMAN: What are they then?

BOY: Exports!

WOMAN: Against artificial preservatives?

BOY: Preservatives? A man must be willing to wait under the sun for the wind to be ripe with rain before whistling his song. For a heart that longs for heat bears the wisdom of mangoes. While a tongue dipped long enough in fermented fish knows sweetness best.

WOMAN: You mean a long history of looking back.

BOY: But who can afford that anymore? We can't afford to be on our island. When a city is only as good as it smells, it cannot afford even the cheapest fermented fish to serve my memory. But you can't afford us being in our mountains. Mountains are still being squeezed for poisonous milk though. . . . (*Sniffs.*) These days, my people only call on the wind for the pleasure of mangoes on our tongue. Because the city can only take what is sweat. (*Sniffs, sniffs, and then smiles.*)

WOMAN: (*Sniffs.*) That's funny. (*Sniffs.*) Not what you said. (*Sniffs.*) Funny, what is that? It can't be the river.

BOY: No, it only means that soon it's gonna rain.

WOMAN: Really? That smell means it's gonna rain?

BOY: It has, actually. But not yet here.

   (*Looks at the view, purses lips as if to whistle but stops.*)

WOMAN: Whistle again then?

BOY: Why don't you just learn?

   (*BOY demonstrates to the WOMAN how to whistle—purses lips, wiggles out tongue, presses the tip against his teeth, and then blows air out. The WOMAN tries but fails, and keeps on trying until she finally can whistle. The BOY and the WOMAN whistle, as if in a trance. The wind sings back at them. Until rain falls on their foreheads. They taste the rain drops.*)

WOMAN: Sweet. Sweat.

BOY: Sweat. Sweet.

(BOY purses his lips, as if to kiss—a siren wails. The "trance" is broken.)

WOMAN: Sweet. Sweat . . . Sorry, emergency! Good morning.

BOY: Good morning!

WOMAN: Can you save the rain for next time?

(The WOMAN rushes to exit. The sound of whistling—in threes, in different pitches, mechanical . . . And then a cold wind blows . . . BOY purses his lips, as if to whistle, sighs instead. It does not rain.)

END OF PLAY

THE DEAL

Javaad Alipoor

Javaad Alipoor is a multi-award-winning playwright, director, filmmaker, and performer. *The Believers Are But Brothers* (2017) opened in Edinburgh, where it won a Fringe First Award, before transferring to London's Bush Theatre, and then going on to an international tour. Javaad adapted the play for the BBC in 2018. The play's sequel, *Rich Kids: A History of Shopping Malls in Tehran* (2019), premiered at the Traverse Theatre. Its London transfer and subsequent national tour were postponed by COVID-19. A new digital version was created for online audiences. This version went on to tour online, including at the Public Theater's Under the Radar Festival, and was selected for the Sundance Film Festival.

Playwright's Statement

The inspiration for this short play is Robert Vitalis's book *America's Kingdom* and the conversations about race and postcolonialism kicked off by the international repercussions of the Black Lives Matter movement.

Note

This is a play for one actor and an audience. The idea is to build the images in the audience's mind and then let them go. As far as sound design goes, you definitely don't have to stick to the music that is explicitly named in the text. In fact you probably shouldn't. The description of the music in the text should contrast with sound, if any is used.

• • •

This is a story about a deal. It's the deal at the heart of the oil industry. It's the deal that used to go like this: Western colonial oil concession; profits in New York, London, or Amsterdam; a cut for a local warlord. Guaranteed production. Iraq. Nigeria. Mexico. Pliant population. Utter destruction of forests and seas. It has a few changes now. Centers of accumulation shift, sovereign wealth funds are established. But the principles remain.

It could be a fictional story. A play or a film. Music and lights. It's got everything: Backstabbing, politics, love interests. But it's not. You know how it ends. Because it ends with the world like it actually is.

This is the story of a little known but real man called Abdullah Tariki. He was, for a few years, the Saudi Minister of Oil. He helped to found OPEC. He died a rich old man in Lebanon.

But in the early 1960s, he was something else. He was a rebel intent on breaking American imperial power in the Middle East, democratizing Saudi Arabia, and giving the wealth of that region to its people.

See what I mean about knowing how the story would end? That's obviously not the ending that we got. He loses, and goes to Lebanon, and makes his money.

If we're going to tell it like a real story, you need to do two things: Imagine you don't know the ending. And imagine that the story I'm telling you isn't just literally true, but something that we can rewrite and reedit.

Imagine the first scene being 1938.

The Arabian desert.

Like retro quality Pathé newsreel. Black and white. A man with a very polished mid-Atlantic accent talks over something that sounds like the theme tune from Lawrence of Arabia.

"This is Dharan, a desert city built by American ingenuity and Arab hospitality." The camera picks out two happy-looking Arab men. "A simple people," the voiceover says. "A way of life unchanged for thousands of years."

And then kicking through the clichéd orientalist strings, the opening riff from Sid Vicious's "My Way." Hard cut from the archive. A camera swoops through the desert and through Dharan. From the manicured lawns of the whites-only quarter, it accelerates through tennis courts, whites-only drinking fountains, out into the cardboard city of the colored quarter.

It lands on an extreme close-up of a young boy's iris. In Abdullah Tariki's 12-year-old eye, we see reflected the whole oil camp: its racial stratification, its burning towers, its American flags, its Saudi secret policemen.

Second Scene.

Texas.

1950.

Eddie Cochrane's "C'mon Everybody" plays over a crackling car radio. The 22-year-old Tariki rubs his sweaty palms together. It's not the Texas heat that's bringing the moisture up but the two white men outside the cinema.

His white date is in front of the cinema entrance arguing with two white men. Telling them he isn't a Mexican, or anything else. He's an Arab. Which means he's a Caucasian, apparently. Not a word he has heard before. In any case, the argument is short. Arab, Mexican, or anything else, he's not getting in the cinema.

As he drives her home, he tells her about Dharan, about his dreams. Asks her if she wants to see it with him one day.

Third Scene.

1955.

Aramco-colored camp, Dharan.

A large tent-like structure. Five dozen Arab workers watching their first film. A white man at the back, keeping a precise eye. On the primitive projector, John Wayne swaggers through an artificial Texas desert that looks as plastic as a shop window selling outdoor wear. Wayne pulls out a shotgun, shoots dead three Comanche, who, to the white man, look awfully like the Arabs watching the film.

The Arab workers cheer Wayne.

The white man breathes a sigh of relief. He gives a message to an Arab boy to take to the office. "Don't worry," it says, "they think they are the cowboys."

Fourth Scene.

1962.

Riyadh.

An Egyptian violin line sweeps down and the crisp Darbuka rhythm of Umm Kulthum's "Alf Leila We Leila" starts up.

A camera follows a Mercedes at street level. Through dusty streets full of Arab men and women in traditional clothes.

It stops. From the back door, two well-dressed American men exit and walk onto the street. The first checks the address. The Aramco executive offers the man from the State Department a cigarette. They smoke.

Tariki, now Oil Minister, sits in his office. Second floor. A fan spins slowly overhead, dragging a slow rhythm.

The radio is reporting news from the palace. The fall of Tariki's allies. Coded of course. But he knows what it means. His junior minister turns to him. Escape plans are ready.

The Americans enter. "Mr. Tariki," says the man from the State Department. "I hope we can find a way out of this regrettable misunderstanding."

"I don't think you misunderstand me at all," answers Tariki.

The State Department man is polite but firm. Unfortunate circumstances. Historically close ties. This is America he is dealing with, not the British Empire. But he must understand, Arabs are not ready for technical jobs. The books cannot be opened to the oil ministry, and, besides, the new king himself has just been on the radio laying out how the talk of unmanaged democracy is a communist plot.

The conversation is long and convoluted. Of the kind conducted by diplomats or gangsters. People who know lives and fortunes turn on the use of a word.

 "Mr. Tariki, we and the US government are determined to help the people of Saudi Arabia reach a modern stage of development. But the facts are clear. Forty years ago, the first king of this country drew up a contract with us. A deal is a deal."

For the first time, in front of these men and his, Tariki loses his temper. "We are the sons of those Indians who sold you Manhattan. And we will renegotiate our deal."

You know how it ends.

A montage. The shimmering opening riff of the Rolling Stones' "Gimme Shelter."

Palace coup. Repentant princes bending the knee to a new king. Aramco executives giving lists of names to Saudi Arabian secret policemen. Desert thugs arriving outside the shacks of trade union organizers in the colored camps. Then OPEC. Deserts made to bloom with sovereign wealth funds. Wherever oil is produced, the integration of a thousand Riyadhs into the global market. Dictatorships, some decrepit monarchies, some republican generals carrying out coups d'état. Gangster economies where closeness to power is capital. Greater and greater consumption. An oil-producing city in the Global South. It could be Baku in the Caucasus, Pitakwa in Nigeria, Basra in Iraq.

In the eyes of a young girl, you see reflected a city, a country, and a world. Abject poverty and ruthless violence in support of the destruction of the world.

Jagger's banshee voice sings the first line.

It's time for a new deal.

END OF PLAY

APOLOGY, MY

Keith Barker

Keith Barker is a member of the Métis Nation of Ontario. He is a playwright, actor, and director from Northwestern Ontario, and the current artistic director at Native Earth Performing Arts. He is the winner of the Dora Mavor Moore Award and the Playwrights Guild's Carol Bolt Award for best new play. He received a Saskatchewan and Area Theatre Award for Excellence in Playwriting for his play *The Hours That Remain*, as well as a Yukon Arts Award for Best Art for Social Change.

Playwright's Statement

This play came out of exchanges I've had with my uncle over the years. He is a fervent climate change denier who believes it is a hoax drummed up by lefty pinkos. This play is me writing out my disillusion by imagining a revelation about the climate crisis through the eyes of a Prime Minister who finds himself on the wrong side of history.

• • •

PRIME MINISTER: I'm sorry. I truly am.

FIXER: You can't say that.

PRIME MINISTER: Why not?

FIXER: You're making it personal. Don't do that.

PRIME MINISTER: It's an apology.

FIXER: You need to think bigger picture here.

PRIME MINISTER: Fine . . . On behalf of the country—

FIXER: The country, the people, whatever you want to call them, are not the ones who are sorry, the government is.

PRIME MINISTER: . . . On behalf of the party—

FIXER: Whoa whoa whoa, it's not one party's fault, it's every party's fault. Got it?

   (PRIME MINISTER sighs.)

PRIME MINISTER: Mr. Speaker, I stand before you today to offer an official apology.

FIXER: There you go.

PRIME MINISTER: The denial of climate change is a sad and regrettable chapter in our history.

FIXER: I like the chapters—That was a sad chapter. This? This is a new chapter.

PRIME MINISTER: In the last hundred-and-fifty years, populations were introduced to widespread electrification, internal combustion engines, the car, and the airplane.

FIXER: Sweet. Keep it in the past, stay away from the future.

PRIME MINISTER: This massive shift to fossil fuels exponentially increased material prosperity and measures of well-being. But we were wrong.

FIXER: We're never wrong.

PRIME MINISTER: It was a mistake.

FIXER: Mistakes are just as bad as being wrong. Neither will get you votes.

PRIME MINISTER: It was regrettable.

FIXER: Mm, better.

PRIME MINISTER: We are past the tipping point of climate change. Now we must deal with the full consequences of government failure.

FIXER: Way too negative.

PRIME MINISTER: Now we must deal with the consequences of inaction . . . and a multigenerational culture of denial to maintain the status quo.

FIXER: Cut the last part.

PRIME MINISTER: I think we need it.

FIXER: And I think we don't. Keep going.

PRIME MINISTER: . . . Unprecedented warming cycles have melted the ice caps, causing the mass extinction of species. The acidification of the oceans has destroyed the majority of marine and mammal food chains. The occurrence of extreme weather events has vastly increased as sea levels continue to rise.

FIXER: You can't say all that.

PRIME MINISTER: People already know this.

FIXER: Then why are we saying it again?

PRIME MINISTER: Because it's true.

FIXER: Truth is overrated.

PRIME MINISTER: Then why am I even giving this speech?

FIXER: Because, politically it's a smart move if we do it right. It also makes you look like a Prime Minister—

PRIME MINISTER: I am the Prime Minister.

FIXER: Yeah, well, you know what I mean.

PRIME MINISTER: I don't think I do.

FIXER: Listen, don't focus on the small stuff. You need to ignore your instincts. Whatever feels right, is wrong. You won't win this if you repeat mistakes.

PRIME MINISTER: Don't put this all on me.

FIXER: Says the guy who stood up in the House of Commons and denied the existence of climate change on the same day scientists announced the Arctic Circle was ice-free.

PRIME MINISTER: They did that on purpose to make me look bad.

FIXER: What, melt the Arctic Circle?

PRIME MINISTER: You know what I mean.

FIXER: I don't think I do.

PRIME MINISTER: You really think you can fix this?

FIXER: What do you think?

PRIME MINISTER: You always answer a question with a question?

FIXER: Only the dumb ones.

PRIME MINISTER: Right . . . Where were we?

FIXER: Somewhere between mass extinction and extreme weather conditions.

PRIME MINISTER: . . . Today, we recognize the denial of climate change was wrong.

FIXER: Not wrong but—

PRIME MINISTER: Regrettable.

FIXER: Beauty.

PRIME MINISTER: I've already said regrettable . . .

FIXER: Yeah, and you're going to say it a hundred more times so get used to it.

PRIME MINISTER: . . . The fossil fuel industry actively misled the public and is largely to blame for the inaction on climate change with capitalism being the driving force.

FIXER: Don't say the C word.

PRIME MINISTER: Why not?

FIXER: You can't be seen placing the blame on industry.

PRIME MINISTER: Just over a hundred companies are responsible for 71 percent of all the global greenhouse gas emissions.

FIXER: That is debatable.

PRIME MINISTER: Not if we're using science it's not.

FIXER: Wow, and where was this guy a few years ago?

PRIME MINISTER: I am trying to make up for my past mistakes.

FIXER: And that, my friend, is how you kill your political career.

PRIME MINISTER: I need to say this.

FIXER: No, you don't. You're talking to the base. Card-carrying members. They voted for you because of your ideology. You can't just bait and switch these folks. Do that and you can kiss the election goodbye.

PRIME MINISTER: You're right. Thank you for that.

FIXER: For what?

PRIME MINISTER: It didn't really hit me until you said my words back to me.

FIXER: What'd I say? Sorry, I've said a lot.

PRIME MINISTER: Mass extinction.

FIXER: Oh come on. I'm just trying to get you reelected here.

PRIME MINISTER: This isn't about politics anymore.

FIXER: Everything is about politics.

PRIME MINISTER: Sorry, but I need to do this.

FIXER: Let me do my job here. I'm a fixer, it's what I'm paid to do. Fix things. And if you want this fixed, Mr. Prime Minister, then you need to start listening to me, pronto. Do. Not. Apologize. These altruistic feelings are fleeting. Trust me. You think you've found some clarity but you haven't. And when those feelings pass, and they will pass, you will regret having made a decision in a moment of weakness. You understand me?

PRIME MINISTER: Perfectly. I think you need to go.

FIXER: You're making a big mistake.

PRIME MINISTER: Maybe, maybe not.

FIXER: Let me help you.

PRIME MINISTER: No, I think you've helped enough. Now if you'll excuse me, I've got a speech to write.

FIXER: Last chance . . . Really? Fine, it's your funeral . . . You know what? I wasn't going vote for you anyways.

PRIME MINISTER: Aww, you broke your own rule.

FIXER: And what is that?

PRIME MINISTER: Don't make it personal.

END OF PLAY

AFFIRMATIONS

Elena Eli Belyea

Elena (or Eli) Belyea (they/she) is a queer playwright, performer, producer, and arts educator from Amiskwaciy-wâskahikan (colonially known as Edmonton) whose plays have been produced across North America. She splits her time between Moh'kins'tis (Calgary), Tkaronto (Toronto), and Tio'tia:ke (Montreal). They are also half of queer sketch comedy duo "Gender? I Hardly Know Them" (on Tiktok and Instagram at @genderihard lyknowthem). Find out more at elenabelyea.com and tinybearjaws.com.

Playwright's Statement

In episode 170 of the podcast *Reply All*, one of the hosts, Alex Goldman, writes a song (entitled "The Wolf Is at the Door") about his feelings of frustration and powerlessness surrounding the climate crisis. In the following episode, his boss, Alex Blumberg, comes on the show to lambast Goldman's song, arguing it was irresponsible to use the show's enormous platform to spread the message that climate change is a lost cause.

I'm thinking about the benefits and disadvantages of writing something "hopeful." Can "hopeful" art actually incite its viewers to action, or does it pacify and promote the status quo? How do we create work that engages honestly with the reality of our circumstances without audiences checking out, convinced it's useless to even try provoking change at an individual level?

Note

Inspired by Mark Ravenhill's *pool (no water)*, this play is written without any stage directions or dialogue tags. I encourage anyone interested in performing it to allocate the text however they like, to as many or as few actors as they wish.*

---

* The following articles are referenced throughout: John Harris, "Our Phones and Gadgets Are Now Endangering the Planet," *Guardian*, July 17, 2018, accessed November 21, 2021, https://www.theguardian.com/commentisfree/2018/jul/17/internet

• • •

aural

auroral zone

spooky dream

glacial hankering

alberta's premier jason kenney

gleams like bratwurst

on fox news

i order flats

of beer off the internet

to press or lower down

the canada-u.s. relationship

in desperate times

depress

the third-largest

oil reserves in the world

according to author james bridle:

"using a tablet or smartphone

to wirelessly watch an hour of video a week

uses roughly the same amount of electricity

as two new domestic fridges"

land

i'm trying to teach

my dog to pee

outside

today's temperature

"extreme cold wind chill between minus forty and minus fifty-five

frostbite can develop in minutes"

he perceives being outdoors

as a kind of punishment

-climate-carbon-footprint-data-centres; and Arwa Mahdawi, "The Real Problem with Your Netflix Addiction? The Carbon Emissions," *Guardian*, February 12, 2020, accessed November 21, 2021, https://www.theguardian.com/commentisfree/2020/feb/12/real-problem-netflix-addiction-arbon-emissions.

"in 2019 netflix's global energy consumption was enough

to power 40,000 american homes

for a year"

sea levels

contain nudity

to avoid mass extinction

madagascar

galapagos

marine turtles

baby seals

not a single one on track to meet their goals

the halifax treaties were a collection of eleven written documents produced between 1760 and 1761 which, amongst other agreements, provided Indigenous peoples the right to fish to put (someone or something) on land from a boat

i'm relieved

to have never ached for a version of my life

with children in it

"the entire communication technology industry could account for up to 14 percent of carbon emissions by 2040"

how are we not

in the streets

about clean drinking water

aching

through the air

on the ground

resting

another surface

the right of peoples to define

their agricultural systems

i make a donation

fret

inflict (a blow) on someone

how the land lies
scroll
the land of the living
i dream of
your sink, full of glass
i dream of
taking you to see
an impassive mountain range
i dream of
being outlived
i fantasize about us embracing
mass inconvenience
dirt
resistance
patience
complication
tomatoes, ripe and
too numerous
too many
to hold

END OF PLAY

THE PENGUIN

Nicolas Billon

Nicolas Billon writes for theatre, television, and film. His work has been produced around the world and garnered many awards, including a Governor General's Literary Award for Drama, a Canadian Screen Award, and a Writers Guild of Canada Screenwriting Award. www.nicolasbillon.com

Playwright's Statement

I am fascinated with the moral gymnastics and cognitive dissonance required to object, on principle, to projects that seek to address climate change with concrete action—like the Green New Deal. That was the seed of this play.

Note

The Penguin is meant to be flexible in terms of performance (IRL, streamed) and casting (age, gender, ethnicity).

• • •

Lights up on THE ACTOR, dressed in a penguin costume.
Sure, there's something comical about this image. Yet the right tone for the play is somewhere in THE ACTOR's combination of earnestness and despondency—like this is an audition piece that garners praise from agents and casting directors, but hasn't ever booked them the part. This may or may not echo the feelings of climate scientists when they contribute their findings to another climate report.

THE ACTOR: Maybe you'll like this story. It's about a penguin. And it has a happy ending.

> *(Shifts, clears throat.)*

OK, so this penguin is waddling along in the Antarctic. Minding his own business, but also checking things out, you know, in the way penguins do. And then he looks up in the distance and sees . . .

(Squints.)

He sees this big white hulking something or other on the horizon. Which, you know, is weird. And the penguin's curious. As penguins naturally are, by the way. So he starts waddling toward the big white hulking something or other to find out what it is, exactly.

As the penguin waddles, he hears a cry: "Hey! Hey there!"

Of course, the penguin wonders if he's the one being spoken to, but he hopes not. Because the voice is high-pitched and screechy. Annoying, you know? So he keeps going—

"Hey! Penguin!"

(Sighs.)

Well poop. The penguin stops, looks around . . . But there's no one.

"Hey!"

The penguin looks up. There's an albatross circling above. A *girl* albatross.

"What do *you* want?" says the penguin. And yes, there's a haughty disdain in his voice. See, the penguin feels like albatrosses are always judging him because, you know, he's a bird but he can't fly. 'Cause he's a penguin.

So, anyway.

The albatross looks down at the penguin (of course it does!) and says, "Where are you going?" To which the penguin, quite reasonably, replies, "That's my business, thank you," and waddles onward.

"Hey! Hold on a minute!"

The penguin looks up again. "What?"

And the albatross, it says, "I only wanted to warn you."

The penguin frowns. "Warn me about what?"

"About the polar bear," says the albatross, indicating the big white hulking something or other.

Now, the penguin doesn't like this one bit. So he broods for a moment and says, "No. That can't be right."

"How so?" squawks the albatross.

"This is Antarctica," says the penguin, brimming with the confidence of someone armed with facts acquired in a poorly phrased Google query. "And in Antarctica, there are no polar bears. They're only found in the Arctic."

Well this shuts the albatross right up.

For a second.

"That may have been true in the past," says the albatross, "but I have a better vantage point, and I'm pretty sure that's a polar bear up ahead."

The penguin scoffs, because . . . Let's be honest?

(Mimics the albatross in a high, whiny voice.)

"I have a better vantage point than you, you flightless little dum-dum . . ."

Anyway.

Then the albatross says, "What do you think it is?"

The penguin squints at the big white hulking something or other—

(Opens their mouth in awe.)

"That's obviously a giant scoop of vanilla ice cream!"

And the penguin is positively vibrating at the thought of eating said giant scoop of vanilla ice cream. So he keeps going, only now, you know, he has a little jump in his waddle.

"Hey!"

(Rolls their eyes.)

"What now!?"

The albatross says, "Look, I'm just trying to help. I'm pretty sure that's a polar bear."

But the penguin knows it isn't. Because it's clearly a giant scoop of vanilla ice cream. So he looks up at the albatross and says, "Prove it."

The albatross ponders a moment then says, "I can't prove it beyond what I can see. But what I see is a polar bear."

It's clear to the penguin that this argument is going nowhere, so he says, "Why don't you go hang yourself on some poor sailor's neck?"

(Grimaces.)

Oh, that is a sick burn. Albatrosses are touchy about these things.

So the albatross flies away.

The penguin experiences a brief pang of guilt, but it goes away when he remembers all the delicious calories that await him.

He darts ahead, beak watering with penguin-drool—

And he reaches the big white hulking something or other—

And to his shock and surprise, it is *not* a giant scoop of vanilla ice cream.

It's a polar bear.

The penguin is upset, because he really doesn't want to admit that the albatross was right.

His fear is short-lived, however, because the polar bear grabs the penguin like it's a stray piece of popcorn chicken and chomps down on him.

Nom nom nom.

> *(Raises their index finger.)*

And this is our happy ending. The penguin, our penguin, is spared the indignity of realizing how irrational it is to deny the existence of a polar bear in Antarctica while simultaneously accepting the presence of a giant scoop of vanilla ice cream on a glacier.

The end.

> *(THE ACTOR takes a bow and then, without any fuss, exits.)*

END OF PLAY

WHEN

Wren Brian

Wren Brian was born and raised in Whitehorse, Yukon, Canada (territory of the Kwanlin Dün and Ta'an Kwäch'än) and is of mostly settler ancestry (seven great-grandparents were white settlers, one was Métis). Wren is dedicated to creating characters that can be played by actors of any gender, ancestry, ability, and/or age. *Anomie* won the 2017 Harry S. Rintoul Award for Best New Manitoba Play, and in 2018 *Bystander* was premiered by Gwaandak Theatre in Whitehorse.

Playwright's Statement

While there were several inspirations for this piece, a primary one was from my time working on *Map of the Land, Map of the Stars* produced by the Yukon theatre company Gwaandak Theatre, co-created by Chris Clarke, Geneviève Doyon, Patti Flather, Andrameda Hunter, Leonard Linklater, Yvette Nolan, Michelle Olson, and Aimée Dawn Robinson. After living down south in a city for several years, getting the chance to come back to the territory of the Kwanlin Dün First Nation and Ta'an Kwäch'än Council, and work on this wonderful project allowed me to process how growing up in the North has influenced (and continues to influence) my views on how humans interact with nature and each other. There is a lot to relearn.

Note

Every effort should be made for the play to be cast primarily, if not entirely, with actors who identify as disabled, female, BIPOC, and/or LGBTQIA2S+.

Two or more voices. New speaker after each new line. Staging is completely up to the artists. May say lines together or apart.

• • •

When . . .

When?

When we . . .

We . . .

When did we?

When did we . . .

When did we forget . . .

Forget what?

We forgot . . .

We're lost . . .

We forgot . . .

Stars

Stars?

Stars

Connections between

Paths, connecting

Roots

Roots

Trees

Connected

In the ground

Rivers

Water

Flowing

Connecting

We forgot

We're lost

When?

A long, long time ago

Not that long

Too long

Not all

Enough

Too many

Too many forgot

The connections

The roots

The waves

The stars

Look up.

Breathe.

Feel.

It's too much

It's amazing

It's dangerous

Yes

Always

Don't forget it

So are we.

We are not separate

We are not better than

It's frightening

We're frightening

Afraid to wake up

Afraid to lose control

We have no control

Nothing has control

When will we remember

When will we accept

Accept what?

We are . . .

We are connected

We are connected

To what?

Everything.

Everything . . .

Every being

Every life

It's wonderful

It's horrifying

No

Yes

We're wonderful

We're horrifying

No

Yes

Stars guide

Get lost in them

Rivers give life

Take it too

Trees clean

Lightning in a forest

Fire

Death

A cycle

It's all connected

We're all connected.

Yes.

All nature.

All the wonder, all the horror

Yes.

We are all connected.

Can't pick and choose

We need to care

How?

Care for . . .

Accept

Care and accept . . . everything

Everything.

Every being.

We're all connected.

We need to care again

We need to accept again

Has to start somewhere

It has

When?

When we . . .

We . . .

When did we?

When did we . . .

When did we remember?

It's hard

It hurts

We did remember

Not all

Not yet

Enough?

Not yet.

When?

We will

How?

We can

We accept

All the wonder

All the horror

All the pain

All the connections.

Look up.

Breathe.

Feel.

Don't be afraid.

Care.

Accept.

Everything.

Every being.

Wake up.

END OF PLAY

MOLONG

Damon Chua

Damon Chua is a New York–based playwright originally from Singapore. Off-Broadway plays include *Film Chinois, Incident at Hidden Temple*, and *The Emperor's Nightingale*. He is published by Samuel French, Smith & Kraus, and Plays for New Audiences. Damon also writes poetry and short stories. He recently worked on a TV series in Malaysia. www.damonchua.com

Playwright's Statement

The Penan people of Malaysia and their traditional ecological knowledge.* Indigenous activist Hindou Oumarou Ibrahim and her TED Talk.** Indigenous peoples make up about 6% of the world population but inhabit more than a quarter of our planet's land area. Harnessing their knowledge and philosophy on sustainability is vital to the future of biodiversity and humankind.

Characters

IBUNDA, an older woman, a person of color.
WATI, a younger woman, a person of color.

Note

"Molong," a Penan word, is pronounced "mo-LONG," with stress on the second syllable. Its meaning will become clear as the play goes along.

• • •

---

* Nadzirah Hosen, Hitoshi Nakamura, and Amran Hamzah, "Adaptation to Climate Change: Does Traditional Ecological Knowledge Hold the Key?," *Sustainability* 12, no. 2 (2020): 676, https://doi.org/10.3390/su12020676.
** Hindou Oumarou Ibrahim, "Indigenous Knowledge Meets Science to Take On Climate Change," TEDWomen 2019, https://www.ted.com/talks/hindou_oumarou_ibrahim_indigenous_knowledge_meets_science_to_take_on_climate_change.

PART ONE

IBUNDA sits in a chair facing the audience. WATI combs IBUNDA's hair. Even though the two are interacting, they exist in separate spheres of being and in different times.

WATI: When she was born, the powers-that-be said she was useless and should be thrown away.

IBUNDA: I was free, roaming the forests, dancing with the trees.

WATI: When she came of age, she was married off to someone who never spoke and never smiled.

IBUNDA: I went to the edge of the realm, saw the sky meeting the vastest ocean.

WATI: When she grew older they moved her to a settlement and cut her off from her land.

IBUNDA: I climbed mountains so high, I reached the top of clouds.

WATI: When she died, no one mourned her passing, no one remembered her stories. Except me.

IBUNDA: I . . .

> *(Beat. WATI begins to hum. It is an ancient tune that conveys all the joys and all the sorrows. Lights change.)*

PART TWO

A time when the two women exist.

IBUNDA: *(Pointing up.)* Look! *(Off of Wati.)* You see them?

WATI: *(She doesn't look up.)* Stars? No.

IBUNDA: I see them.

WATI: In your imagination.

IBUNDA: *(After a beat.)* Are you suggesting . . .

WATI: There are no stars.

IBUNDA: *(Unsure.)* But . . . what's that, then?

WATI: Remember the men with their machines and bulldozers and chainsaws?

IBUNDA: . . . Maybe.

WATI: They came and started cutting down the trees?

IBUNDA: . . . Maybe.

WATI: They burned the forests to make room for their own trees?

IBUNDA: . . . Why would they do that?

WATI: That's what they do. The forests burned. Sky filled with smoke and ash. Do you remember?

IBUNDA: I remember when morning mists shrouded saplings and undergrowth and revealed fruits and flowers when the sun rose.

WATI: That's gone.

IBUNDA: Gone?

WATI: No more mists. And no stars . . . because of the smoke and ash.

IBUNDA: Really? (*She looks up and tries to ask the stars.*) Is that true?

(*There is no answer. Lights change.*)

PART THREE

When IBUNDA was younger.

IBUNDA: (*To audience.*) When the scientists came, I thought it was my way out. Out of the clutches of the powers-that-be. So I told them everything I knew. I told them the ways of the trees and the ways of nature. I told them how the color of the sky changed and what it meant. I told them why the sizes of fruits and leaves determined everything. And of course, I told them about *molong*.

(*Beat.*)

Molong. There is no "us," there is no "them." We live in balance with everything. If we take, we give back. If we take more, we give back more. We know we'll be here for a long time, so we plan ahead.

(*Beat.*)

At first the scientists were confused, not sure what to think. Then they realized—*we may not understand this "molong" thing, but the rest of it . . . it's USABLE knowledge.* So they recorded, learned, applied. They put me on TV. My name appeared in magazines. Newspapers. Important documents. No longer useless.

> *(Beat.)*

But . . . things changed.

> *(IBUNDA seems lost in thoughts.)*

WATI: What happened?

> *(We're back in the same time period as Part Two.)*

IBUNDA: You know what happened.

WATI: Tell them.

IBUNDA: What's the use?

WATI: (*To audience.*) I came with the scientists—a hired help. Straightaway, I knew this was special.

IBUNDA: You knew nothing. You were so young.

WATI: (*Ignoring her, to audience.*) The problem was—nature was no longer our friend. Temperatures rose; the rains didn't come; everything went awry.

IBUNDA: We tried to—

WATI: (*Interjecting.*) The color of the sky—different.

IBUNDA: We tried to—

WATI: (*Interjecting.*) Leaves, fruits—irregular.

IBUNDA: We tried to—

WATI: (*Interjecting.*) No one could tell anything anymore. It was . . .

> *(As WATI thinks of the right word . . .)*

IBUNDA: Nature was speaking another language—one too new to understand. We . . . *I* . . . was useless once more.

WATI: No.

IBUNDA: *Please.* (*Then:*) Are they coming back?

WATI: Always the same question. (*Off of IBUNDA.*) You know the answer.

IBUNDA: See?

WATI: Come, let me comb your hair.

> (*After a moment of hesitation, IBUNDA sits down, assuming the same position as at the top of the play. As WATI combs, she hums another ancient melody.*)

IBUNDA: If only . . .

> (*Beat.*)

WATI: What?

IBUNDA: . . . Nothing.

WATI: (*To audience.*) She is the last of her people. When she's gone, what of her stories? What of *molong*?

IBUNDA: You know nothing about *molong.*

WATI: (*To audience.*) This much I know—the scientists were only interested in facts and figures. Things that can be measured. But *molong* . . . (*Off of IBUNDA, to IBUNDA:*) It's what makes the facts and figures . . . *dance*, right?

> (*IBUNDA shrugs, but she seems to be agreeing.*)

WATI: (*To audience.*) That's something we agree on. The only thing we agree on.

IBUNDA: (*Looking up suddenly.*) Isn't that . . . (*Getting excited.*) A star! (*To WATI.*) Look. (*No immediate response.*) LOOK!

> (*WATI finally looks. She searches the sky, looking at every corner. As she does that . . . IBUNDA gets up and begins to dance. Soundlessly. Simply. Beautifully. Lights fade.*)

END OF PLAY

THE PAGEANT

Paula Cizmar

Paula Cizmar is an award-winning playwright and librettist whose work, which explores the events challenging us as humans, has been produced all over the world. She is the librettist for *A Hole in the Sky*, a mini eco-opera (with composer Guang Yang) performed at the Natural History Museum of Los Angeles County, and the initiator of Sacrifice Zone: Los Angeles, a multimedia project that highlights how environmental justice is a human rights issue. www.paulacizmar.net

Playwright's Statement

Most of us know deep in our bones that we have to protect the earth, but what stops us is the hard work that must be put into the effort. Then there are the fear tactics used by certain politicians who say that climate change activists just want to take away our ice cream and our cars, and force us to ride around in high-speed trains "powered by unicorn tears." But suppose we get to a place where everyone finally agrees to make change—and it happens? And it's successful! Imagine a future where we save the earth. That's where this play came from—a future where environmental justice wins.

TIME

The Future.

• • •

GAIA and GAI-ETTE gather to plan the annual Pageant . . .

GAIA: I'm just saying that we have done it the same way for 50 years so could we please just be a little more original this time—

GAI-ETTE: Fine, be original. But you can't mess with the parts that people love—

GAIA: It's not about whether they love it, it's about whether it's right—

(GAIALEE rushes in, impatient.)

GAIALEE: Hey, hi, sorry, late, I've only got a half hour so could we—

GAIA: We don't have a quorum.

GAI-ETTE: We're not going to get a quorum. The last time we had a quorum we voted to not bother to have a quorum ever again.

GAIALEE: No one wants to come to these meetings. Whole thing is boring.

GAIA: So we'll fix it—

GAI-ETTE: How? You want to take out the part that is the most fun!

GAIALEE: Start the damned meeting!

(GAI-ETTE gives up and pounds the gavel.)

GAI-ETTE: Whatever. *(Starting the official chant.)* Oh Earth Oh Moon Oh Sun. Gather we all.

GAIA and GAIALEE: We are gathered.

GAI-ETTE: Today, we come to you humbly on this, the uh—

GAIALEE: Could we skip the official mumble-stuff and just get to the business at hand—

GAI-ETTE: —this, the uh, 145th day of the 56th year of the New Green World Order—

GAIA: Say the old-fashioned date, too.

GAIALEE: Why?

GAIA: I just think it's nice. And ceremonial.

GAI-ETTE: Now I have to calculate—Uh. Uh. OK, we are gathered this 145th day . . . uh, May 26, of the old-era year, uh, uh, the year 2091, to plan our annual Pageant of The New Green Planet and Civic Solar Responsibility Light Show . . . Um, who's reading the agenda—?

GAIALEE: We all read it before we got here. Get down to business.

GAIA: Fine. I move we retire the Unicorn Tears segment.

GAI-ETTE: No.

GAIA: It's not truthful and it's giving kids the wrong idea—

GAIALEE: Kids *love* that part—

GAIA: Yes, just like they love the Tooth Fairy and Santa Claus, but it gives them a false sense of—

GAI-ETTE: Can't they have some fun? Can't they be kids for a while and not pay attention to dire predictions or worry about—

GAIA: History has shown us what happens when we don't pay attention to the signs of—

GAIALEE: Ohmygod, do you never have a moment when you just chill?

GAIA: I'm just saying, the Pageant needs to be meaningful. To remind everyone how we got here. All the changes in human behavior. It was not easy.

GAIALEE: That part was especially not easy.

GAIA: So to include a section where everybody was given the mission to collect unicorn tears so that the high-speed, pollution-free trains could run on time—. That's misleading.

GAI-ETTE: That part is sooooo beautiful. When the tiny children wear their twinkly flowy robes and go up to the adults in the audience with little solar battery-powered sparkle lights and say, Are you the unicorn? Do you have any tears for me? Do you have any tears for the future? And then they sing that beautiful song in 15-part harmony. There's usually not a dry eye in the house.

GAIALEE: Yes, all those tears, which the kids collect in their little star-power jars . . .

GAI-ETTE: So that we don't have to burn fossil fuels and so that the earth's air quality is pristine and everything is run on renewable energy.

GAIA: Stop stop stop! That's not how it happened so why do we want kids to think that it did!

GAIALEE: Well, you gotta inspire them—

GAIA: As if the reciting of the Honors of the Elders is not inspiring—

GAI-ETTE: OMG, no one wants to sit there and listen to the 125-year-old from San Pedro, California, drone on about the old days when she would have asthma attacks from the idling trucks at the port and then, miraculously, her asthma was cured when electric vehicles were—

GAIALEE: Or the 132-year-old who claims he worked in a coal mine—

GAIA: No, that was his grandfather. He never worked in a coal mine—his family left Kentucky when he was three. That's why he's still alive.

GAIALEE: I think they all take supplements. Imagine living longer than 115.

GAIA: It's inspiring. And we have to do the Earth-U-Love Creed and pledge to always remember all the important—

GAI-ETTE: I love doing the Creed. "Oh Earth, I believe in sustaining you with my efforts and if I should ever for a second forget the dates of your liberation starting with . . . uh . . . May . . . uh . . ." Um . . . you know, I don't say it much anymore. I have to look up the dates.

GAIA: OMG, you don't know. April 1, 2031! The day of the last piece of coal! July 5, 2033, the day that every person on the planet had access to clean water! January 1, 2035, the day we converted to the new calendar for the New Green World Order.

GAI-ETTE: So many numbers. It's hard to remember. And boring. And then there's the Starvation Diary—

GAIALEE: Such a downer. Why do I always have to be the one who has to perform that every year?

GAIA: It's a reminder! Of the time when only some people had enough to eat.

GAI-ETTE: That's why we need the Unicorn Tears section. Because the rest of this is so depressing.

GAIA: Oh, wake up. The whole unicorn tears thing was a joke. It was some sneering, smart-alecky remark made by some climate change denier politician! The early Pageant organizers put it in because it was supposed to be satire!

GAI-ETTE: But the children—

GAIA: The children don't get satire. The children need to know how everyone on this planet pulled together, how nations—even nations that *hated* each other—and people, young old rich poor, finally were at a place where they had no choice but to agree to make *changes* in their lives—

GAIALEE: Well, in all honesty, most of them were near death—

GAIA: But they finally did and we created a new green order for a new green planet and lo and behold people actually got jobs creating this new green earth, and people were no longer stuck with toxic waste dumps in their neighborhoods or food deserts or skies full of smog, and people started to trust, and it was hard work, and everyone had to be involved, and that was hard to do, to get *everyone* involved, but they did, they pitched in and—now here we are, on an earth that survived, and the planet isn't dying anymore. So we celebrate that. With the Pageant. We celebrate *that*. The effort. Not a fantasy.

GAI-ETTE: Can't we keep the Unicorn Tears part and the song, just as a little, you know, fun part—which we can label *fun* and say over and over again this is not *real*—

GAIALEE: That ruins it for the kids.

GAI-ETTE: And then just pass out a little flyer that has all the boring stuff?

GAIA: And who exactly is going to read the flyer? They're all just going to sing the Unicorn Tears song and forget everything else.

GAIALEE: Yeah. I guess. Damn. I hate when you're right.

GAI-ETTE: Oh, not you too!

GAIALEE: We have to perform the boring stuff. We just do.

GAI-ETTE: I just love that little Unicorn Tears song so much . . .

GAIA: I know. I know you do. But it's time to make sure the children know the truth of how we got here.

GAIALEE: And it wasn't magic.

GAI-ETTE: No. It wasn't. I know. (*Sighs.*) OK. So who's going to contact the old folks for the reciting of the Honors of the Elders . . .

GAIALEE: And why don't they come to these damned meetings?

GAIA: Oh, sweetie. They already paid their dues . . .

(*The GAIAS get to work. Lights fade.*)

END OF PLAY

DREAM/REMEMBER

Hanna Cormick

Hanna Cormick is a Finnish Australian with Sámi ancestors, living in Ngunnawal country. She works across the fields of performance art and curation, and crip activism. Her recent performance artwork, *The Mermaid*, was featured at the 2020 Sydney Festival and was nominated for the 2018 Disability Leadership Institute award (Arts) and the Chief Minister's award (Young Leader). Her current practice is a reclamation of body through radical visibility.

Playwright's Statement

When I tried to imagine a path to my ideal green justice-led future, it wasn't as easy as I anticipated. In the age of capitalism, dreaming and hope have become subversive acts; the status quo is adept at clipping the wings of dreams and squashing fantasies, making it hard for us to imagine the tangible path between where we are and where we want to get to. But there are fragments we do know: ideas that ignite our hearts, or fill us with unexpected hope, clues from the past, from earlier decades' or centuries' ways of living, or Indigenous ways of living, new systems we are starting to integrate, or fundamental values that we want to live by; maybe time is a bit fluid and there are lots of clues to what we are yearning for hiding inside our bodies, our unvoiced wishes, our ancestral sensations, that can be "remembered"— reaching beyond what we already know to touch the things that lie just outside the edges of our imaginative map. I wanted to create a ritual to allow sacred space for that dreaming/remembering, and to feel the potency of imagining and moving forward into unknown territories as a collective act.

A participatory ritual of mass dreaming, a guided visualization, a choreography, a story, or any of the things in between.

Note

For one or many performers.

Lie down and lead a guided visualization. Make it a podcast, make it a dance track.

Or dance it as a choreographic score.

Or dream it. Or perform it like a play. Or read it as a bedtime story.

Go do it for real: step into a lake, or ocean water, or a field, or the imagined lake of a stage.

This is a flexible script—

Attribute text how you wish, among one or many.

Let the text of dreaming-remembering flow, overlapping one another, if you wish, and be free for you or the audience to add your own future-memories.

Let the places and references be switched for your own, if you wish.

Any words may be translated into first, second, or third person text.

Any words may be translated into movement or image instead of spoken.

If you enact this as a participatory event, ensure you build time and space for audience after-care; a space to safely return (and dry off, if necessary), maybe share experiences or connect, or to sit and reflect.

• • •

We have come
Gathered at the side of the lake
And my toes are sinking into the coffee-black sludge
It's cold and thick
It stains our skin in tiny speckles up our calves
Itching with small insects

Holding each other's hands, or wherever we hold each other with whatever we hold with
I think the line stretches around the whole four-kilometer perimeter
A full circle
Elsewhere, other gatherings dip their feet
In the scratch of sand before the curling lip and salt tang of waves
Or pebbles that push into the muscles of your soles

With insistence and enduring grace
Or jagged edges that spur your step into the water

The whole planet over, we gather
Just like us who encircle this lake
To enact a ritual of dreaming—no—
. . . Remembering
Remembering forward to what has not yet happened

A tender tightening against my palm: we have begun

The very edge of the water
Was sharp
As an intake of breath

And the thick silt caresses
Our toes
As it melts off
Under the lapping
Water's tongue

Water that gripped around the ankle
Pulling gently
Because we lingered still in the shallow
No one leading, leading each other
Led by the lake
So many of us, side by side

The submerged part of your body is gliding slow into sinking
And the other part of you still rising upwards in this world of above

Listening for the tinsel rustle and chimes of the birch leaves quivering in a
channel of wind
Trying to catch the half whispers
Attuning to the language
You had forgotten
You had never yet learned
But which that dreaming part of you
Still half almost remembers

Don't you feel that?
Like something
Maybe not your own memory

Maybe something
Older
I don't know how to name it
The language was stolen
But I feel it
You do, too
We feel it in the way the old order didn't fit and our spirits twitched and
struggled against it
We recognise when a thought approaches it, and tears and laughter
suddenly spill into your mouth out of nowhere
We sense it like something glimpsed by the back of your head, whispered
from behind the curve of your ear

Together
Dreaming back or remembering forward
At the edge of history
Outside the border of imagination

The slip of a fish through your hand in the water
Quick and
Gone

Listen
Listen
Listen
Step deeper
I chose this lake because it is from my homeland
By the farmhouse in the forest on the land where I was born

I chose this lake because I was thinking
Of learning what wild things are carried in my blood that are not disease,
but memory and ritual
To remember the scent of pine needles, and the taste of birch tree flesh, the
sweet blood of cloudberries, the comfort of the color of snow at the blue
hour

I'm thinking of growing out my roots
I'm thinking of letting the other roots reach in through my walls, opening
cracks through which to connect

Knee-deep in the water
I try to shuffle off my fear of cliché

With some half-joke about
Middle-aged bourgeois women reconnecting with ancestry
A young Noongar woman, to my right in the circle, in a calmness that lands
so gently that it cuts right through the clamor of my shame says:
That's the colonizer's narrative

My embarrassment doesn't disappear, but it falls back like an echo on the
shoreline
Accept
That on the way to where we are going, I will appear foolish
That, as someone with colonizer's blood mingled in my veins, there's no
graceful way out of this place
Go through the mud
You will slip and fall, accept the dirt on your face
Some might be graceful, but not you
But keep going
Stepping forward
stepping with whatever you step with

Because some of us in the circle don't walk
And I don't walk well or far
And I leave my wheelchair at the edge of the lake
Not because I don't still need it
—there's no miracle story here—
Except the miracle that my body is as welcome in this lake as any other body
That my crutches help lift me in the water
And when they cease to, that I'm supported by the multitangle of arms of
people around me
And the lake itself
That we all together, and with the lake too, support any body however it
needs to be supported
And holding each other up
Doesn't feel heavy at all, it feels like an embrace
Because there is no right way to be in the lake, except to be in it together

We go deeper
The shock of the water surprises sounds out of our mouths
We start to remember
Or we forget to forget

Snippets of memory-dreams
Jumping into the air:
You say your granddaughter has gone to **** to study earth advocacy
You say the glyphosate reparations built organic gardens for each village in
****

How the boots of your lover tread dust from the solar farm through the
house

There's a moment where I
Think about turning back
I wonder if other people linger on the shore
Or didn't come out here into the middle of the forest to walk into a cold lake
with no purpose
Except
What?
That's the colonizer's narrative

That hope must be
Piecemeal, small, achievable
And fully laid out as a plan before you embark

Keep stepping forward

The cold is lifting our voices out of us
Unexpectedly
At our hips
The woman next to me starts laughing hysterically from the cold water
In between shrieks of laughter she starts to
Spill out words about how she'd always wanted to keep bees
How she now tended to hives built in her apartment complex garden
Free housing pods built during the climate refugee reform
That sat near a ring of blossoming fruit trees where the bees would dance
around each morning
And in spring, she'd sit with her coffee, watching the slow dance of them
visiting the flowers
Dipping heads up to their waists in yellow pollen dust
And in summer the hot smell of the fruit in the evening
would be full in the air
As small children climbed and clung in the branches, throwing small fruit
down to each other

As they taught each other words from their own languages for the sweet tasting gifts
Exchanging taste and tongue

A whisper ripples down the line
A child over on the eastern flank of the circle
Has begun talking about Universal Basic Services and the demonetisation of labor

A man to the west is remembering the patients' strike, where he and other nurses and unwaged carers helped barricade city intersections, and the sick and injured stared down the unmoving cars

Someone remembers when their company's plastic permit was revoked

There's a secret bubbling to the south about the Robin Hood rebellion, and the billionaire bosses, bankers, and oil-barons whose heads were hoisted high and their accounts drained dry

Someone remembers the rewilding of Berlin, and the surprise glimpses of the plants and predators that reclaimed the deasphalted streets

And land return and reparations
Running swift alongside
The language reclamation, when we scrubbed the
Scars off our maps
And gave the old names back to the land

And then we slowed down
Because progress doesn't mean speed
And the wind blows around us quick like change
But our movement, as a species, through the day
We can slow all that right
Right
.

.

Down

We slowed down
We took time
We gave time
We spent our attention, our care
We no longer counted cost using money
We no longer counted growth using money

An older woman, who I think I maybe recognize, her shawl billows up
around her shoulders in the water
And she is singing the wounds of the land

To grieve what was taken, stolen, hurt
To grieve the trees empty of lichen, the snow empty of the reindeer's tread
And I didn't see those things but I feel like they are pieces of meat carved
out of my own heart
It feels like the hurt was done to me too
We all recognize the grief we feel for the earth
That we have pretended was an empathy
But was really a very intimate and personal heartbreak
A betrayal
We each felt
We each were harmed by
And reaching through the water, we place our hands on the cracks in each
other's hearts
And we cry together
Salt water flowing into the cold freshwater lake
Because both our hope and our grief must be supported together

And water under our noses
With those petrol-tasting coughs
When you almost inhale
Do you remember what's beneath
In the dark water under your feet?
When it felt like the whole sky had been poured down into the mouth of the
mountain
And you lay cradled in the serene vastness?

At first it seemed uncomfortable

But it's not uncomfortable
Just different
We held each other and stepped forward

Trying to dream
Trying to remember
You talked about the solar farm dust on your lover's boots

END OF PLAY

BOOK OF G

Nelson Diaz-Marcano

Nelson Diaz-Marcano is a Puerto Rican, New York City–based theater-maker, activist, and community leader who serves as the literary manager of the Latinx Playwright Circle, as well as the Community Outreach Coordinator for Atlantic Theater Company. His plays have been developed by Clubbed Thumb, Ensemble Studio Theatre, The Lark, Vision Latino Theater Company, Milagro Theatre, The William Inge Theatre Festival, Classical Theatre of Harlem, and The Parsnip Ship, among others.

Playwright's Statement

What inspired me to write this play was the question of how I would envision a world in which the Green New Deal would exist. I couldn't see it. As a person obsessed with sci-fi and magic, the Green New Deal sounds too much like a deus ex machina device, a too-good-to-be-true solution to tie up loose ends. The only way I could make sense of the last four years and the Green New Deal was to see it as a narrative series made to entertain those who do not have to live it. And most importantly, to see what happens when your values and your art have to coexist.

• • •

A woman comes in, dressed as anybody, at a time no one knows, yet feels familiar—current and past.

The woman seems tired as she waters plants. She looks at the sky before taking a peek down. She sighs as if the ground she looks at was the sky instead.

Suddenly a book is thrown past her and it falls on the hole.

The woman sees the book, then looks back. She is not surprised to see who is there. Z, a young, nonbinary individual comes in, hand over their mouth in disbelief.

Z: Sorry, ma'

MOTHER: Hmm-hmm.

Z: It's just like—

MOTHER: What?

Z: That Green New Deal, really?!

MOTHER: Yeah—

Z: That's the best Millennial could come up with?!

MOTHER: Call him Milli, he doesn't like the full name.

Z: It's another crappy *deus ex machina* cliffhanger that really creates more problems than not.

MOTHER: How so?

Z: How am I supposed to write the next chapter in the Book of Generations series if they are giving me such—

MOTHER: They all do it. Xennial didn't give much for Millennial to work with. A global recession—and let's not forget X just up and left after he started the Persian Gulf War and never finished it. At least Milli is giving you—

Z: A fix-it-all solution.

MOTHER: Well—

Z: Let's get racism and social restructuring together—

MOTHER: One does feed the other.

Z: Oh great, let's also bring up the fact that the planet is dying and tackle all that eco-babble here like the planet dying hasn't been the biggest threat since Sibling Greatest Generation wrote the World War II chapter.

MOTHER: Z, Sibling GG created a whole reset with that chapter.

Z: How am I supposed to do this, ma'?

MOTHER: With patience.

Z: Patience?! None of my Siblings have written something that has led to me having patience. What they have written until now has left us with Milli having to come up with the fix-all Green New Deal because nothing else can tie up the millions of loose threads, save us from the messy situations and downright stupid decisions that Siblings Boomer, X, and Xennial created from Sibling GG's foundation. Milli is trying out of nowhere to steer the course of this series but—

MOTHER: But—

Z: But if the Green New Deal is it, maybe this Book of Generations series needs to go.

MOTHER: Ok.

(*MOTHER smiles.*)

Z: Ok?

MOTHER: If you don't think you can make something good out of it maybe this series needs to end. Time, your father, has been saying for years that this series is a cruel exercise anyways.

Z: Yet we keep writing it.

MOTHER: The gods love it the more drama it has.

Z: Is not sustainable!

MOTHER: Yet each one of them gives us more of their humans each year because they can't get enough.

Z: What if I just write something boring?

MOTHER: Boring?

Z: What if humanity gets it together and starts working toward betterment?

MOTHER: That's an idea. One I heard many times.

Z: Many times?

MOTHER: Oh yeah—You know how everyone hates Boomer? They started with dreams of creating the best set of humans too.

Z: Oh please, they are the ones that created the main issue now.

MOTHER: But it started the same way. Everyone praises GG, but forgets GG ended his chapter with the beginning of the Cold War and the rise of communism. Boomer also was mad at GG and dreamed of a better world. But the thing is, Boomer never asked Greatest G why? They just got mad. Boomer had started the same way, mad at Sibling Great D for leaving him with the rise of the Third Reich as his big cliffhanger, yet it led to World War II. Without the endless wars that GG left Boomer with, the cultural revolution wouldn't have happened. The Civil Rights Movement, the—

Z: Yet here we are.

MOTHER: Yes, a step closer to that better world.

Z: How?! We are killing it.

MOTHER: Maybe so, but that chapter is for you to write.

Z: Great, I'm just left with the modern rise of white supremacy and a Green New Deal as a Band-Aid.

MOTHER: Or is it a plot device? A starter? The Book of Generations is a long series, my offspring. Many cycles, many recycled plots, many stories left unfinished or unexplored. Maybe the answers lie in looking at those. In history.

> (*Z looks defiantly, but can't keep it up for long. They then look longingly to where they threw the book.*)

Z: I guess you can say at least the planet is being talked about more.

MOTHER: Yes, all of them have focused so much on the social aspects, they have neglected the earth.

Z: How?

MOTHER: By giving them the least of development. Now we can't ignore it no more.

Z: No not that—how do I make sure I don't fall for the same trap when I grow older?

> (*MOTHER tries to look for an answer but shrugs at the end.*)

Z: Great, so the Green New Deal . . .

MOTHER: Unravel it.

Z: Right.

MOTHER: You are still young, the answers may not be obvious yet.

Z: Fine, fine, I'll go and try to figure this whole thing out.

MOTHER: That's my kid.

Z: But—

MOTHER: You always have your buts—

Z: If Father Time thinks this is such a cruel exercise, why keep it going?

MOTHER: Because I tell him so. It's our responsibility, after creating all these characters, to guide them to a great conclusion. Where they need to be.

Z: And where is that?

MOTHER: I don't know, you tell me.

(Z takes a second and like a petulant child, they throw their arms in the air.)

Z: Fine! But if I see Milli—

MOTHER: Send them my love.

Z: Oh I will. That and some more!

(Z stomps out. MOTHER laughs.)

MOTHER: Another one ends, and another begins. What says you, Time, do we make it better this time?

(She snickers, finishes watering the plants.)

MOTHER: We'll see.

(A crying baby is heard.)

MOTHER: There's Alpha just in time. I'm coming!

(She laughs, leaves the watering can, and as she starts making sounds to the baby, the plants start to shine.)

END OF PLAY

HOW TO HOLD WATER: A SPELL FOR ADAPTIVE LIVING

Erika Dickerson-Despenza

Erika Dickerson-Despenza is a poet-playwright and cultural-memory worker from Chicago, Illinois. Awards: Susan Smith Blackburn Prize Finalist (2021), Laurents/Hatcher Foundation Award (2020), Thom Thomas Award (2020), Lilly Award (2020), Barrie and Bernice Stavis Award (2020), Grist 50 Fixer (2020), Princess Grace Playwriting Award (2019). Currently, Erika is developing a ten-play Katrina Cycle, including *hieroglyph* and *shadow/land*, focused on the effects of Hurricane Katrina and its state-sanctioned, man-made disaster rippling in and beyond New Orleans.

Playwright's Statement

how to hold water: a spell for adaptive living was inspired by the Greater New Orleans Urban Water Plan, "Living With Water." The play offers a very introductory answer to the question: What is a queer Black socialist feminist response to climate change in New Orleans? I weave science fiction and a re/visioning of the Yoruba orisha, Oshun, within the work to offer a vision of an abolitionist ecology and to urge us to see climate change action as spiritual work.

Characters

SHUN (shoon), an ageless, beautiful Black woman cancer survivor dressed in the finest yellow-gold and K&B purple. a peacock feather ornaments her clothes. she is the City's mirror.

FLO, late teens or older. a keeper and conjurer. wears all white. shun's
daughter.

Setting

new orleans. june. the year 2050.

• • •

*a beautified excavated waterway & public park. the grass is a brilliant emerald
jewel beneath FLO's bare feet. SHUN sits on a bench applying makeup in a gold
compact mirror. a canopy of strong oak shields her face from the sun or makes
the skin between slits of shadow gleam all the more.*

FLO: you a story

SHUN: i aint / honest! /
used to be a wall there /
concrete

FLO: a concrete wall? / to hold back water? /
didn't they know water aint never honored no boundaries?

SHUN: she was not a welcomed guest

FLO: that don't make sense / the city is a sun belt island /
water will be here long after we gone / we the guests

SHUN: ev'ry time they erected one of them floodwalls the concrete started
crackin & my cancer come back

FLO: what the floodwalls got to do with yr cancer?

SHUN: yr guess bout good as mine / doctors down at charity said it was
some kind of rare alkali-aggregate reaction / they hadn't seen nothin like it
before / called it "concrete cancer" / made the skin all cross my body a veiny
breach / split open / but i never bled / just had water pourin right out my
cracks / naturally i was dehydrated all the time / couldn't bear a noonday
sun in those days

(SHUN basks in the sunlight & stretches her mouth into a wide grin.)

FLO: so the walls come down & bam / you was healed? / just like that?

SHUN: well the floodwalls aint just come down themselves / after we abolished the military & established the community nonviolent defense force / the people vowed to stop makin an enemy outta water / built rain gardens / bulldozed the floodwalls / made these water gardens & pretty lil waterways / the more the people made room for the water / the more they saw her beauty / the more my skin stopped bucklin under itself / started to scab / heal

(FLO starts dancing. she is a woman making room for something greater than herself, but very much like herself: feminine, divine, fluid.)

SHUN: what are you doin?

FLO: choreographin a spell

SHUN: a spell?

FLO: for the future / so they will know what to do in some other place when somebody's body is grievin the water / that's what it sound like was happenin to you / you was grievin the water & the people aint know a sure remedy / but you was healed in the process of another healin / we gotta make a record / draft a spell so they know for sure next time / which is this time right now someplace else / & if they forget the words / or healin cant be spoken of in that place then they can move the spell through their hips / wind it round their shoulders & stomp it out of their feet & it'll still work

(FLO begins her sacred work. new, exacting movements find her with each line.)

FLO: how to hold water / a spell for adaptive livin /
when the ground puckers beneath yr feet / thank the earth
for its warnin / wipe *drain-pipe-pump* from yr memory /
eat a bitter leaf to thwart its return / place a spoonful
of raw honey under yr tongue / chant *detain-infiltrate-filter*
five times / offer a peacock feather to sweet water /
cup yr hands round her mouth & see her
quickly escape your grasp / this is how to hold water:
dont / let water hold you

(SHUN has disappeared. the waterway glistens & SHUN's peacock feather & mirror are left at the mouth of the water. FLO dances & chants.)

FLO: *you are welcome*
you are welcome
you are welcome here / oshun
we make room
we make room
we make room

END OF PLAY

THE PERSISTENCE OF POSSIBILITY

Karen Elias

Karen Elias is a writer/activist living in rural Pennsylvania whose plays make use of the intersections between myth, ideology, and history to raise awareness about the climate crisis. She produced a Climate Change Theatre Action event, "Act Like Our Lives Depend On It!," in cooperation with her local Millbrook Playhouse in 2019.

Playwright's Statement

This play has three sources of inspiration: the near-destruction of Paradise, California, by fire in 2018; the Sumerian myth of "Inanna's Descent to the Underworld,"* which gave me the characters of the Earth Mother and her flies; and the bravery and passion of today's young climate activists.**

Characters

NARRATOR
ERESHKIGAL, Queen of the Underworld
FLIES, young actors (can be male or female, any race or ethnicity) who are
    dressed as flies, with large eyes and wings, as though costumes for a play

Setting

The Heart of the Earth

---

* See *Inanna, Queen of Heaven and Earth, Her Stories and Hymns from Sumer* by Diane Wolkstein and Samuel Noah Kramer (New York: Harper and Row, 1983).
** The discussion of the Sunrise protest is taken from Varshini Prakash's essay, "We Are Sunrise," from *All We Can Save: Truth, Courage, and Solutions for the Climate Crisis*, edited by Ayana Elizabeth Johnson and Katharine K. Wilkinson (New York: One World, 2020).

Time

The Present

. . .

NARRATOR: On the morning of November 8, 2018, a faulty power line belonging to the electric service provider Pacific Gas and Electric caused a power outage four miles east of Paradise, California, a region desiccated by months of drought. A fire that started on a canyon ledge was inaccessible to fire trucks. And the wind, described as "roaring like a jet engine," drove the fire toward town. One onlooker saw a "bulging whirlwind of flame and smoke that was sucking debris from the ground, setting it alight and rocketing it into the sky . . . It sounded like a freight train going around," she said. "There was nothing earthly about it." The fire, considered the deadliest in 100 years, would claim 85 lives in Paradise and destroy 90 percent of the town.

(The following is set in the heart of the earth where ERESHKIGAL, the Underworld's queen, is in mourning. The FLIES, sent by the God of Wisdom, have slipped through the gates of the Underworld to bear witness to her pain.)

ERESHKIGAL: Oh! My children!

FLIES: (*Mirroring.*) Oh! Your children!

ERESHKIGAL: Oh! My careless children!

FLIES: Oh! Your careless children!

(Gradually the sound of wildfires grows louder in this next section, followed by the noise of helicopters overhead.)

FLY ONE: I was excited. I was going to be in a play. But by first period the smoke was so bad, we had to come in from the playground. It looked like the sun was setting, even though the day had just begun. Ms. Patterson called our parents to come pick us up, but ours didn't answer. They couldn't be reached.

FLY TWO: She gave us snacks and played Simon Says with us. Then someone came in to say the buses were waiting and we had to hurry. Outside the school there was smoke and darkness. And wind. It looked like midnight. When we went around the corner, we saw there were no buses. They had already left.

ERESHKIGAL: Oh! My blustering winds, my ragged breath!

FLIES: Oh! Your blustering winds, your ragged breath!

FLY ONE: Ms. Patterson flagged down someone she knew, a lady named Penny.

FLY TWO: She had a big car. We piled in.

FLY ONE: The road was packed with cars. Everyone was on the road. We could hardly move.

FLY TWO: The fire was catching up to us. I looked out the window and saw embers flying on the wind like falling snow. I saw the trees. They were lighting each other on fire, one after the other. Too fast.

ERESHKIGAL: Oh! My scattered bones, my running feet!

FLIES: Oh! Your scattered bones, your running feet!

FLY ONE: We had the air conditioning on in the car. But the windows were burning hot. Penny said not to touch them. She yelled at us.

FLY TWO: In front of us, cars were empty and on fire. We couldn't move. Penny pounded on the steering wheel. She shouted, "Go! Go! Goddammit, go!"

ERESHKIGAL: Oh! My raging fires, my blistering flesh!

FLIES: Oh! Your raging fires, your blistering flesh!

FLY ONE: Ms. Patterson was saying "Please, oh please," over and over.

FLY TWO: But then a bulldozer came. It pushed the empty cars out of the way and made a path. Penny said, "We're stepping on it!"

FLY ONE: We made it out of there. It took three hours.

FLY TWO: That night we saw on TV that our school had burned to the ground.

ERESHKIGAL: Oh! My breaking heart!

FLIES: Oh! Our breaking hearts!

ERESHKIGAL: (*Looks at the FLIES.*) I know who you are. You are the creatures who see from many angles. You see the discarded scrap and the begging bowl. The bubble wrap caught in the foam and the ocean itself. The sweat on the skin from aspiration, the salt on the skin from fear. You are the ones who fly through the cracks, the annoying ones, the messengers. Go out from here. Tell my children Paradise is burning. Persist until they pay attention. Persist until they pour out of their houses and into the streets, demanding change. Now go! Hurry! Before it's too late!

NARRATOR: In November 2018, as images of the California fires blazed on congressional TVs, 200 youth activists from the Sunrise Movement poured into Nancy Pelosi's office, like flies, to demand that the Democratic Party support the Green New Deal. Young activists, in the United States and elsewhere, thereby moved the issue of climate change to the top of our national agenda. Three months later, in February 2019, an historic Green New Deal resolution was introduced that defined the terms of governmental climate action and made such action a real possibility. (*Beat.*) It's a beginning. Go. Hurry. It's not too late.

END OF PLAY

US IN THE PAST

Nathan Ellis

Nathan Ellis is from the United Kingdom and is based between London and Berlin. He was a member of the Royal Court Invitation Writers' Supergroup 2018–2019 led by Alice Birch and Ali Mcdowall. His plays include *No One Is Coming to Save You* (published by Oberon) and *work.txt*. In 2020, his play *SUPER HIGH RESOLUTION* was short-listed for the Verity Bargate Award.

Playwright's Statement

The inspiration for the play is the exciting impossibility of imagining together: the simple knowledge that what I see in my head when I say "bridge" is different to what you see. Plays are obviously live objects, but this is trying to be as present tense as possible, trying to build a real sense of a live, unrepeatable experience shared by a group. It's loosely based on Brecht's *Lehrstücke* so if you're interested in this kind of work, that's a good place to go looking.

Note

The play is performed by a group of people, sight unseen, all together. It doesn't require performers—it just requires the audience to speak together—so it's very free how you manage it. It's about bridges and working together.

You could send the text of the play as a PDF or you could project it line-by-line. Probably don't print it—I'm sure there are lots of other imaginative solutions to getting a crowd to speak as a group. Try to make it as accessible as possible and don't stress if you want to change any of the words I've written here to make it feel more comfortable.

You might need someone to set out some rules at the beginning, depending on how the group works out, but in my experience with these kinds of things, people are happy to work together when they're clear about what they're up against. Have fun: don't be afraid that it won't work.

• • •

ONE PERSON SAYS THIS OUT LOUD:
Once upon a time,
On a day much like today,
In a place much like this one.
A group of people,
Human
Beings,
Joined together to speak as one.

EVERYONE READS THIS OUT LOUD TOGETHER:
They spoke the same words
At the same time.
Words they'd never read before
But had decided to read out loud.
And decided to tell a story.

A CONFIDENT PERSON SAYS THIS:
I don't like this.
I'd rather we spoke separately.

EVERYONE SAYS THIS:
Why?

THE CONFIDENT PERSON SAYS THIS:
Well, it's always frustrating talking as a group,
And some people aren't talking at all,
I don't see why we can't just read in our heads.

A PERSON WHO LOVES A THEATRICAL EXPERIMENT SAYS THIS:
I think it's fun!
It's so modern!

A PERSON WHO LIKES TRADITIONAL THEATRE SAYS THIS:
I hope it's not long.

A HELPFUL WOMAN SAYS THIS:
I understand this sort of thing isn't for everyone,
But it's short,
It won't take long,
And when we're done,
We can go back to talking as individuals.

EVERYONE SAYS THIS:
OH.
KAY.

   (A pause.)

A GEMINI SAYS THIS:
I wonder what the story is?

   (A pause.)

A MARRIED PERSON SAYS THIS:
One day some people decided to build a bridge
To get from
A
To
B.
They set about it very carefully.
On a very hot day
When the river was low
And the sun was high and bold in the sky,
A group of people toiled in the sun
Trying to figure out how the heck to get the stones to stay upright on top of
each other,
Patting each other on the back whenever things went well,
Being very dramatic and angry when things didn't go well,
And by the end of a few days,
They had a bridge
Connecting
A
To

A PERSON WITH KIDS SAYS THIS:
B.
That's how bridges get made.
Someone decides they need to get something from A to B,
And imagines a world where A is connected to B.
And then a lot of people work very hard to make that happen.

A PERSON WHO OWNS A LOT OF BOOKS SAYS THIS:
The oldest bridge in the world still
in use is from 850 BC.

It is still standing in Izmir, in Turkey.
It is a stone bridge, with a big arch,
In the hot sun.
850 BC—I don't need to tell you clever people—
Was when Homer, the Greek poet, was alive.
And he was from Izmir,
So, we can imagine Homer,
With his big beard because he was so old and wise,
Walking over this stone bridge
On a really very hot day.

A PERSON WHO KNOWS NOTHING ABOUT HOMER SAYS THIS:
The people who built
the bridge in Izmir
Were doing it for very practical reasons:
A to B.
There was no bit in their minds that said
"In nearly 3,000 years, a person who owns a lot of books will tell a group of
people about this bridge."
Nobody thought that, as they lugged the huge stones
And did all the things that people do to build a bridge
"Imagine if this bridge were here in 3,000 years."
It would be really weird if someone had thought that
Or said that out loud.
Everyone would have laughed and thought that was really weird.
Particularly Homer.
Because he had a great sense of humor
And was always laughing at other people and cracking great jokes.
Probably.

TWO PEOPLE WHO KNOW EACH OTHER SAY THIS TOGETHER:
The people who built
the bridge in Izmir,
2,850 years ago,
Weren't trying to solve a crisis.
They were trying to make things better,
Easier.
Get from
A
To
B.

AN OLDER PERSON SAYS THIS:
I crossed the bridge in Izmir once.
On a sunny day.
I don't mean I crossed it in 850 BC.
I am not that old.
I crossed the bridge a few years ago on holiday.
It was fine.
The fridge magnet I got was not very nice.

AN OPTIMIST SAYS THIS:
A bridge is an imaginative object.
We can all imagine bridges in our minds
And these bridges might never have existed,
But their ability to be imagined is transformative.
And what we know from the bridge at Izmir
Is that bridges last a very long time.
There are all sorts of boring, practical desires.

A PERSON WHO NEEDS A HAIRCUT SAYS THIS:
I need a haircut,
On the other side of that river.

A PERSON WHO IS IN LOVE SAYS THIS:
I need to see my partner,
On the other side of that river.

A PERSON WHO WANTS THE WORLD TO CHANGE SAYS THIS:
Perhaps the world is
completely different,
On the other side of that river.

THE OPTIMIST SAYS THIS:
And those kinds of boring,
Practical desires
To build bridges
Can lead us forwards.

A PERSON WHO OFTEN REMEMBERS THEIR DREAMS SAYS THIS:
Imagine it is 2,870 years
In the future
And a group of human people
Meet as a group
And agree that they need a new bridge.

And they will look at the bridges,
The practical decisions
We have taken right now,
Us in the past,
Them in the future.
Imagine what they might say.

EVERYONE SAYS THIS TOGETHER:
Once upon a time,
On a day much like today,
In a place much like this one,
A group of people,
Human
Beings,
Joined together to speak as one.
To speak the same words
At the same time.
Words they'd never read before
But had decided to read out loud.
We come at the end of a line of
100 billion people.
10,000 generations of human beings
And all their collective work.
And at the end of that line is us.
And it is up to us whether there will be a bridge
Or not.
All we have to do
Is imagine.

> *(Everyone imagines the same bridge*
> *3,000 years in the future.*
> *They can see the hot sun on the bridge*
> *And the beautiful way the people of the future will marvel at it.*
> *They will be impressed by our foresight*
> *And our ability to work together,*
> *And the people in the future will think about us in the past*
> *And want to show they are impressed.*
> *So they will clap.*
> *Everyone applauds.)*

END OF PLAY

MIZHAKWAD
(THE SKY IS CLEAR)

Dylan Thomas Elwood

Dylan Thomas Elwood is Turtle Mountain Chippewa. He has been a member of Red Eagle Soaring (RES) Native Youth Theatre, located in Seattle, Washington, for sixteen years. He has acted in and cowritten numerous productions and engaged with the Seattle Native community, culminating in the premiere of his production *Killer Whale and the Black Rush* at ACT Theatre in August 2019. He currently serves RES and YTT (Yesterday-Today-Tomorrow) as Artistic Associate.

Playwright's Statement

My inspiration for this work comes from a place of deep-seated anxiety and dread. The Earth is changing, and perhaps not taking us with her. We are living each day in a slow, sliding apocalypse, one that Indigenous people have grown all too accustomed to. Unless we embrace our connection with our land and our animal cousins, the snow will blow on each of our graves, and the dollar sign will be our collective epitaph.

Characters

COYOTE, male.
SUN, female.
BLACK SNAKE, any gender.
RAVEN, female.
SUIT, male.

. . .

Lights up on a twisted, decayed forest clearing. Fireflies hang in the air, giving off a faint blue glow. The trees dotted around the stage are skeletal, heavy with black moss and dripping oil. The ground is cracked and barren.

COYOTE sits on his knees center stage, his head hung in sorrow. He wears tattered leather clothes, a beaded choker, and fur over his sleeves. He gradually lifts his head, staring into the audience.

COYOTE: It was all a long dream. A wish. A promise. Soft grass underfoot. Crisp air on my face. The warm kiss of that lucky old Sun.

> *(SUN enters stage right. She wears a brilliant yellow dress, sparkling with crystals and shards of mirror. She dances a slow step toward COYOTE. He does not react.)*

COYOTE: But one day, even old Sun cast her gaze away in shame. She took a look over Turtle Island, and screamed out, "how could it come to this?"

> *(SUN stops her dance and looks around the trees. She grabs her head and shrieks, falling to her knees.)*

SUN: HOW COULD IT COME TO THIS?

COYOTE: The Black Snake covered Sun's eyes, tried to quiet her cries, and now all that falls on us is venomous rain.

> *(BLACK SNAKE enters stage right. They are a mass of torn black and gray fabric, gloved and clawed hands, tentacles and smoke. They wrap their arms around SUN's head lovingly, and slowly tear her offstage right.)*

COYOTE: When Sun went away for the winter, she took all her warmth with her. Where once the rivers ran, now they crawled, bubbling and sour. The grasses bent sideways and curled up brown. The trees fell around their roots, and made their quiet exit.

> *(RAVEN enters stage left with a limp. She wears gray and dark blue scarves, with red paint spiraling her cheeks. She kneels to the ground, lifting stagnant water to her mouth. She winces as it touches her lips, and begins to retch silently.*
>
> *BLACK SNAKE enters stage right, drifting around the stage in a slow, crooked dance. They curl around RAVEN's back, massaging her shoulders. Their touch seems to drain RAVEN's energy, and she begins to droop over. BLACK SNAKE releases her, and runs their hands over the trees.)*

COYOTE: The Black Snake took us all in its coil; its scales touched the sky, its fangs pierced the water. It doesn't mean us harm, it truly never did. It is like a child, unknowing of the pain its power can cause. But its thirst is insatiable, its belly aches unrelenting. And it feeds on our negative thoughts, our greed and malicious urges.

(BLACK SNAKE wafts behind COYOTE, planting a small kiss on the top of his forehead.)

COYOTE: Its breath . . . fills this land with sorrow. Our sorrow is the mother of hate, and hate is the little brother of war.

(BLACK SNAKE caresses COYOTE's forehead and lies down in front of him, running their fingers along his arms and chest.)

COYOTE: But we are not at war with the poison water, or the white frost, or the choking air. We are at war with ourselves.

(SUIT comes running onstage right. He wears tattered, oil-streaked Wall Street attire. He carries a metal pipe and lunges at RAVEN. RAVEN shrieks a war cry and rises to meet him. SUIT swings the pipe at her but she catches it, and a tug of war ensues over the weapon. BLACK SNAKE rises up beside COYOTE, watching the melee, clapping their hands with glee.)

COYOTE: Please . . . how could it come to this?

(RAVEN knocks SUIT to his back and begins bludgeoning him with the pipe. BLACK SNAKE gets to their feet and dances around the scene, their movements growing chaotic, following no rhythm or beat.)

COYOTE: Is there still time? (Beat.) STOP! PLEASE STOP!

(RAVEN stops her assault and turns to COYOTE, panting. BLACK SNAKE abruptly stops their dance, confused. COYOTE shakily rises to his feet, turning to RAVEN.)

COYOTE: Please . . . it's not too late. It can't be.

(RAVEN drops the metal pipe to the stage. SUIT gasps and holds his chest. RAVEN approaches COYOTE and embraces him tightly.)

RAVEN: I'm sorry, old friend.

COYOTE: Don't be, my love. We will know that blue again. Mizhakwad, can't you see it?

(RAVEN turns to look stage right.)

RAVEN: I . . . I can't! I can't see a thing!

COYOTE: Look my love, she's come to see us again.

(SUN gently enters stage right, carrying a luminous torch. It radiates light across the stage. RAVEN turns to face SUN. COYOTE holds RAVEN around her waist, hugging her close. SUIT rises to a sitting position, amazed by the light.

BLACK SNAKE stomps in fury, running to COYOTE and RAVEN, trying desperately to pry them apart with their clawed hands. The two won't budge.

SUN holds a hand out to SUIT and lifts him to his feet. She holds the torch out to him, and he cautiously takes it.

In a fury, BLACK SNAKE rushes at SUIT. SUN claps her hands at BLACK SNAKE. THUNDERCLAP!

BLACK SNAKE is thrown to their back. COYOTE and RAVEN hold their hands out to SUIT. He slowly approaches them. They step to either side of him, kneeling down, and raising their hands in gratitude. SUIT's shoulders begin to quake as he falls into sobs. SUN comes up behind SUIT and holds him in a motherly embrace.)

SUIT: I'm sorry, I'm so sorry . . .

COYOTE: It's alright. The Black Snake has not yet awakened. See to it their eyes stay closed.

(SUIT leans his head into SUN's neck.)

SUN: Do not be afraid.

END OF PLAY

MOO! BE QUIET! LAMBCHOP'S SECRET MISSION TO STEAL EVERY COW IN THE WORLD

Alister Emerson

Alister Emerson is a playwright and the artistic director of Duck Bunny Theatre, a small but feisty theatre company using satirical humor to comment on the absurdity of corporate stupidity, greed, and corruption. His recent plays include *The Fridge, Six Polar Bears Fell Out of the Sky This Morning*, and *Ed Sheeran Tastes Like Chicken*, a play about the plight of the endangered Māui dolphins which debuted at the Nelson Fringe Festival and was short-listed for the NZ Playmarket Plays for the Young.

Playwright's Statement

Those who are observant may have spotted that "Moo! Be Quiet!" is another way of saying "Shut up, cow!" This play was inspired by the courage and work of Alexandria Ocasio-Cortez in the face of resistance and opposition. I have seen countless speakers (typically middle-aged white men) trying to justify their position and desperate to cling to the status quo. Typically, the conservative position attempts to oversimplify and reduce ideas down to a sounding board that they can beat on to drum up fear about what might be lost instead of focusing on what might be gained. The rallying war cry against the Green New Deal was crystallized around fear of losing hamburgers, ice creams, and jet travel.

One of the US Senators opposing the Green New Deal summed up the fears of the conservative position by saying the resolution was an opportunity for the left to "implement their radical vision for humanity." Little did he realize that those with a hope for the future don't see that as a threat but rather as an opportunity to mobilize our economy around the needs of the planet rather than the pockets of corporations and the mega-rich.

Characters

LAMBCHOP (DEREK), keen, a little bit likable but not so bright.
CELINE, Lambchop's feisty, intelligent, and strong-willed friend.
SPECIAL AGENT SNOWFLAKE, a severe and officious government-type.
SPECIAL AGENT MULLET, another severe and officious government-type.
BARRY, Lambchop's gruff and no-nonsense father.
SYLVIA, Lambchop's concerned mother.
DAISY, the cow. (This may be either a sound effect or a character,
    depending on the director's preference.)

• • •

The play begins with the sound of two people, LAMBCHOP and CELINE, struggling to sneak a cow, DAISY into the house; the audience hear banging and crashing, an occasional "Moo!" of protest from the cow, a vase being broken. The director can choose to stage this so that the audience sees the action, or have the voices from offstage, or show just the actors struggling with a cow we never see in the wings . . .

LAMBCHOP: Come on Daisy . . . get in there . . .

DAISY: Mooooooo!

LAMBCHOP: Move your rump! Are you gonna help, Celine? Can you push harder?

CELINE: Shush! Be quiet, Lambchop.

DAISY: Mooooooo!

LAMBCHOP: Daisy!

CELINE: Come on girl . . . You've just got to speak to her nicely.

LAMBCHOP: Nicely? It's just a walking hamburger. Get up there, go on, get!

DAISY: Moooooo! (*Accompanied by the sound of DAISY smashing a large vase.*)

CELINE: Look what you made her do. Come on girl, don't listen to him, he's a nasty man. Come on, who's a pretty girl? See, she likes that. You have to treat a girl with respect.

LAMBCHOP: (*Childishly mocking Celine.*) "Who's a pretty girl? You have to treat a girl with respect." Get up the stairs . . . you heffalump.

DAISY: Moooooo!

LAMBCHOP: Oww! She just bit me.

CELINE: Good girl, Daisy.

> (*Lights down on the LAMBCHOP and DAISY scene. Lights come up on SPECIAL AGENT SNOWFLAKE and SPECIAL AGENT MULLET as they step forward and address the audience.*)

SPECIAL AGENT SNOWFLAKE: March 16 started like any regular shift. At 0200 hours, Special Agent Mullet and myself, Special Agent Snowflake, responded to a Code 10-91 BK, that is a Bovine Kidnapping, and arrived in the neighborhood of Cherrywood Avenue to begin surveillance. Special Agent Mullet proceeded to record audio from the subject's house, poured her regulation soy-mocha-latte skim, stirred the drink three-and-a-half times in a clockwise direction, adjusted her waistcoat buttons, began consuming her beverage, and remarked that the evening was feeling humid and the full moon was shining bright. At 02:06, Special Agent Mullet finished her caffeinated beverage. When we heard the perps trying to coax a cow up the stairs, we knew that it was time to act. Begin transcript of follow-up interview with the parents of the offender, one Lambchop.

> (*Lights up on BARRY and SYLVIA, seated side by side on a sofa in their lounge, being interrogated by SPECIAL AGENT SNOWFLAKE and SPECIAL AGENT MULLET.*)

BARRY: Lambchop was not the brightest bulb in the packet.

SYLVIA: Don't call him Lambchop, dear, his name is Derek. You know I don't like it when you call him Lambchop, it makes him sound like a TV dinner.

BARRY: Better than Meathead, that boy is an idiot.

SYLVIA: Please, Barry, he's your son too.

BARRY: Don't remind me, Sylvia. Maybe I dropped him on his head as a baby one time too many.

SYLVIA: Don't joke about things like that, Barry. Barry is joking, right, Barry?

BARRY: Whoever said that men should bathe babies needs their head examined. They're slippery little buggers when they're soapy. Makes more sense to hold onto them with BBQ tongs, but Sylvia said, no Barry, it'll traumatize him. Make him afraid of BBQ sauce and potato salad for the rest of his life.

SYLVIA: Barry . . . I don't think the nice people want to hear about BBQ sauce and potato salad. Perhaps you should tell them what we found.

BARRY: I was . . . until someone interrupted me.

SYLVIA: No need to get snippy.

BARRY: Are you going to keep interrupting?

SYLVIA: No, dear.

BARRY: Two days ago, Lambchop did something . . .

SYLVIA: Derek.

BARRY: Sylvia!

SYLVIA: It's Derek, dear.

BARRY: Two days ago . . . Derek did something monumentally stupid, even by his standards. Apparently, the boy convinced his best friend to help him steal a cow and to make matters worse, they decided to hide it in his bedroom.

SYLVIA: And it wasn't the only one. Who knew they had six cows up there by the time we found out. Six cows . . .

> (As SYLVIA breaks down in tears and is comforted by BARRY, the focus shifts to LAMBCHOP leaning on the outside of the door to his room with CELINE. LAMBCHOP is staring in disbelief as occasional crashing noises and mooing can be heard from behind the door. As the scene progresses,

the noises from the bedroom become minimal so as not to be a distraction for the audience.)

CELINE: I can't believe you wanted to bring the cows into your house.

LAMBCHOP: We should've smuggled them into your house, it's closer to the paddock we stole the cows from.

CELINE: No, mum would've thrown a fit.

LAMBCHOP: Is she allergic to milk?

CELINE: No.

LAMBCHOP: Cheese?

CELINE: No.

LAMBCHOP: Hamburgers?

CELINE: No, you idiot, she'd freak if we turned our house into Old MacDonald's farm. Maybe you need to tell me what you are planning on doing with all of these cows in your bedroom?

LAMBCHOP: (*Breaking the fourth wall and looking directly at the audience.*) Do you think it is reasonable to expect them to believe that you have helped me to steal six cows, a task that has probably taken us about three hours, and never once during that time did it cross your mind to ask me why we were stealing the cows?

CELINE: Well, this is only a five-minute play and they weren't here when we started stealing the cows. So, they don't understand you are planning to steal all the cows in the world because you are convinced that the Green New Deal means no more cows for anyone and no more ice cream or hamburgers. I thought I would give you a chance to tell them some important exposition . . .

LAMBCHOP: Oh yes, good, good, they probably need a bit of exposition to make sense of the story.

CELINE: (*Returning to the reality of the present moment.*) So, Lambchop, what are you planning on doing with all of these cows in your bedroom?

LAMBCHOP: I think they know now.

CELINE: No, you need to say it.

LAMBCHOP: Ok, I am planning to steal all the cows in the world because I'm convinced that the Green New Deal means no more cows for anyone and no more ice cream or hamburgers.

CELINE: I don't think it says that.

LAMBCHOP: Yeah, it does. And that they are going to confiscate all planes and make us ride around on high-speed rail powered by unicorn tears.

CELINE: Ummmm . . . I don't think so.

LAMBCHOP: Yeah? What about cow farts? They destroy the planet. No cow farts means no cows. No cows, no ice cream, and no hamburgers.

CELINE: The big idea is to rethink the way we do stuff in more sustainable ways. Hopefully reducing climate damage and addressing social injustice at the same time.

LAMBCHOP: But, I love cow farts.

CELINE: Really?

LAMBCHOP: Yes. Cow farts are one of my basic human rights to enjoy. They can't take that away from me.

CELINE: You know cows belch more than they fart? Ninety to ninety-five percent of the methane emissions escape as burps because they are closer to the start of the digestive system.

LAMBCHOP: Aha! Your greeny mates are scared the cows will kill us all. The Green New Deal says we are doomed to live on fish and soybeans. You can't milk a fish, you know. I've tried.

CELINE: I think you are missing the point here. Maybe there's a better way to make ice cream and hamburgers just as delicious without cows. Or maybe there's just a smarter way of producing the same goodies with cows that doesn't destroy the planet so much. Go on, tell me your genius plan one more time.

LAMBCHOP: For the last time, I am going to steal all the cows in the world. And it's my right because I love cow farts. According to you, they are an endangered species Mrs.-cows-only-fart-5%. I have six cows, only one billion four hundred ninety-nine million nine hundred ninety-nine thousand nine hundred ninety-four to go.

CELINE: Sounds kinda stupid when you say it out loud. I helped you steal the cows because I'm your friend, but I'm gonna leave you to it. Good luck with all of those cows, Buffalo Bill. I don't think you've thought this through.

(*CELINE exits. As LAMBCHOP becomes more worked up, the cows in the bedroom become more and more agitated, and the noises from within become louder and more destructive.*)

LAMBCHOP: (*Muttering to himself.*) You're right, we're gonna need a bigger boat. I can fit four more cows in the bathroom and 25 in the garage. (*Shouting after Celine.*) I don't need your help! I'll start a blog. I'll message people on Twitter and Instagram and on TikTok. We'll see who's laughing when everyone has 150 cows in their house and you have none. Thanks for nothing, loser. You're not my friend anymore. The cows are my only real friends. They have four stomachs, you know, that's four times more love. The average life expectancy for a cow is 25 years. A friend for life! Cows are forever pets. A cow stands up and lays down about 14 times a day, did you know that? People say that you can't make a cow go downstairs but you can with a whip and a cattle prod. And you can't milk a fish or a chicken!

(*The mooing becomes a cacophony of moos, and the sounds of cows slamming into the door and furniture being broken rise to a crescendo as the lights fade to black.*)

END OF PLAY

INITIATION

Angella Emurwon

Angella Emurwon is an award-winning Ugandan playwright, filmmaker, and dramaturg. Angella lives and works in Tororo, Uganda.

Playwright's Statement

We have run out of time.

Climate change scientists and activists are not talking about implementing solutions that secure some distant future. We are fighting for the hope and future of All Life that is on the planet right now. It is now time for radical measures that, hopefully, buy us time and set us up to make better decisions for lasting recovery and change.

Initiation is a conversation with the near future when a Global Green New Deal means we've gained a little more time on the clock to make things better.

It is ritual. It is reflection. It is hope.

• • •

A woman kneels, hands deep in a mound of earth, rich, alive. Two or three young shoots peep through at the edges of the mound. Dead leaves and stems peep through as she works the earth.

Don't be afraid. Come here to me.
Mmhmm . . . ? Come.
Your limbs have grown strong.
Still.
Yet,
You've been tasked to find your footing in an in-between time.
Past exploits and exploitations no longer serve a world brought to its knees.
And the future, a fledgling wing, on which the hopes of All are buoyed.

Come, heart of my heart.
Come put your hand on this earth, let your fingers sink deep.
Lower your head, listen, allow the pulsating silence to train your hearing.
Breathe deep, expand your chest, and make room for all the work that must
be yours.
Behold the battleground and the spoils.

Battle one:
It was not our portion that wrought this devastating decay.
Not on us to bear the impossible burden
And render the statistic one in one, inevitable.
Not us who forced-fed the poison that was to make us "civilized"
Now ailing, are led back to a cure that once was all we knew.

Battle two:
True . . . this earth is our home, all of us.
True . . . this battle is on us, all of us.
Then let us fight together as peers.
Do not our commanders drink at the same fountain of greed and
corruption?
Do not our commanders deserve the same sins with which to repent?
Let us burn and build, and with it grow our capacity to fight as all have
done.
Let all our warrior garments weigh the same.

But,
As battles were spoken and prides were enraged,
The earth unpacked itself of all options.
It shut down convenient exits and arguments,
Armed itself with wind, and water, pestilence, and plague
And, tired of listening, took the Future off the table.

This is not a storyteller's song.
No.
Do not wait to hear the name of some hero, some legend, some icon
For indeed, you are the hero, and here we are still, in the midst of the
journey.

As recent as last night's dream.
As fantastic as dreams can often be
We had no choice. We took a stand!

Yes. It was not we who wrought this devastating decay
But, heart of my heart
It was we who held the key that would buy all the world more time
We, on this continent.
With more recent remembrances and practices of a life and world shared,
and—
With available global knowledge and technology that would enable us to
rebuild,
Differently, new and better systems, for better lives, justice, and equality for
all.

We remembered our own terrible mistakes.
We did not need to prove our value by making more.
It would not be less of an exploit to put aside hard-won advancements
If less meant that we would gain more time for all of us.

This earth, this beautiful planet, and all the life that lives here
Is a thing of Utmost Wonder.
Here, heart of my heart.
Close your hand around this fist of dirt.
Dark, rich, sacred.
Brimming with hope.
Promising a future.

I have called you here, heart of my heart,
Not to pass the work of keeping this earth alive to you,
But to ask you to put your hands in the dirt
And do the work of keeping the earth alive with me.

END OF PLAY

ALL ITS TAINTED GLORY

Georgina HL Escobar

Georgina HL Escobar is a playwright and director from Ciudad Juárez, Mexico. She is a MacDowell Fellow, Djerassi Resident, and a recipient of the Kennedy Center Darrell Ayers Playwriting Award. Her work has been featured in the Kilroys List, The Texas Review, *Lighting The Way*, Los Bárbaros, McSweeney's Anthology, and New Passport Press. Her plays have been produced across the United States and internationally in Mexico, Denmark, and Sweden.

Playwright's Statement

In the video "A Message from the Future" by Representative Alexandria Ocasio-Cortez and Canadian author and activist Naomi Klein, Rep. Ocasio-Cortez closes with, "We can be whatever we have the courage to see." Oscar Wilde has a quote that says, "It takes great courage to see the world in all its tainted glory, and still to love it." I wanted to juxtapose the elements of "seeing" from the point of view of a hopeful romantic and a cynic in order to scratch at the root of *tainting* narratives of progress, for profit.

• • •

ALAN: Don't do that.

REBECCA: Do what?

ALAN: Pretend.

REBECCA: Pretend? You mean imagine?

ALAN: Oh same, same. Same thing.

REBECCA: I don't think that's—

ALAN: Same thing.

REBECCA: Uh, no.

ALAN: Rebecca, with all due respect—

REBECCA: Alright—

ALAN: With all due respect, to pretend that you know what you're talking about—

REBECCA: I do know what I'm talking about.

ALAN: Fantasy is not—

REBECCA: It's hardly fantasy, it's imagination. It's literally the first step towards realization.

(She looks for something on her phone, a web page.)

ALAN: You might be too young to understand—

REBECCA: Well I'm forty, so.

ALAN: But to guide and "imagine" a restructuring of education and the future of this school without the facts, the data—

REBECCA: Ah here it is. "Imagination: noun— the faculty or action of forming new ideas, or concepts of external objects not present to the senses."

ALAN: Not present to the senses. Fantasy.

REBECCA: Do you love your children?

ALAN: Excuse me?

REBECCA: I assume you do—what is love?

ALAN: I'm not following.

REBECCA: Is it a concept not present to the senses?

ALAN: No, of course it's present to the senses, I kiss, I hug, I say it.

REBECCA: Indeed, that is the action that follows, that *stems* from the love but is the kiss itself, *love*? Do you love your job?

ALAN: Yes.

REBECCA: Do you kiss it then?

ALAN: . . . Where are you going with this?

REBECCA: What gives you permission to act outwardly what you feel and see inwardly?

ALAN: Not imagination.

REBECCA: "It is difficult to get a man to understand something when his salary depends upon his not understanding it."

ALAN: What?

REBECCA: Upton Sinclair.

ALAN: My salary depends on me absolutely understanding things, with facts.

REBECCA: Facts are the fruit, imagination is the seed. You're trying to understand something that has not yet undergone its maturity, so it is my job to speculate.

ALAN: Your job is to teach art to our elementary school students.

REBECCA: But that *does* create jobs.

ALAN: We don't know that.

REBECCA: Do you remember that movie, *The Fifth Element*?

ALAN: I don't watch sci-fi.

REBECCA: Oh, but you *do* know what I'm talking about.

ALAN: Never seen it. I have an 11:00 a.m., can we wrap this up, please?

(REBECCA demonstrates a scene from the movie. She takes ALAN's coffee cup and chucks it across the room. It smashes into pieces as it hits a wall.)

ALAN: What in the world is the matter with you?!

(Alan's Secretary, LULU, enters.)

LULU: Is everything okay, Sir—Oh! Look here. A mess!

ALAN: I'm sorry Lulu, Ms. Robles was *just* leaving and she . . .

LULU: No matter, it'll be tidy in a jiffy.

(She exits. Silence. They watch her return with a broom and dustpan.)

ALAN: No, you don't have to do that, I can—

LULU: Oh please, Alan. It gives me something to do. I mean no offense but your phone has been as silent as a bank on Superbowl Sunday. (*She cleans.*) I've archived, reorganized, stapled random things, and organized your email thrice over. This is a good feeling. (*She looks at him.*) To feel useful for once. You know, ever since cellular phones and laptops—well, you know—the job of the secy is well . . . Obsolete. (*Is she about to cry?*)

ALAN: Lulu, I . . .

LULU: It's quite alright. It's fine, really. I love it. I love this job. I love . . . feeling useful.

REBECCA: How long have you two—

LULU: I've been his secy for 27 years. And counting! Unless you've come here today to sell him a robot for a secretary, ha ha ha . . . haha . . . ?

REBECCA: No. On the contrary. I'm trying to remind Alan here of the importance of Love and Imagination.

ALAN: Idealism, really.

LULU: Oh, that's nice. Well. I'll let you to it. Thank you. I mean. I'll be out here. I mean. Call me if you need a thing.

　　(*LULU exits.*)

ALAN: I had no idea she was so affected.

REBECCA: Lulu and millions of others in this country who have lost their jobs in our extractive economy . . . But imagine, Alan. Imagine giving them something new to do. Something that could also be beneficial for us. It's a win win.

ALAN: I still don't understand what this has to do with our students.

REBECCA: *Imagine* we create "ideation forums." *Imagine* Tuesdays becoming a day where the school suspends all "schooling" and allows the kids to imagine new futures, new jobs, new technologies. *Imagine* that we stop *teaching* old models and repeating old mistakes and enhance their imaginations and their ability to *see* what they want to see realized. Make kids *excited* to engage in creative problem-solving to help our climate cr—

ALAN: How do I present that to the parents?

REBECCA: Smash some coffee cups maybe?

ALAN: It was a vague concept materialized; I must admit.

REBECCA: Everything is vague until we have the courage to name it. To see it. To create it.

(*Silence.*)

ALAN: If I didn't know any better, I'd think you're an educator.

REBECCA: (*Smiles.*) Anyway. I do hope you like it, it was a joy to make.

(*REBECCA hands ALAN a canvas. She's painted a portrait of his cat.*)

ALAN: Looks just like Sargent Dojo.

REBECCA: I'm glad. (*Beat.*) In the movie, the glass breaking is to make a point. A point that destruction creates work, that war is money, that chaos brings prosperity.

ALAN: Oh?

REBECCA: But I disagree. I think drastically, yes. Destruction creates jobs, but can't we imagine creation doing the same? We can teach the kids that creating new viable solutions for our climate problem, for society, for the things they want to see changed starts with *creation* and imagination—not destruction.

ALAN: So in that case, had you not shattered the coffee cup—

REBECCA: You'd've never known how incredibly bored and unhappy your secy is.

ALAN: True. But?

REBECCA: To prove my point, I would have called her in here and asked her to spend the day redecorating your office.

ALAN: I see.

REBECCA: That's good. That's very good. That's super good. Indeed, "We can be whatever we have the courage to see."

(*They share a smile.*)

END OF PLAY

ALL OF US WERE BORN IN THE CRISIS

David Finnigan

David Finnigan is a writer and theatre-maker from Ngunawal country. David works with Earth scientists to produce theatre about climate and global change. He has written plays including *Kill Climate Deniers* and *You're Safe Til 2024*. David is a Fellow of the Churchill Foundation, a member of science-theatre ensemble Boho, and an associate of UK theatre ensemble Coney. Website: davidfinig.com. Newsletter: davidfinnigan.substack.com.

Note

This is a true story, and I trust you to perform it however you choose, whatever you feel, there are no wrong moves.

• • •

75,000 years ago the Toba volcano in Indonesia erupted.

This is the biggest volcano eruption in human history. The mountain rumbled for decades beforehand, and then exploded—and kept exploding, for two weeks straight.

Something of that scale is beyond comparison. Three thousand cubic kilometers of rock blown into the sky. Ten million tonnes per second. A wave of lava and poisonous gas covering 30,000 square kilometers. Most of India and Pakistan, covered in ash three-meters thick. The largest tsunami humanity has ever seen.

And the mushroom cloud darkened the sky over the whole earth, until the middle of the day was as dark as night under the full moon. For years.

And that two years of darkness, that two years without sun, was the start of 2,000 years of relentless freezing winter and drought. The coldest period of the ice age. The seas shrank by hundreds of meters, most of the world's fresh water froze as ice in the poles, and ecosystems across the planet collapsed.

Around that time, we nearly went extinct. Genetic analysis says that around 70,000 to 80,000 years ago, humans were reduced to 15,000 individuals, maybe fewer. Some scientists believe that this eruption caused this genetic bottleneck—that Toba almost wiped humanity out altogether.

That tiny group of survivors was hidden in the Ethiopian highlands, and they had a very tough time of it.

My great-grandparents were there, yours too. Everyone in the whole world traces their family tree back to this one community of a few thousand struggling humans. All of humanity in one small town's worth of people, maybe ten high schools.

How did we survive? We don't know. Maybe your great-grandparents helped my great-grandparents, maybe the other way around. But we got through it.

And our numbers slowly grew, and the weather warmed, and generation by generation, century by century, we spread out from there. Walking along mountain ridges, through valleys, down to the water's edge. We lit fires on the beach and watched the surf. We crept across the face of the planet. And we forgot, as much as an animal forgets.

But remember this: when we were down to the last survivors, when the sky was black with ash and the ground was frozen and we were sick with hunger and thirst,

there were people who gave up
there were people who lied and stole and took more than their share
there were people who said the future was not worth fighting for

and there were people who kept pushing
and there were people who laughed and told funny stories to help keep spirits up
and there were people who gave what they had
and there were people who helped.

Even in that moment, there were people who were selfish and there were people who were kind.

We've been here before and we'll be here again
And all of this is your heritage and my heritage too.

And the waves still crash on the sand
leaving bubbles of foam as the water draws back.

END OF PLAY

HELEN'S HANGOUT

Patti Flather

Patti Flather is an award-winning writer and theatre artist in Whitehorse, Yukon, Canada. Patti's play *Paradise* toured nationally and is published with Playwrights Canada Press. Her fiction collection *Such A Lovely Afternoon* is forthcoming with Inanna Publications in 2022. Recent collaborations include the radio play series *Ndoo Tr'eedyaa Gogwaandak—Vuntut Gwitchin Stories* at vuntutstories.ca (Vuntut Gwitchin Government/Gwaandak Theatre). Patti is of settler ancestry and grateful to live as an uninvited guest on Kwanlin Dün First Nation and Ta'an Kwäch'än territory.

Playwright's Statement

I live in Canada's North. My inspiration springs from the climate emergency's extreme impacts on the northern environment and remote Indigenous communities, the desperate need for affordable housing, the urgency to transition away from fossil fuels and reduce our demands on the earth. I found hope in visions for a Green New Deal, and in the many people and groups already putting these ideas into practice. My dreams include greater social justice, Indigenous and community-led solutions, fostering people's connections with each other and the earth, and leaders stepping up to truly address our climate crisis, for our children, grandchildren, and future generations all over the planet.

Characters

JULE, late thirties or older.
BERT, fifties or older.
BETSY, sixties or older.
WILLOW, late teens or twenties.
CHASE, thirties or older.

Setting

Summer 2031, Whitehorse, Canada.

Notes

Characters are of Yukon Indigenous ancestry, settler ancestry, and/or a mix-ture, representing a cross-section of Yukon's First Peoples and diverse settler population. For example, elder Betsy could be First Nations, or deeply con-nected with the community. Casting may be tailored to your country/region, where possible reflecting First Peoples and various settlers; casting non-Indigenous actors to portray Indigenous characters is not appropriate.

Approach Willow's drumming as a simple, strong, clear heartbeat. Wil-low's song is not intended to represent any Yukon First Nation's culture and traditions. Approach Willow's song as one individual's unique offering, rather than attempting to be culturally specific and replicate a particular Yukon First Nations song. These are owned by individuals, families, clans, and moieties within various Nations; they must not be used without permission.

Pronunciations: Southern Tutchone words have pronouncers in brackets next to them.

Learn more about Kwanlin Dün First Nation,* Ta'an Kwäch'än Council,** and Southern Tutchone language.***

• • •

A drumbeat, strong like a heartbeat. Lights up. A flurry of activity and final touches in preparation for an outdoor ceremony in a housing project's commu-nal green space, with decorations inspired by Yukon land, salmon, wildlife. JULE seats BETSY. BERT rehearses with a bizarre contraption.

A clang and crash; JULE trips over BERT's large, recycled, homemade musical contraption.

JULE: Ow, shit, Bert, what the, is that a, god no . . .

BERT: A waffle iron from the Robinson free store, five sizes of tin cans, this one from Riverside Grocery had a whole chicken in it! A rusty chainsaw from my cabin out by Keno, oh and an old vibrator from my ex . . .

---

* https://www.kwanlindun.com/
** http://taan.ca/
*** https://taan.ca/southern-tutchone-taan-dialect-language-app/; http://ynlc.ca/languages/stutchone.html

JULE: Oh my. That's disturbing but creative. Did you get an arts grant for that?

BERT: I applied but, no. They're biased against geriatric prospectors.

JULE: Next time. Orchestra, just, keep your . . . instruments off the footpath. Stand by in the community garden—not by the arugula, Bert! In the gazebo.

BERT: Gotcha.

JULE: Here's your tea, Bets.

BETSY: You sweetheart.

CHASE: (*Doing a sound check.*) Test, test.

WILLOW: I can't find my drum. I literally just had it.

JULE: Willow! It's on that bench.

WILLOW: I'm kind of nervous.

JULE: This is about our home.

WILLOW/JULE: Food shelter culture. Water earth sky.

JULE: Good?

WILLOW: Yeah.

JULE: Stand by at the medicine garden, you're after Grandma Betsy. Then it's Helen's Hangout Orchestra. Get your earplugs ready.

WILLOW: Mom!

JULE: Did I just say that out loud . . .

CHASE: Jule. Where's my notes?

JULE: Seriously? You've been talking about this in your sleep since before the last sea ice.

BERT: Right on, you two. Ten frickin' years, eh. A lot of campfires, beers, and tears.

JULE: It wasn't easy. When we lost the salmon . . . shit.

BERT: Jeez, that was tough. Ocean warm as soup.

WILLOW: Hello. Can we start? It's going to pour again. I really don't want it ruining my drum.

CHASE: Ok, ok. (*He starts.*) Hey everyone, I'm Chase. Welcome to Helen's Hangout for this historic ceremony, celebrating our community. Built by us, for us. Hopefully, crews get the mudslides cleared and reopen the Alaska Highway. But, happy to report no flooded basements here.

JULE: I thought the last few summers were torrential but . . . maybe we can tell the sky that Canada finally got our emissions down.

CHASE: Totally. It's hard to believe it's been 10 years since we broke ground here, coming out of the pandemic into the Green New Deal. Together with you, First Nations and community partners, like a lot of housing projects here in the territory, and coast to coast to coast.

JULE: 2021. Gee, that was an amazing time. The Just Recovery protests, people just on fire calling for a real shift. Saying to hell with the old normal. Building on so much passion, Black Lives Matter, Indigenous Climate Action, social justice, earth justice.

(*The crowd whoops.*)

JULE: I meet this underemployed carpenter sleeping in a van by the river . . .

CHASE: And you, Jule, super-smart. Trying to connect affordable housing and energy transition and top climate standards, wow.

JULE: Meanwhile scrounging for my next house-sit. Oh. Land acknowledgment!

CHASE: Right. We acknowledge with deep gratitude that we are gathered here next to Chu Nínkwän (CHOO NIN-KWUN), the Yukon River, and that we live and breathe and benefit on the traditional territory of the Kwanlin Dün (KWON-LIN DUN) First Nation and Ta'an Kwäch'än (TAH-ON KWOCH-UN) Council. Both self-governing Nations who have cared for this territory for millennia. Stewards of this land. And that's what we're striving to continue, for next generations.

JULE: I'd like to invite up Betsy, our Elder-in-residence at Helen's Hangout.

BETSY: How are you all doing?

WILLOW: Awesome, Betsy!

(More whoops from crowd.)

BETSY: Thank you. You know, it was 20 years ago in June 2011, just upriver from here, when my old friend Helen Hollywood put up her tent on the Yukon legislature lawn. That Helen. Feisty as heck. Along with her friend Linda, Helen began the Tent City protest to demand decent housing.

BERT: Tent City, yeah Helen!

BETSY: Back then, lots of people couldn't find a place to live. Indigenous people. Young folks. Artists. People on that minimum wage. I don't have to tell you, it's expensive up North. And ever since the gold rush, First Nation families got pushed away from the river, into the swampland to make way for the newcomers. So it's really good what you've done. This place to live together, using less energy. A daycare for the little ones learning Southern Tutchone, the Indigenous language rooted right here in this place. Our garden full of vegetables. And good building jobs for the young ones. I love it here. Oh, I'm so proud of you. Well. That's all I wanted to say.

JULE: Shäw níthän, Betsy. Now we've got a couple from the team here, who also happen to be performers. It's the Yukon, right? Culture in our DNA. Willow. Bert.

WILLOW: Hi. It's been incredible figuring out how to use renewable energy from the sun and the wind and the earth with that geothermal down below us.

BERT: I'm living proof you can teach an old dog new tricks.

WILLOW: And a young dog old tricks, right Bert?

BERT: Don't befuddle me, Willow.

WILLOW: I would never.

BERT: A miner and prospector learning about green energy. This rockhound still gets out hunting for nuggets but we've been a good team, eh, you an' me, Willow.

WILLOW: I do a mean solar panel install.

BERT: Units all shapes and sizes, for singles and bachelors and old farts like me.

WILLOW: And families.

BERT: Built to last and stay dry. Insulated for 40 below.

WILLOW: Building a place like this, taking as little as possible from the land, it gives me hope.

(Beat). I remember the salmon from when I was a kid. They still swam up the river here. This is for them. The salmon *will* come back.

> *(WILLOW drums a heartbeat on her hand drum and vocalizes a brief, haunting tune.)*

WILLOW: Thank you.

> *(Applause, whoops.)*

JULE: And now for our very own, one-of-a-kind, Helen's Hangout Orchestra. Take it away, Bert.

BERT: Okie-doke. Chase?

CHASE: Yup.

WILLOW: Earplugs.

JULE: Right.

BERT: One, two . . .

> *(A cacophony erupts from Bert, Chase, and the motley Helen's Hangout Orchestra.)*

END OF PLAY

THE OYSTERS

Miranda Rose Hall

Miranda Rose Hall's works include *Plot Points in Our Sexual Development* (LCT3/Lincoln Center Theater, finalist for the 2019 Lambda Literary Award in Drama), *The Hour of Great Mercy* (Diversionary Theater, 2019 San Diego Critics Circle Award for Outstanding New Play), *A Play for the Living in a Time of Extinction* (Baltimore Center Stage), and *The Kind Ones* (Magic Theatre). She is a graduate of Georgetown University and the Yale School of Drama.

Playwright's Statement

I grew up in Baltimore, Maryland, and I have been thinking a lot about the plight of oysters in the Chesapeake Bay. I felt inspired to imagine a story that could pay homage to these amazing creatures and advocate for the health of our bay.

Characters

A chorus of oysters, as many as you please. Assign the lines as you see fit.

Place

The Chesapeake Bay

• • •

THE OYSTERS are asleep.
The waters of the bay swish around them.
Perhaps there is oyster music that plays throughout this play.
THE OYSTERS wake up.

THE OYSTERS: Good morning, oysters!
Good morning, oysters!
It is today, and we are alive!
We are alive in the Chesapeake Bay,
water of the centuries.
We wish to start our day,
but wait!
What is this?!
One oyster among us appears to be overcome with fear!

(*We see ONE OYSTER who appears to be overcome with fear.*)

THE OYSTERS: Oh, poor little oyster, what is the matter?

ONE OYSTER: I have had a terrible vision
of the total disappearance of oysters!
A bay with no oysters!
A world with no oysters!

THE OYSTERS: Poor little oyster!
We must renew you!
What do we do!

(*A brief oyster conference.*)

THE OYSTERS: We shall present a magnificent ritual!
The Oyster Story, why not?!
Do we have what is needed?
Oysters, ready?
Begin!

(*The OYSTERS begin an oyster dance. How does an oyster dance? Have fun! Perhaps part of their ritual is sung, or chanted, however you want to do it. Have fun!*)

THE OYSTERS: We are Eastern Oysters,
ancient bivalve mollusks!
We have shells!
We make reefs!
We live to do our work!
What is an oyster's work?
To live together in giant communities,
to filter water, breathing in, breathing out!

To help small creatures,
to protect our young,
to avoid being eaten by seabirds, ah!
To avoid being eaten by crabs, ah!
To avoid being eaten by flatworms, ah!
And yet,
we know that we all must eat,
we all must hunt,
and survive.
Oh, but what is the balance of survival?
The ongoing quest of our lives!

We are Eastern Oysters,
ancient bivalve mollusks!
We have survived for thousands of years,
years of turmoil and strife.
For centuries, we were undisturbed,
we filtered the water,
we cleaned the bay,
we protected the waters for millions of creatures,
until the invasion
of settler industry
nearly wiped us out.
Harvesting, harvesting, overharvesting!
Humans racing from reef to reef,
wrenching us from our homes by the hundreds,
the thousands,
the millions!
Selling us, eating us on the shore,
throwing our shells in landfills,
in mountains of waste and decay,
far from the bay,
directing their runoff into our waters,
harvesting our fellow creatures,
polluting the homes of fellow creatures!
We mourn for those we have lost:
the rockfish, the crabs, the grasses, the sponges,
we mourn for our young, who were killed by disease,
we mourn for our old, who never grew old,
we mourn for all oysters who were torn from the reef,

for the water that clouded,
the water that warmed,
we mourn for the water that teemed with life,
life that was gone in a century!
Diminished in a century!
Diminished by human industry!
Some days the pain of such reminiscing
can paralyze the mouth!
The heart!
The hinge of an ancient bivalve shell—
oh, how do we go on?
Oh, dear!
Oh, dear!
Can we go on!

(A brief moment in which they may not be able to go on.)

ONE OYSTER: Oh no!
The oysters who tried to help me are overcome with fear!
What have I done?
My fear has frozen them!
Oh how can I help my reef!
I shall try to do what they did for me,
I shall try to summon my courage and love.
Oh, oyster heart of mine!
Where is the love that can help overcome
this overwhelming fear?!

(ONE OYSTER prepares to summon love for the oyster community.)

ONE OYSTER: I am one little oyster!
I am part of the web of life!
I am part of the web of millions of years
of beautiful, beautiful life!
I am an Eastern Oyster,
an ancient bivalve mollusk,
and though I don't know what the hour will bring,
what the day will bring,
what the future will bring,
I go on for love of all oysters!
We must go on for love of each other!

We go on for love of the water!
We shall band together and filter the bay,
how else could we possibly fill the day?
We do what we can! What else can we do?
Oysters! Hey Oysters, I'm talking to you!

THE OYSTERS: Yes!
Your courage renews our souls!
Your love renews our purpose!
We are Eastern Oysters,
ancient bivalve mollusks!
We give thanks for our lives,
we give thanks for each other,
we give thanks for our love of the Chesapeake water!
We give thanks for the hope of a Great Restoration,
a Great Conservation,
for a future all creatures can dare to imagine!
Where the waters are warming, but they are clearer,
where the shoreline recedes, but we are alive!
Where industries of land and water
can work together for a common good!
There is no such thing as a total reversal,
but there is such a thing as renewal of life!
Oysters, fish, waters, grasses,
there is such a thing as renewal of life!
Thank you, young oyster, for helping all oysters!
And so our day begins!
Oysters! Begin!

(The oyster dance settles into a gentle breathing.
They filter the bay.
The bay pulses with life.)

END OF PLAY

CONFESSIONS OF THE LITTLE MATCH GIRL TO THE STAR

Kamil Haque

Kamil Haque is the founder and artistic director of Haque Centre of Acting & Creativity (HCAC), Singapore's first professional acting studio for everyone. As Asia's only experienced coach of the Lee Strasberg method of acting, he has coached actors for the stage and screen, including for major Hollywood films. Using theatre and storytelling techniques, Kamil's work also includes training corporate leaders and employees. A Singaporean of multiethnic origin, Kamil has produced, directed, and acted in several award-winning and critically acclaimed productions in Singapore, the United States, Malaysia, and Australia.

Playwright's Statement

I chose to fracture a fairy tale, a nursery rhyme, and the calling out of "mama," common symbols of innocence, to create the spine of this piece. To create the heart and soul, I examined and extracted text from Greta Thunberg's speech at the 2019 UN Climate Summit and from George Floyd's final moments in 2020. I wanted to explore how two people on opposite ends of the age and racial spectrum express grief and anguish at their circumstances. How might their spirit and the spirit of their message live on, literally and metaphorically?

• • •

A match is struck to illuminate the LITTLE MATCH GIRL as she looks up.

THE LITTLE MATCH GIRL: Twinkle, twinkle, little star, how I wonder what I am doing here?

I shouldn't be here. It's 8:46 p.m. Just two matches left and it's too late to get shelter. Stars light your fires, make me forget the cold lies I was told. The cold eyes that looked anywhere but at me. Make me forget the cold icy grip that tightens.

("Mama" is meant to mimic the sound of a heartbeat that is weakening with every mention.)

Mama, mama, mama, mama . . . . ma . . . ma . . . . . . ma . . . . ma

Are you up there in the stars? I remember those fairy tales you used to read me. Always ending with "happily ever after." But things turned out so different. I was meant to be in school, grow big and strong and tall so I could look after you one day. I was meant to be anywhere but burying my dreams for a better life with you. It's hard to shine when your spirit lives outside your body six feet underground. My dreams and childhood, stolen. I tell myself "happily ever after" is if you still feel your heartbeat. It's all wrong.

(A second match is struck to illuminate the LITTLE MATCH GIRL.)

All I see is a world already burning. A world of people suffering. People dying. Entire ecosystems collapsing. A world where the only fairy tale is the gospel according to money. When I go, who will even notice but the stars? Look, the clock is inching closer to doomsday. I don't want to believe that the world is evil. I don't want to be angry. I don't want to fight anymore. I'm so tired. My body aches. I feel drained. My arms hurt. I've grasped at straws for too long. My fingers. Each finger has a separate sensation. Why can't I feel my fing— . . .

Mama . . . mama . . . . . . ma . . . ma . . . . ma . . . . ma . . . . . . ma . . . . ma

Why did I waste all that time begging people to listen? I'll probably just die this way. I'm through. My stomach hurts. My neck hurts. Everything hurts. I feel so betrayed. This was meant to be my time to shine. Instead, here I am cowering in the darkness. Meek is the earth that I have inherited. Without any money to my name, age in my face, and agency in my spirit, I'm just another number. Tomorrow if the world wakes up, maybe change will come, whether people like it or not.

(The last match is struck to illuminate the LITTLE MATCH GIRL. Try to time the duration of the flame to end with the last "ma." More "ma" may be added if necessary to time it with the end of the flame.)

One last attempt to be seen. Stars, shine your light for the travelers in the dark night of the soul. The ones after me, oh my God. I can't believe this. I believe this. I can't breathe. I can't breathe. I can't breathe.

(Sung quietly to put herself at peace.)

Twinkle, twinkle, little star, how I wonder what . . .

Mama . . . . ma . . . . . . ma . . . . ma . . . .

END OF PLAY

A WINDOW

Whiti Hereaka

Whiti Hereaka is an award-winning novelist and playwright of Ngāti Tūwharetoa, Te Arawa, Ngāti Whakaue, Tuhourangi, Tainui, and Pākehā descent, from Aotearoa/New Zealand. She holds a masters in Creative Writing (Scriptwriting) from the International Institute of Modern Letters. She is the author of three novels: *The Graphologist's Apprentice*, *Bugs*, and *Legacy*. Her fourth novel, *Kurangaituku*, was published in 2021 and has been shortlisted for the Jann Medlicott prize for Fiction in the Ockham New Zealand Book Awards 2022.

Playwright's Statement

A Window is almost as much a response to the provocation as it is to the Green New Deal. To write the play I had to put aside my annoyance at the US-centric theme (which assumes that the New Deal is familiar and has relevance to the rest of the world) and found that my annoyance only grew when researching the Green New Deal. It is not radical, nor do I believe it sufficient to address any of the problems facing our global community—instead, it is a pallid retooling of the same systems that got us into the problems we now face.

Characters

FOOTE, put upon.
HART, means well.
HAND, invisible.

Notes

About Foote, the box, and The New Box.

A contortionist would be ideal for the role of FOOTE—if their proportions are a surprise in relation to the box, it would be delightful.

The box should be able to fit FOOTE inside—but it should be small enough that the audience wonders how FOOTE can fit inside it.

The New Box can be made physically using flats or metaphorically using lights. When "built," it should be big enough for both FOOTE and HART to move around inside, but not comfortably—it is a squeeze for them both.

• • •

A box. It is big enough to fit a person, but not comfortably. It is solid and the audience cannot see into it.

The box has a lid that opens so that FOOTE is out of the audience's sightlines. The lid can be opened from within, and it opens and shuts rhythmically as if the box itself is breathing. It is as if the box is a living creature on stage.

The box should be low enough that HART can (eventually) sit on it.

HAND stands, unmoving, with their back to the audience.

Enter HART, head tilted up, one hand pinching their nose. Under their other arm, they carry a set of blueprints.

HART sets the blueprints on top of the box and, still pinching their nose, pats their pockets looking for a tissue.

The lid of the box opens and FOOTE holds out a tissue.

HART takes the tissue and dabs their bloody nose.

HART: Thank you.

HAND: HART!

   (HART yelps, drops the tissue, and blood gushes from their nose.)

HART: Oh! I didn't see you there, Hand.

   (HAND waves away HART's words.)

HART: I've finished the plans, I have them here . . . they were here a minute ago . . .

HAND: Plans? What plans?

HART: The plans you wanted to see . . .

HAND: I didn't ask to see plans . . .

HART: (*Over.*) . . . You did ask to see . . . the plans for . . .

HAND: Plans for what?!

FOOTE: (*Inside the box.*) For the box.

HAND: What box? We have a box!

(*HAND opens the lid of the box and bellows at FOOTE.*)

HAND: And what do YOU know about it anyway? It doesn't concern you.

HART: Well, it sort of does . . .

HAND: How on earth would it [concern] . . .

HART: Foote is in the box . . .

(*HART sniffles and pinches their nose.*)

HAND: Exactly. Someone in the box has no idea about boxes, do they?

(*HAND opens the lid.*)

HAND: (*To FOOTE.*) Have you ever been out of the box?

FOOTE: No.

HAND: Have you ever seen another box?

FOOTE: No.

(*HAND closes the lid.*)

HAND: You see? Foote has no idea about boxes, sure, they are in a box but being in a thing does not make you an expert in the thing you're in—you see? I, on the other hand, come from a long line of box procurers, I have knowledge about boxes that goes back generations and that knowledge was passed down Hand to Hand. There is nothing about boxes that I don't know. I know a good box when I see one. This fine box . . . (*HAND kicks the box. FOOTE groans.*) . . . was handed to me by Grandfather Hand . . .

HART: Your grandfather made this box?

HAND: Hands don't make boxes, we procure them.

(*HART lets go of their nose. Bleeds.*)

HART: Well, then—I have a box to show you.

HAND: A box, you say? Then why were we bothering about old Foote here . . .

(FOOTE opens the lid, waves a tissue.)

HAND: You see? They surrender!

(HART takes the tissue, dabs their nose.)

HART: (*To FOOTE.*) Thank you.

(HART unfurls the plans on top of the box. HAND snatches the plans.)

HAND: I know a good box when I see one . . .

(HART gently takes the plans from HAND and turns them the right way up.)

HAND: . . . and this is a great box.

(As HART speaks to the audience, HAND is to the side with the plans, directing unseen builders. HART speaks over the sound of construction.)

HART: I saw this as an opportunity to reimagine what a box could be. What do we need from a box? How do we make a box that will take us into the future? What is a box ? It is a thing that contains space, and that's what someone like Foote wants, isn't it? Space?

(HAND and FOOTE speak over each other. HART ignores both.)

HAND: What does it matter what Foote wants?

FOOTE: Actually, I'd quite like . . .

HART: So I started with the idea of space—but there are constraints on pure space, right? It is a *box* after all . . .

(HAND and FOOTE speak over each other.)

HAND: Too right, it's a bloody box . . .

FOOTE: Does it have to be, though?

HART: Come on. We can't think outside of a box, can we?

(HAND and HART laugh.)

HAND: Can you imagine?

HART: No. I really can't.

(HART sits on the box, dabs their nose. As HART speaks, FOOTE tries to open the lid and becomes more frantic as time goes on.)

HART: I came from a box myself, you know.

HAND: And look at you now.

HART: Yes. Look at me now. I've worked hard and followed my dreams and look where I am.

HAND: Self-made. All of this is because of you. You should be proud.

HART: I should. I am proud.

(The structure of the New Box now surrounds HART and the box. HAND is on the outside of the New Box. The New Box fits snugly around the old box.)

HAND: It's a fine box.

(HART stands up and looks around.)

HART: It is a fine box.

(HART opens the lid of the box and offers their hand to FOOTE. FOOTE climbs out of the box, stretches their neck.)

HAND: Mind your heads!

(The lid of the New Box is lowered. HART and FOOTE cannot stand in the New Box without slouching.)

HART: There's no need to thank me.

FOOTE: Thank you?

HART: You're welcome.

FOOTE: It's . . . a box.

HART: It has a window.

(FOOTE sits next to HART on the box. They both stare out the window.)

END OF PLAY

LIFEDAY

Jessica Huang

Jessica Huang is a playwright based in New York, from Minnesota. Her work has been commissioned by Audible, Ars Nova, History Theater, Manhattan Theatre Club, Mixed Blood Theatre, Timeline Theater, Theater Masters, and Theater Mu, and includes *The Paper Dreams of Harry Chin* (2018 Barry and Bernice Stavis Award, 2017 Kilroys List), *Mother of Exiles* (2020 Rosa Parks Playwriting Award, 2020 Paul Stephen Lim Playwriting Award, 2020 Kendeda Prize Finalist), *Transmissions in Advance of the Second Great Dying*, and *Purple Cloud*. She is a graduate of the Playwrights Program at Juilliard.

Playwright's Statement

I'm continually inspired by *Project Drawdown: The Most Comprehensive Plan Ever Proposed to Reverse Global Warming*, edited by Paul Hawken, especially Hawken's beautiful quote from the introduction: "The buildup of greenhouse gasses we experience today occurred in the absence of human understanding; our ancestors were innocent of the damage they were doing. That can tempt us to believe that global warming is something that is happening *to* us—that we are victims of a fate that was determined by actions that precede us. If we change the preposition and consider that global warming is happening *for* us—an atmospheric transformation that inspires us to change and reimagine everything we make and do—we begin to live in a different world. We take 100 percent responsibility and stop blaming others. We see global warming not as an inevitability but as an invitation to build, innovate, and effect change, a pathway that awakens creativity, compassion, and genius."

Characters

AUNTIE, nonwhite. Aged.

• • •

AUNTIE has gathered us for Lifeday.

It is possible she has gathered us in person

and also possible that we have been gathered on a streaming platform.

It doesn't matter—we are gathered just the same.

Before the play begins, there are a few items that the audience should have accessible:

- *Something living (a plant, a pet)*
- *Something recycled or eco friendly or zero waste*
- *Something to write on*
- *Something to write with*
- *Something sweet*

AUNTIE: Is everyone here?
Yes yes—I can see you can you see me?
Babygirl put that down
we'll get to our sweets in a second
Does everyone have what they need?
Well go on and get em
No go on I'll wait
—Huh?
—Junior we do this every year
Can anyone tell him?
Anyone?

   (A deep sigh.)

No no no
wait
come back
We celebrate Lifeday on *[today's date]* every year
Sweetpotato you even said it's your favorite holiday
can you tell me why?
Can anyone tell me why
—You can go get them in a second
—I'll tell you when
No listen
Though it might be hard to believe

we didn't always have what we have now
—Don't roll your eyes Babygirl, listen
There was a time when we heated our homes with natural gas
and cooled our food and our bodies with hydrofluorocarbons
The fuel we used to get from A to B?
Petroleum
Laugh if you want to
I was there
I saw it
I did it
—Well I couldn't help it Junior it was back then
There was a time when
even if you did everything you could possibly think of
you used green cleaning products and recycled your gray water
you were still given your liquids in single use plastic
and oil companies got more tax breaks than teachers
and of course
there was convenience
"What is to be done?"
I wrung my hands
and ordered takeout
"The world is set up for me to fail!"
Six days out of the week I ordered from Amazon dot com
and then on the seventh day
I called my college and asked them to divest from fossil fuels
This was Good
Decidedly so
Because capitalism is motivating
and because
through hard work and privilege
I had found a way to eek out some power
I had a college to call
stocks of my own to divest
access to the articles that told me I should
and the power to choose
but my beautiful sister
your Ama
had nothing
but ritual
Yes—Ama who started Lifeday

In her house every dish washed was washed without waste
every meal eaten was savored
She watered the plants in the morning
and composted her food waste in the evening
ate vegan and local and homegrown
and even though it wasn't convenient
it also didn't decrease the heat
or lower the oceans
or change the carbon count either
All that it did
was change her
and it changed Ama totally
Which is why
we still celebrate Lifeday
even now
even after aquaculture
and the high speed trains
and 100% renewable energy
and green refrigeration
and carbon captured
and sequestered
and ___ [an aspect of the company's vision for our brilliant green future]___
and ___ [another aspect of the company's vision for our brilliant green future]___
and ___ [another aspect of the company's vision for our brilliant green future]___
and dead zones repopulated
and family planning for all
We celebrate
because without celebrating
we forget
We say the government should
and we grill a steak from who knows where
We say our children will
as we vote war instead
Ama changed her life
in order to put LIFE in the center
And now we do too
so we always remember
Okay?

Now
Junior
and anyone else who needs to—
go get something living. A plant. A cat.
No no I'll wait
—

Now hold that life
—gently Sweetpotato
and say thank you
—

Go on let's say it
—

Thank you
for reminding me that I am not the only species that matters
Thank you for helping me practice
taking care
—

Now let's gather our reusable sponge
our upcycled bag
our vegan dinner
Hold it with love and appreciation
Say thank you
Thank you
for helping me keep this fight
center in my mind
and in my pocketbook
Now take the paper
and write an intention
a new commitment we will take no matter how small
no matter how many important articles say it too will be ineffective
This isn't for them
it's for us
a mark of our devotion
our conviction
our care
a centering
so that when given a choice
we will remember not to hesitate
when given a vote
we will know what to do

Write it down
—

—

—

Read it again
—

—

And to seal it in
—that's right Babygirl
it's finally time
eat something sweet
savor this pleasure
know our enjoyment
See?
See my beloved ones?
This is what it means
to be present to life

END OF PLAY

FUCAWWWFFF

Faezeh Jalali

Faezeh Jalali is the founder and artistic director of FATS Thearts, Mumbai. She is an actor, director, writer, and producer. She has lived in Mumbai, India, all her life except for six years of graduate studies in the United States. She is of Iranian descent. She has written and directed plays including *777* (devised with an ensemble cast), *Shikhandi: The Story of the Inbetweens*, *Bone of Contention in Cosmopolitan Cooperative Society*, and *Afterlies*.

Playwright's Statement

This play is inspired by the crows that come to our kitchen window every day. They prefer meat but sometimes take bread depending on which family member makes the offering. Crows are fascinating to me because of their superior intelligence. In India, especially in Mumbai, we have an abundance of crows. The cawing of crows is a normal part of our soundscape. In India, it is also believed that your ancestors come as crows so one must feed them. The play has not much to do with all of this, but for the fact that I am fascinated by crows.

Characters

CROW 1
CROW 2
A PIGEON
WOMAN'S VOICE
The PIGEON and the WOMAN'S VOICE can be performed by the same
   person.

• • •

Two crows cawing at a kitchen window. A piece of fat is thrown. They fight for it. CROW 2 gets it. CROW 1 is pissed. There is cacophonous cawing in the background throughout the piece. The cawing stops completely at the end.

CROW 1: This is my window, ok. (*CROW 2 is chomping on the meat, unaffected.*) The kitchen window is mine! The living room balcony is yours.

CROW 2: What's yours is mine!

CROW 1: Exactly, you stole the balcony from me and now when there is fleshier feed at the kitchen, you want the kitchen window! Shoo!

CROW 2: You can't shoo me, I'm a crow like you!

CROW 1: Go eat breadcrumbs on the balcony! You chose the balcony.

CROW 2: But now I want the kitchen window.

CROW 1: You can't have what you want when you want it after displacing others!

CROW 2: She's cooking chicken, I love chicken!

CROW 1: Fuck CAWWWW off, you scavenger!

WOMAN'S VOICE: Shut up both of you! Shoo! Shoo!

> (*The crows fly off and rush to another window, out of which another piece of meat flies out. This time CROW 1 catches it in its beak mid-air. CROW 1 caws in victory and the meat falls from its mouth. Both crows swoop down to grab it as it lands on the garage roof. Both crows are hopping around the meat like the game "dog and the bone").*

CROW 1: Get away from here. This is my place!

CROW 2: Now it's mine!

CROW 1: This piece of meat flew straight into my plate! You go find yourself another home to scavenge at!

CROW 2: I'm here now and I'm going to take what I get.

CROW 1: Well, that's pretty desperate.

CROW 2: Aren't we all desperate?

CROW 1: Desperate enough to deny our fellow crows what is rightfully theirs?

CROW 2: Where else in this neighborhood are you getting meat to eat? Just a handful of people privileged enough to buy meat now that cow, goat, and chicken populations have dwindled . . .

CROW 1: I . . . don't know where . . .

CROW 2: You don't know because you got lucky and got homes where meat was thrown at you almost every day. The rest of us are scavenging and getting rotten carrots at best.

CROW 1: No wonder the rest of the crows were circling . . . (*Looks up at the rest of the crows and shouts:*) Stay away! Shoooo!

CROW 2: Crows don't shoo other crows! It's bad etiquette! Besides, buddy, you're lucky the vultures and hawks have left the city or you'd have stiff competition there!

CROW 1: Yeah! Those mothers are vicious!

CROW 2: Now you only have the pigeons.

CROW 1: The stupid pigeons are vegetarian.

CROW 2: Pigeons are not stupid, don't be mistaken. They've adapted to becoming scavengers too, just like me and you!

CROW 1: Are you serious?

(*A wild PIGEON swoops down and tears the piece of meat from CROW 1's beak.*)

CROW 1: What the fuck? What are we going to do?

CROW 2: It's a bird-eat-bird world.

CROW 1: Damn you, pigeons!!

CROW 2: But you see, they have no grains left to eat so they are looking for meat, or like I said, taking what they can get.

CROW 1: Just when I thought there were only crows left in the neighborhood.

CROW 2: There might be only crows left if we don't smarten up. We'll be feeding off each other's carcasses soon enough. Unless we move.

CROW 1: Move to where?

CROW 2: Papaya county.

(*CROW 1 caws boisterously, as if laughing.*)

CROW 2: Caw caw caw . . . laugh all you want. You will remain a scavenging crow, sitting here waiting for luck to throw you a piece of meat to fight over . . . Papaya county is the place to be.

CROW 1: Sounds like some stupid utopia. Where everyone is happy and there's plenty for all.

CROW 2: It's true, though! The rivers flow, clean and serene. Farms don't have scarecrows.

CROW 1: What are we doing here, then?

CROW 2: Exactly what I'm sayin'! Let's get to the better place and rest! Eat without having to fight for each morsel!

CROW 1: No! I mean, how could there be a place where there are no crows to scare?!

CROW 2: It's pretty peaceful, I hear! Wanna take a trip there?

CROW 1: I would go and take over!

CROW 2: This is exactly why we are never invited! Because of stupid crows like you! You stay here and wait for your small pieces of meat. I'm off with those who want to join me!

CROW 1: This is the one time I don't have to compete with the bullies of the sky, the vultures, hawks, and eagles. I can rule!!!

CROW 2: I'm off! Who wants to join me?

(*A lot of cawing. The cacophony of cawing slowly fades away. CROW 1 is left circling in silence.*)

END OF PLAY

LISTEN TO VANESSA NAKATE

Aleya Kassam

Aleya Kassam is a Kenyan feminist, storyteller, writer, and performer whose work has been published and performed around the world. She is widely experimental; from page to stage, screen to speaker, micro-fiction to memory poems, docu-theatre to participatory filmmaking, she loves to play with how people experience story. As the "A" from The LAM Sisterhood, she fills the world with stories for African women to feel seen, heard, and beloved, like the award-winning *Brazen Edition*.

Playwright's Statement

In 2020, five young climate justice activists from around the world attended the World Economic Forum in Davos, Switzerland, to speak truth to the power lent to global leaders. In the media that followed, one of these activists' presence was erased and her voice silenced—the only African in the group. Her name is Vanessa Nakate. This piece is for her, in her honor, and in gratitude to her and the other young African women fighting for the people and planet.

Characters

TELLER(S) and SIGN LANGUAGE INTERPRETER(S), this can be one
    person, or multiple tellers and sign language interpreters.
VOICE(S), speak Vanessa Nakate's words out loud. Ideally, the VOICES
    should be picked from the audience. You have creative liberty about how
    many voices, and how to do this—whether you prearrange it, give the
    quotes to people beforehand, or invite people in the moment. However, if
    the teller chooses to speak these words themselves, they must be read out
    loud from a script to indicate they are direct quotes.

Notes

The storytelling must have sign language interpretation. You can choose whether the sign language interpreter leads the story and the teller translates the sign language, or whether it happens the other way around.

This is a storytelling piece, with its lineage in the oral storytelling practices shared in much of Kenya. There is no fourth wall. The teller(s) are not performing but sharing—the story is brought alive as much by the teller(s) as by the audience. The teller(s) should have fun, engage the audience, animate the imagery, trust the words, become vessel(s) to the story, and listen . . .

In preparation for this piece, the teller(s) should explore and research the ways in which they can bring sound and movement alive in the telling (e.g., what does a locust swarm sound like, how can they create those sounds with their bodies, and how can the sounds be echoed and amplified when also done by the audience).

Here is an invocation by one African woman to another. I share these words in the hope that they prepare the teller(s) in the ways they prepared me when writing this piece:

> *I remember that I have something to say. I hold onto that and the words show up.*
>
> —Laura Ekumbo to Sitawa Namwalie, 2021

• • •

TELLER: Hadithi Hadithi . . .?

> *(Wait for the audience to respond with "Hadithi Njoo!" It is ok if they don't, because you are teaching them how to call for stories.)*

TELLER: When I say "Hadithi Hadithi," you say "Hadithi Njoo" (*rhymes with fro*). Hadithi Hadithi, story story . . . Hadithi Njoo, story come. This is how we call for stories, and as your storyteller, I need your help calling for the story. Will you help?

> *(Make space for the audience to respond.)*

TELLER: Hadithi Hadithi?

> *(The audience responds "Hadithi Njoo!" Help them if they are shy. You can use the "Hadithi Hadithi" call and response whenever you need to energize the audience.)*

TELLER: As most stories do, this one starts a long long long time ago. But we will catch it on a December day in 2018, in Kampala, Uganda. On that day, a 22-year-old young woman named Vanessa Nakate was feeling very very very hot . . . so hot that she . . .

(The TELLER is unable to hear the story.)

TELLER: . . . Vanessa Nakate was feeling very very very hot . . . so hot that she . . .

(The story is not coming.)

TELLER: The story is not coming. Hadithi Hadithi?

(The audience responds "Hadithi Njoo!" The teller has a realization.)

TELLER: Wait! This story will not come unless we listen to Vanessa's words.

(The teller invites Vanessa's words to be read.)

VOICE: I asked my uncle to tell me how hot it was 20 years earlier. He told me he thought it was much hotter now.

TELLER: It was hot! The kind where you sweat from places you didn't even know you could sweat from . . . and it wasn't just the heat.

(The TELLER makes the sound of rain, and encourages the audience to join in and amplify the sound.)

TELLER: Let's listen to what Vanessa had to say.

VOICE: It's quite dangerous to walk when it has just finished raining, because you never know where you could fall in a ditch filled with water.

TELLER: Vanessa was curious . . .

VOICE: Climate change really caught my eye because in school, it is taught as something that we don't have to worry about, something that is coming in the far future. I decided to read more. That is how I found out about the Fridays for Future climate strikes.

TELLER: Vanessa prepared her placard, and stood outside the Ugandan Parliament, on strike.
By herself.
For hours.

VOICE: Seeing millions of young people from different parts of the world doing these climate strikes was very inspiring for me because I knew that I wasn't alone.

TELLER: She went back the next Friday. And the next. And the next . . . By then, she was no longer standing by herself.

VOICE: At first, I thought I was fighting to save a tree. Then I thought I was fighting to save a rainforest. Now I realize I am fighting for humanity.

TELLER: Hadithi Hadithi?

(The audience responds "Hadithi Njoo!")

TELLER: Then . . .

(The TELLER makes the sound of a locust swarm and encourages the audience to join.)

VOICE: Locusts invasion in East Africa is threatening the availability of food. They have come after the torrential rains.

(The TELLER increases the volume of the sound of the locust swarm.)

VOICE: How can we achieve zero hunger if climate change is leaving millions of people with nothing to eat? We are going to see disaster after disaster, challenge after challenge, suffering after suffering if nothing is done about this.

TELLER: Vanessa Nakate had something to say.

VOICE: There was the World Economic Forum's annual meeting in Davos, Switzerland, in January where myself and other climate activists took the personal decision to sleep in tents as a statement to global leaders and governments. We wanted leaders to know that they have to make uncomfortable decisions, like giving up on the fossil fuel industry.

VOICE: The people and planet must come first.

TELLER: Vanessa was one of five climate activists on the Davos stage speaking. But in the photo that came out after, there were only four. All European. All white.

VOICE: You didn't just erase a photo. You erased a continent.

TELLER: But Vanessa Nakate refuses to be silenced.

TELLER: Hadithi Hadithi?

(The audience responds "Hadithi Njoo!")

TELLER: Listen to Vanessa Nakate.

VOICE: Historically, Africa has only contributed 3% of global greenhouse gas emissions. Countries in the Global South are suffering the most as a result of climate change, but have contributed the least.

VOICE: And yet, money still pours in from abroad to fund the burning of fossil fuels in Africa.

VOICE: Breaking news: We cannot eat coal or drink oil.

TELLER: Hadithi Hadithi?

(The audience responds "Hadithi Njoo!")

TELLER: Listen.

VOICE: To truly understand this problem, we must listen to the voices of those suffering, both around the world and at home.

VOICE: Everyone must be involved in the process.

VOICE: We can all do something; we can rewrite the story.

TELLER: Hadithi Hadithi?

(The audience responds "Hadithi Njoo!")

TELLER: You want to know how? Listen to Vanessa Nakate.

VOICE: Young women are the light this world needs right now.

VOICE: Young women are the solution the world needs right now.

VOICE: There is power in our voices.

VOICE: There is power in our activism.

TELLER: Listen to Vanessa Nakate.

END OF PLAY

TRUTH OR SOMETHING LIKE IT . . .

Nikhil Katara

Nikhil Katara is from Mumbai, India. He started his journey in theatre with his own production titled *The Unveiling*. He has a degree in philosophy from the Mumbai University and has written for the *One India One People Magazine*, *Free Press Journal*, and the journal *Sambhashan* on a regular basis. He teaches the B.Voc course Theatre & Stagecraft at Wilson College. He is the artistic director of Readings in the Shed and has directed and cowritten the play *The Bose Legacy*.

Playwright's Statement

> *One of the first conditions of happiness is that the link between man and nature shall not be broken.*
>
> —Leo Tolstoy

When the pandemic arrived in India, the government took measures to control it. That meant the country had to be put under lockdown, and people had to stay home. But India is a unique country. The cities are built by migrants who come from different states. When the lockdown came, the buses and trains were shut. Some villages were hundreds of kilometers away. Since the migrants had no means to sustain themselves, no homes to stay in, and they lacked hope, many of them preferred to walk home. When the old couldn't walk, their family members came to rescue them. There was an episode of a woman who cycled 1,200 kilometers to save her father. Their long journeys were reminiscent of the Dandi March that Gandhi took during India's freedom struggle. I wondered that it was highly probable to see someone like the Mahatma walking in the midst of the thousands of migrants as they went back home. The play stemmed from this episode, and the thought of what would happen when the climate crisis takes root. What would happen if more people were displaced? The scale of that, for a country like India, can't be measured.

Note

The playwright encourages the dramatists to perform the stage directions through shadow theatre, puppets, and object theatre.

• • •

Shadows pass by. Hundreds of shadows walk across the streets. They are full of people's shadows. Not one face can be seen. Not one can be recognised. Through the shadows we see a woman, VIDYA, who is walking confusedly in the village. She seems worried. In a parallel world, we see GHANSHYAM, walking confusedly too; they both are mirror images of each other. He falls and injures himself. He is in pain as the shadows rise and fall like waves. GHANSHYAM stands again and limps through the many under-construction roads, now abandoned; under-construction buildings, incomplete; and traffic lights, blinking. The sirens can be heard in the background. VIDYA picks up her phone and dials her father. They have a conversation. We can't hear them. But the fear in them is evident.
Fade Out.
The light fades in.
We see VIDYA cycling.
Fade out.
The light fades in.
We see her cycling through the shadows.
Fade out.
The light fades in.
We see her tired and stopping to grab a glass of water.
Fade out.
The light fades in.
We see her reading the billboards and using her dupatta as a mask.
Fade out.
The light fades in.
We see her exhausted and on the verge of tears.
Fade out.
The light fades in.
We see her frustrated with the broken chain of the cycle.
Fade out.

The light fades in.
We see her finally making her way into the city.

VIDYA: Baba! Baba!

(*She speaks in an incomprehensible manner as the shadows around her rise and fall. The lights fade in. They fade out. They fade in and fade out again. She faints. Her eyes open slowly. We see MOHAN coming to help her. He is very old. He has a long stick in his hand, and is bespectacled. He also has a chaddar [shawl] draped over him that goes around his body and covers his face.*)

MOHAN: Are you ok?

VIDYA: I . . . I thought you were my father.

MOHAN: (*Laughs.*) It happens. Many people confuse me for their father.

VIDYA: You look strangely familiar.

MOHAN: Here, drink some water.

VIDYA: (*Drinks. Coughs out the water.*) Is this the city?

MOHAN: It looks like the city. It smells like the city too.

VIDYA: I am finding it hard to breathe here.

MOHAN: (*Laughs.*) You know that tells me you are not from here. If you were, you'd be used to this air by now . . .

VIDYA: Yes, I am not. I am from the village.

MOHAN: But how did you come here? They have locked the state borders, haven't they?

VIDYA: I cycled.

MOHAN: You cycled here?

VIDYA: Yes.

MOHAN: For how long?

VIDYA: For about 600 kilometers . . .

MOHAN: Mohan, that's my name, and you?

VIDYA: I am Vidya. I am here to take Baba home. I believe there was a lockdown because of the new disease, and there was no way to go back. My Baba works here.

MOHAN: Oh! Really. What does he do?

VIDYA: Small jobs. He rides the rickshaw. He also takes up some construction work.

MOHAN: He builds the city?

VIDYA: (*Laughs.*) You can say that.

MOHAN: Come, let's go look for your father.

> (*VIDYA looks around. The shadows entwine with the other shadows, moving in a strange manner. MOHAN rides pillion. They keep speaking as they ride together. They go past the shadows of people walking.*)

MOHAN: Thousands are walking home. Thousands.

VIDYA: This city is ruthless.

MOHAN: Cities like this one are formed by the blood and sweat of the people who inhabit them. Some are visible and some are invisible to our eyes.

VIDYA: How do you help so many people together?

MOHAN: By starting with one . . . You started with your father.

VIDYA: Would God forgive me if I didn't?

MOHAN: To a people famished, the only acceptable form in which God can dare appear is as work and the promise of food as wages.

VIDYA: For anyone who'd see them walking, would feel . . . God is dead.

MOHAN: Truth is God. Can truth die?

VIDYA: This Truth is disturbing.

MOHAN: It most certainly is. But Truth affects everything. It is affecting our environment, our health, our education systems. How long can we ignore it, before it comes and meets us here, like this? Can we hide it?

> (*Pause. VIDYA looks around and halts.*)

MOHAN: What are you looking at?

VIDYA: That.

MOHAN: The windmill? Or the solar panels?

VIDYA: What are those?

MOHAN: Energy.

VIDYA: I haven't seen them yet. In our village I think they use . . .

MOHAN: Fossil fuel?

VIDYA: Yes.

MOHAN: Things will change now. Our country has strong plans. You see these forms of energy are special, Vidya. They cause no pollution.

VIDYA: And will that help?

MOHAN: It is a great step. A positive step. If this takes root, then everything will become better. The air would be breathable. The water drinkable.

VIDYA: They should put more of these things everywhere. What are they waiting for?

MOHAN: It will come soon. I think India plans to double these in the next few years.

VIDYA: These developments are great. But there is a gap somewhere.

MOHAN: What do you mean?

VIDYA: I always feel that in the village, where I stay, things reach us later. My father, and many other people who are capable of contributing, don't really get the right opportunities. Look at the situation now. Do we exist? Why did no one think about us when they had such a lockdown? Why did they not think about how we would go home?

MOHAN: I know. These big changes and plans are meaningful only when everyone takes part on the journey. Not just a few billionaires.

VIDYA: What's a billionaire?

MOHAN: Someone who has 1,000,000,000 rupees in their bank.

VIDYA: (*Shocked.*) That is a lot of money. I had only 2,000 and I spent them buying this cycle.

MOHAN: Well, it was a good deal, given the circumstances.

VIDYA: How do these big people with big money make these big plans?

MOHAN: Who told you only big people with big money make the big plans?

VIDYA: Then who else would?

MOHAN: A dedicated government does, an interested group of people who are concerned about the future does. Sometimes little children do too . . .

VIDYA: Children? You are joking?

MOHAN: No. I am serious. In fact, young girls like you came together for the cause of climate change. There are so many examples. The biggest conversation in the world right now is around the Green New Deal and it is led by a young politician.

VIDYA: Is this some sort of new law?

MOHAN: It isn't just some new law. It is something worth fighting for. The future. The scientists think there is little time before climate change will destroy the planet. If things continue this way, cities like Mumbai will be lost under water in a few decades.

VIDYA: If that happens, where will the people go? There will be so many who will be trapped like my father is right now. No. No. No. That can't happen. What can I do?

MOHAN: Think.

VIDYA: Am I capable?

MOHAN: You most certainly are . . .

(*VIDYA is confused.*)

MOHAN: No ordinary person cycles 600 kilometers on the national highways of India to save someone's life.

VIDYA: 604 now. Four kilometers have passed with you riding pillion.

MOHAN: (*Laughs.*) And quite an effortless ride it is.

VIDYA: Oh! Look there, that is my father. We've found him!

(She is ecstatic. They stop.)

MOHAN: Now I think I should get off. I need to make room for your father.

VIDYA: It was nice speaking to you.

MOHAN: I will remember this conversation. Take care on your way back home.

VIDYA: The journey doesn't end there.

MOHAN: I know. You are one for the long road.

VIDYA: As long as I have my cycle, I'll keep going.

MOHAN: I am sure you will.

(MOHAN offers his blessings, and smiles. He slowly begins to walk as the shadows make way for him. VIDYA watches as the silhouette of the old man with the long stick grows smaller and smaller, until it merges with the other shadows.)

END OF PLAY

FRIENDS FOR LIFE

Himali Kothari

Writer-Editor **Himali Kothari** loves being led on a merry chase by words, as long as she can eventually get the better of them. A believer in the power of words to effect change, it is what she seeks to do in her own small way.

Playwright's Statement

The Green New Deal is about inclusiveness. It is about involving more groups and perhaps those categories of humans who may not have been considered potential contributors towards creating global change. When I chanced upon the stories of "Jal Sahelis," it struck an immediate chord. In Hindi, "jal" means water and "saheli" means friend, thus "jal sahelis" are friends of water.

The initiative that started with a small group of women in a village in central India has now extended to over 200 villages and brought 700 women in its fold. These women have taken on the task of enabling availability of drinking water and water for irrigation in this arid region. From building dams, cutting through hills, and repairing water pumps to mobilizing the community to participate in this endeavor, the stories of these women fascinated me. In a society where a woman's role as a change-maker is often overlooked, to see these women assert themselves as ambassadors of change not just within their community but also at the global level is heartening.

Characters

NAVYA, a young woman in her twenties. She is dressed in a saree with a drape covering her head. Her saree is a vibrant color but a little stained with dirt, like the clothes of someone who has been doing manual labor.

AMMA, a woman in her fifties. She could have a couple of earthen pots at her feet. She is dressed in a saree with a drape covering her head. Her saree is of a similar hue as NAVYA's but much faded from use, something that has seen better days.

Setting

An arid landscape

• • •

The two women are at opposite ends of the stage, largely unaware of each other. They could be standing or sitting on chairs facing the audience. Occasionally, when one is speaking, the other could get up or move forward and look at a specific point. They address the audience.

AMMA: (*Looking skyward.*) Anytime now.

NAVYA: (*Looking at a spot beyond the audience.*) Anytime now.

(*A few moments pass as they continue to each look at their specific points.*)

AMMA: (*Wiping the sweat off her face with the end of her saree.*) It's hot, huh? Hottest summer yet, they say in the village. How hot? Let's see . . . (*thinking*) A month ago, I would get water from the village well. And then two weeks ago, I let my bucket in and heard the clang of the metal on the parched bottom. That dreaded sound. I have been hearing that clang for a few decades now. But, it still hurts the ear, every year. It's come sooner this year than the last. I peered over the edge, hoping. Not a drop left. Had it seeped through and run off elsewhere? (*Pause. Shoulders droop.*) I would have to make my way to the pond on the other side of the hill. The rain clouds were not here yet. I had hoped that it would be a few days before I would have to start walking all the way there. But, pots have to be filled. Food has to be cooked. So, I hoisted both my pots on my head and took off.

NAVYA: It's not new, you know, this walk for water. I have been doing it since I was a little girl. Towards the end of summer, the walk would take so long, I would have to miss school. Frankly, that bit I didn't mind. (*Giggles. Pause. NAVYA grows thoughtful.*) I never understood it. This wait. Endless staring towards the heavens. Walk and wait. Wait and walk. The longer the wait, the longer the walk. And every year, both were getting longer.

AMMA: That was two weeks ago. One look inside and I knew that this pond had a few days left. It was already many inches below the dark line that the water had left when it was full. And, when I leaned into it and narrowed my eyes, I could see the bottom. This was not going to last very long. What next? How far to the next one? (*Pause.*) There was some excitement at the village when I got there. My heart skipped a beat. Had we been showered with a miracle? Had the well filled up? I peered in. No. Nothing. Some man was standing by it, speaking in a loud voice—"tubewell"—"dam"—"freshwater." He seemed familiar. Had he been here before?

NAVYA: They come every four years. Walk through our village in their starched white shirts, smiles stretched across their faces, hands folded. Long speeches filled with promises would echo through the village. And then silence. Silence and swirling clouds of dust as they retreated.

(*Pause.*)

AMMA: The sky was a different shade yesterday. A little less blue. The sun didn't bounce off the earth as hard. I was so sure yesterday would be the day. The clouds would burst and I would line up the pots outside my house and wait for them to fill up. But, no, nothing. And at the pond, when I scooped my bucket in, it scraped the bottom. Another week, if we are lucky. "No, no . . . don't think about that," I told myself. By then, for sure . . .

(*She looks skyward, craning her neck.*)

NAVYA: Enough. I was done with the waiting. Nobody was going to sort this out for us. Fetching the water was our job after all, and you know what they say: Don't send a man to do a woman's job. I rounded up friends, and they rounded up a few more. I had a plan. Water flows so why are we foolishly walking to it? We are not going to the water I told them, the water is going to come to us.

(*AMMA scoffs and pointedly looks up at the sky. NAVYA ignores her.*)

NAVYA: It was not easy. But, it's done now. Anytime now . . .

(*She looks towards her point beyond the audience.*

Long pause, during which NAVYA continues to look at her point and AMMA continues to look skyward.

The gurgling sound of water followed by a little gush, like water bursting through a newly laid pipe. NAVYA jumps up and down and claps her hands in glee. AMMA looks at her, bamboozled by her actions.)

AMMA: What's wrong with you, girl? Have you gone mad?

NAVYA: It's here Amma, it's here!

AMMA: (*Craning high towards the sky*) Where? Where?

(*NAVYA holds AMMA by the shoulders. She turns her to look at the point where she had been looking throughout the play and points.*)

NAVYA: There, Amma, look! There!

(*AMMA looks at the spot. The gurgling sound of the water becomes louder. Bewilderment slowly changes to joy on AMMA's face. NAVYA grabs AMMA by the wrists and holding her hands compels her to spin around in a couple of circles, like two little girls playing. When they stop, they stand shoulder to shoulder, embracing each other in a side-hug, huge smiles on their faces, tears running down their cheeks, and stare steadfast at that spot.*)

END OF PLAY

DREAMSONG

Heidi Kraay

Heidi Kraay pulls myth, metaphor, and monsters together to discover connections across difference. Her plays include *Unwind: Hindsight is 2020*, *see in the dark*, *How To Hide Your Monster*, co-devised plays, one-acts, short plays, and plays for young audiences. Her work has been presented where she lives in Boise, Idaho, as well as regionally, in New York City, and internationally. Heidi holds an MFA from California Institute of Integral Studies. She is a member of the Dramatists Guild of America.

Playwright's Statement

Like many big ideas, the theme "Envisioning a Global Green New Deal" got me thinking from a childlike perspective in order to see into it more clearly and from the gut. Inspired by Representative Alexandria Ocasio-Cortez, I stuck onto the question—what is the future we want?—and gravitated toward her words that "we can be whatever we have the courage to see."

Characters

AZ, male, 11, Berry's best friend. Science nerd.
BERRY, female, 12, Az's best friend. Tomboy-ish.

Notes

The kids can be played by adults.
Multiracial casting is supported, but Az and Berry are preferably not white.
A slash (/) indicates where the next speech begins.

• • •

The California Coast, near a small town in the Redwoods. August, twilight.

The sound of distant fire shifts into lapping ocean waves. On the shore stands AZ, facing the water, sing/chanting to something deep below.

AZ: Grow
Grow like rainbows
Grow like moonbeams
Grow like love—

    (BERRY enters, running.)

BERRY: Az! There you are! We've been looking all over—. What in hell are you doing?

AZ: Hi, Berry

BERRY: Hi, Berry? You piece of—. Got everyone worried sick looking, we're s'posed to be packing and this is how you spend our last chance to hang out? Staring at the sea?

AZ: We'll see each other again—

BERRY: Insta doesn't count. Long way from Oakland to Michigan.

AZ: That's why I have to bring her out tonight.

BERRY: Who?

AZ: The creature. My Lito was the last to see her.
A summer night like this, when he was just my age. Ma told me, like he told her.

BERRY: Aw hell, Az . . .

AZ: The night he had to migrate from his family's home, he saw the creature.
Gave him courage for the journey. Called her the Dream Saver.
We call her out from the water now, we'll get what we need to go on.

BERRY: Smoke's really got to you this season huh? I know we're dealing with a lot, but—

AZ: Just has to be good enough cause, and we'll see her magnificent, ancient neck rise up—

BERRY: Thought you were into science, not this / crap.

AZ: Cryptozoology has lots of scientific basis.

BERRY: Come on, Az, yer mom's going nuts.

AZ: She should know I'm here. This full moon, electric air, our great need tonight—.
The conditions are just right—

BERRY: Right for what?! My dad's out fighting this fire, we lost our house, I'm sleeping on your floor, tomorrow I gotta go live with my aunt and start a new school—are you listening?

AZ: Yes! Ma lost her shop, fire's taking everything—they're evacuating our whole town!

BERRY: Welcome back to the living! So / let's get back—

AZ: *So* we have to call her out *now*. To get our home back. Stop the fires, not just here.
All of California, the whole northwest.

BERRY: Why stop there? Ask Dino Dragon to stop the droughts, hurricanes, bring world peace—

AZ: Now you're getting it!

BERRY: Are you losing it?!

AZ: Beryl!

BERRY: Azure!

AZ: We can be whatever we have the courage to see.
And if we see it with clear eyes, ask for it with brave hearts, and she approves—

BERRY: She'll make all our dreams come true? Like some fairy godmother under the sea?

AZ: Not exactly. But if she shows herself, we'll know our dreams are possible.
We can pull together and maybe have the courage to keep going.
If you're not willing to try, leave me alone. You're killing the vibe.

BERRY: Okay! I'll be quiet, but I'm not leaving without you.

AZ: Don't be quiet . . . What's the future you want? Come on, imagine. See it!

BERRY: This is such a—. Alright, Dad and I get our house back. Like you said.

AZ: Good. And?

BERRY: And? My aunt in Flint . . . can trust her water again. Everyone gets clean water.

AZ: Keep going, what else?

BERRY: And I dunno . . . the fires stop raging so we can stay here. Everyone has a job . . . and we take care of the ones who can't work. Grown up leaders and rich people stop playing games with our planet, and us. Nobody's hungry. Nobody has to leave their home, but when they do, they're welcome where they wanna go. We get the global temperatures down, like Mrs. Thatcher said, so the polar bears stop drowning. And nobody's sick, the air's clean . . .

AZ: (*Sing/chanting.*) Grow . . .	BERRY: (*Building intensity.*) Ice caps
Grow like rainbows	stop melting
Grow like moonbeams	Rainforests stop burning
Grow like love	Islands stop washing away
Grow	People like us make a difference
	And they treat us like we matter

(The oceans start to churn.)

BERRY: What's that?!

AZ: Don't stop, keep seeing it, sing with me!

AZ: Grow	BERRY: . . . Grow
Grow like rainbows	. . . like . . . bows
Grow like moonbeams	Grow . . . moonbeams
Grow like love	. . . like
Grow	This is bull—

(The sound of earth cracking, water rushing.)

BERRY: What's happening!? Earthquake?!

AZ: You're safe, keep singing!

AZ: Creature of the deep!	BERRY: Grow
We're united in our dreams.	Grow like rainbows
Committed to make them true.	Grow like moonbeams
Will you show us we have a chance?	Grow like love
That it's possible to teach the world	Grow
to love the world	Grow like rainbows
so we can all heal?	Grow like moonbeams—

(An eruption, like a chasm opening. Singing stops.)

AZ: Look!

BERRY: I am!

(Their eyes lock with something beyond.)

BERRY: It's / giant.

AZ: . . . perfect, look at her neck.

BERRY: It's glowing! What's it gonna / do—

AZ: Thank you, creature of the deep! We welcome you and your great wisdom!

(A giant splashing. The children duck.)

BERRY: It's . . . gone.

AZ: She did . . . what we needed.

BERRY: What? Just . . . showed up and left? Can't even prove it was here! Did that happen?

AZ: I . . . I know what to do now. And I know we can. Help me?

BERRY: Well . . . Of course . . .

AZ: Could take a lifetime.

BERRY: So . . . how do we start?

(Their eyes stay with the sea, forever changed.)

END OF PLAY

2079

Camila Le-bert

Camila Le-bert is a Chilean American playwright living between Santiago, Chile, and Long Beach, California. She is a graduate of the MFA in Playwriting from Columbia University and in Acting from Universidad de Chile. Her works include *CHAN!* (developed with the Royal Court Theatre), *LATINO*, *Trío*, *La Guagua*, *Mis Tres Hermanas*, and *Chicos Tóxicos*. Her play *Comunidad* was featured in the Delirios en Cautiverio at the Chilean National Theatre in 2020. She is the founder and director of the Lápiz de Mina women's playwriting festival.

Playwright's Statement

The inspiration for this play is a mix of utter despair and anxiety on the subject of climate change, the abysmal pain of losing many loved ones last year, and the hope brought about by the 2018 social uprising in Chile, when "Chile despertó," Chile awakened, and we found a collective struggle and unity calling for a change of everything. The system that had made us feel like we had failed had, in fact, failed us, and we came together, as never before, to bring it down. Now, in the throes of writing a new constitution we continue, once again, to struggle to keep the power with the people and away from the oligarchy, the one percent.

• • •

When I was a kid, I was a member of the Junior World Wildlife Fund. Every month I'd get a magazine with a little black and white bear and some monkeys, a dolphin, a cheetah. I always liked cheetahs.

I was never a girl scout but I had my little black and white bear badge and I felt like I had a duty to protect the planet. A lone ranger. If I saw someone throwing a piece of garbage on the floor I would yell: LITTER!

LITTER!

It was like a capital sin. I guess. I wasn't really raised in the church. My family was more along the lines of nonpracticing Marxists if you really get down to it.

LITTER!

But I imagine that's how religious people feel about sin. Going against the divine. LITTER!

You're killing the whales!

The cheetahs! The little black and white bears!

I would run to pick up the trash and hold on to it until I found a garbage can and my mission was accomplished.

I threw out my grandma's cigarettes too. My kid mind could not understand how someone could purposefully kill themselves every day. She wanted to kill me. I think she wanted to strangle her little gringa granddaughter for being so fucking McGruff. I had been brainwashed by the empire, she must have thought. But cigarettes were the least of her problems. She had survived the fight for a fair world and the violent backlash of the elite and its military minions, exile, the destruction of her country, and her dreams, and now that I'm older I see the lure of a little death. Life is exhausting.

My grandfather died last year at 97.

If I lived to be 97, I would have to wait until 2079 to die. 2079.

Chile has the fourth highest suicide rate in the Americas. You know who kills themselves more?

Men over 70.

Death is everywhere.

You know what pension the state gives you in Chile?

158,339 pesos a month. 223 dollars and 96 cents. A month.

That's what you get when you have no savings.

Like me. Like most of my friends.

I don't want to make it to 2079.

I've been to the cemetery so much, I have a regular spot in the parking lot.

Not a lot in the graveyard.

I don't own anything.

I always wanted my own apartment but I've been living as an *allegada* since 2018. *Allegada* is what we call people in Chile who live in someone else's house because they either can't afford their own place or a catastrophe has taken their house. An earthquake, a tsunami, a fire, a mudslide. We have a lot of *allegados*. A lot of people crammed together. And a lot of natural disasters. We are also the birthplace of neoliberalism a.k.a. capitalism that respects no one and no thing. They sold everything: schools, water, gas, the phone company, the roads. You can't walk a block around your house in Chile without someone charging you for something. They also call it entrepreneurship.

We faked it so long we actually thought we made it.

Now we're going to bury neoliberalism.

We are leaving our little apartments and we are taking back the streets.

These are our roads. This is our water. And this is our air.

And it isn't woo. I am not a hippie. And it is not impossible.

We can share. We can stop pretending we are going to be one of them because we're not.

We are all one paycheck away.

I'll meet you halfway. There are other ways to do things. We just proved it!

And we'll find García Lorca in the watermelons. And we will do more than just survive. And we won't believe the lies because we will know better, we, dare I say it, will have class consciousness and we will tell them to trickle down their own economics.

We won't have to break our souls smiling for a tip.

You won't have to wait for me to be good, because we won't depend on charity or crowdfunding support to pay for life-threatening surgery because we will all take care of each other.

We don't want things back to normal.

My friends can make a difference. Take back the internet. Copy or die. Free the pdfs.

I got you.

It wasn't depression, it was capitalism.

Huddled masses, broken bones, making herstory.

For all of those who came before me, we can do it.

Things change.

I don't regret throwing out Nena's cigarettes.

It's been a while since I saw someone throw garbage on the ground. Litter bugs are going extinct.

And the white and black bears are still around.

Let's check out 2079.

END OF PLAY

GET ME TO THE SIXTH FLOOR

Philip Luswata

Philip Luswata is an accomplished theatre and arts development and interactive communications professional with over twenty years of experience. Philip is the founder and director of the Theatre Factory at the National Theatre in Kampala. He lectures in theatre and film at Makerere University and is a highly rated and respected performer and creative artist in Uganda and East Africa.

Playwright's Statement

Ugandan churches have grown really rich and are investing heavily in industry outside tithe. As participants in the abuse of the environment and professed servers of the people, they must take responsibility for the struggle for a greener Uganda.

• • •

The lobby of a high-rise building: a table is placed at the entrance at which sits a disinterested woman, HENRIETTA, in a security uniform. Somewhere at the back is a huge trash can. A sign with an arrow reads, "CHURCH SANCTUARY." Variously placed around the lobby are posters advertising five products by the Church and their fancy taglines ("Messiah Faith Healing Clinic and Pharmacy: For Everlasting Life," "Brethren Holy Rice Enterprise: The Grain on Good Soil," "Salvation Mineral Water: Quench Your Spirit," "Apostle Plastics and Packaging: Bundle your Blessings," and "His Blessed Grace Bakery: The Hidden Treasure"). Enter MARIAM, a diminutive, colorful, and very fussy-looking woman.

MARIAM: I want to get to the sixth floor.

HENRIETTA: Go to the sixth floor.

MARIAM: You are security. You don't want to know why I'm going to the sixth floor?

HENRIETTA: Are you the first person to go to the sixth floor? This is a public building! Anyone can go up and come down as they want! So go!

MARIAM: But do others go up and down for the same reason as I am?

HENRIETTA: Brother Pius! Please come and show this one out.

(*BROTHER PIUS, also in uniform, enters from the sanctuary.*)

MARIAM: "Please come and show this one out" and I go where? I came here to be listened to! Out there is a disaster! Storms! Heat waves . . . floods . . . droughts . . . people are suffering out there! I am here to talk to people who should listen!

PIUS: Miss . . .

MARIAM: Global Warming . . .

PIUS: Miss Global Warming . . .

MARIAM: Don't be silly! I am Mariam! Miss Mariam! (*She prowls around them.*) But I want to talk to the people here about global warming . . . (*She moves and shouts towards the church sanctuary.*) Every person who has more than 10 people who sit and listen to them every week must know that they have the responsibility to talk to their listeners about global warming . . . (*PIUS and HENRIETTA panic and hurry to pull her away.*) The Bishop, and others in privileged positions like him, can no longer shield themselves behind the excuse that "Global what?! That's difficult English to explain." We live it! We feel it every day! So we should be able to talk about global warming in vernacular by now!

PIUS: Miss Mariam, go to a government building with your chatter. This here is a church investment. Out of his love, our Bishop of the Living Waters has invested heavily in business and industry to make local people richer.

(*He offers a proud tour of the posters.*)

Messiah Faith Healing Clinic and Pharmacy: For Everlasting Life; Brethren Holy Rice Enterprise: The Grain on Good Soil; Salvation Mineral Water: Quench Your Spirit; Apostle Plastics and Packaging: Bundle your Blessings;

His Blessed Grace Bakery: The Hidden Treasure . . . What does any of this have to do with your global warming, heat waves, floods, and droughts? Go back to whoever sent you, and let them know they have lost!

MARIAM: When the well from which you draw this Salvation Mineral Water dries up, will it be government to suffer? Listen . . . (*They listen . . . The buzz of an engine in the distance.*) Engines . . . burning fuel to bake His Blessed Grace Bread . . . We want to eat bread to stay alive, but conveniently ignore the fact that the process of making it releases fumes into the atmosphere that are increasing greenhouse gasses.

PIUS: Sister Henrietta, I am leaving you with your Professor. Too much English . . .

HENRIETTA: Throw her out!

(*MARIAM follows PIUS menacingly.*)

MARIAM: Throw me out as you throw out your "I don't care" attitude too! The developments roaring under this building are part of many others around the world doing the same, at this very minute . . . all using energy formed from dead animals and plants. (*Pause.*) We thank the dead for their sacrifice . . . but we have overexploited their indulgence. As they decayed for centuries . . . now because of "development" we are burning these extracted fossils . . . more gasses in the atmosphere, more heat is trapped than we need . . . wet places are becoming wetter . . . dry places are becoming drier . . . even the dead are confused. What is it that the living want?

(*PIUS is fed up. He grabs her suddenly and dumps her into the big trash can.*)

PIUS: I don't like mad people! That woman has smeared mud on the sacrifices of the Bishop! In Luke 17, Verse 1, Jesus said to his disciples, "It is inevitable that stumbling blocks come, but woe to him through whom they come!" She has got what she deserves! Trying to fight development!

MARIAM: (*She shouts out from the trash can.*) But can development be sweet and bitter at the same time?

PIUS: Garbage talking!

HENRIETTA: Listen to that garbage, Brother Pius. I have been listening and thinking . . . Bishop says that all the water on earth today was created on the first day of creating the world. Not a drop has ever been added or lost.

PIUS: Our Lord is an awesome God.

HENRIETTA: This water comes down as rain, flows into the rivers, lakes, oceans and swamps, then goes back up as vapor to return as water again . . . If it returns, it means there is somewhere where it stops when it goes up. A place it can't cross. A border between our world and the universe . . . since it can't go beyond, it returns after forming into water . . . So, now these fumes from Bishop's factories . . . these . . . what . . .

MARIAM: (*From the trash.*) Carbon dioxide . . .

PIUS: What is wrong with you?! Did they give you a tongue to terrorize others?

HENRIETTA: Those carbon . . . whatever . . . that are released when we burn our factory fuels . . . where do they go . . .? Up. And what do they come back down as? We know water goes up as vapor and returns as rain. But those fumes . . . you can even see them going up. What do they come back down as? Have you ever seen them returning?

PIUS: No.

HENRIETTA: They stay up there . . . and stay up there . . . without coming down! Even now we are adding to them as we bake the bread. As we make plastics . . . as we bottle water. . . so much is going on right now that is increasing those fumes going up! Something not good is happening up there, Brother Pius, for sure.

PIUS: Sister Henrietta, wake up! This is where we are working. Now you want us to go to the Bishop and bite the hand that feeds us?

MARIAM: It is not about him alone! It is about Bishop and others with influence like him. We need leadership today!

HENRIETTA: Brother Pius, remove the woman from the garbage.

   (*PIUS complies.*)

MARIAM: We are the earth's waste . . . oil and coal when we decay. This is what we are burning to produce energy. As we burn, we emit these gasses faster than Mother Earth needs them. There is excess and scarcity at the same time.

HENRIETTA: Me, I am going to tell Bishop! He should switch off his engines today! He should think of another type of electricity for the factories! The leaders should be the ones to show the way!

PIUS: You try your madness and you will see me! For me, I still need this job!

MARIAM: In your own small way, Brother Pius, try and be mad. Think of energy that is affordable and not becoming more expensive by the day. Think of energy that is always there and that you can access. Is this ever a possibility?

(They give him time to think it over. He bursts out laughing. They let him have his fill.)

MARIAM: It is a possibility. The free wind . . . the sun . . . cheaper energy that is renewable and everlasting. We defeat the dangerous effects of climate change. We ensure economic growth that will not be interrupted. Employment for you will be abundant and guaranteed and you can talk of a future for your children.

(It is HENRIETTA's turn to laugh at Pius.)

HENRIETTA: Brother Pius! Now you are asking yourself why you laughed so loud!

PIUS: Sister Henrietta . . . we learn something new every day.

HENRIETTA: We better learn. If what this woman is saying is correct, people will die from lack of food because of the effects of climate change as a result of the gasses . . . People will be killing each other as they fight for things we need that will become scarce. These greenhouse gasses will finish everything.

PIUS: You said you were going where?

MARIAM: The Sixth Floor . . .

END OF PLAY

COST

Zizi Majid

Zizi Majid is a Malay Singaporean playwright based in New York City whose plays advocate for a shared humanity. Her award-winning plays have been staged in New York City, Singapore, and China. For five years, Zizi was artistic director of Teater Ekamatra (Singapore), successfully breaking into the mainstream during her tenure, tripling audiences, and garnering multiple awards. She is the recipient of a Young Artist Award from the National Arts Council, Singapore, and a fellow of WP Theater's 2020–2022 Lab, NYC. She holds an MFA in Playwriting from Columbia University.

Playwright's Statement

An enduring fact of climate change is that those who are least responsible bear the brunt of its consequences. In this play, I imagine what it would be like if there had been some positive progress made vis-à-vis the Green New Deal and private nonprofits had persuaded global carbon emitters to cut financial risk associated with climate catastrophe. Yet there would still be those in the developing world dealing with the consequences of calamitous energy production.

Characters

ASHOK MELWANI, mid-to-late 40s, Indian American, CEO of EcoInvest.
CHRISTINE MELWANI, *née* Jones, early 40s, white American, Ashok's wife.
BENJY MELWANI, early 20s, Indian, Ashok's son from his first marriage.

• • •

SCENE 1

2025. A luxury suite in the most exclusive hotel in Mumbai, India. ASHOK and CHRISTINE are in formal evening dress.

CHRISTINE: Do that last bit again.

ASHOK: What last bit?

CHRISTINE: The carbon reduction yada yada.

ASHOK: Right. (*Clears his throat.*) The levels of carbon reduction we have managed to hold companies accountable for have far exceeded expectations. The strong partnership—

CHRISTINE: Symbiotic—symbiotic's better.

ASHOK: The symbiotic partnership between EcoInvest and the Indian government has made all this possible. Who would have thought that an investor-driven, climate-focused nonprofit from New York—

CHRISTINE: That's a hell of a mouthful.

ASHOK: It's how we brand ourselves.

CHRISTINE: It's confusing, it's stumbly, it's crud—

ASHOK: It's what I do.

    (*CHRISTINE waves her hand, nonchalantly.*)

ASHOK: Who would have thought that an investor-driven, climate-focused nonprofit from New York could have such real-world climate impact?

    (*CHRISTINE has lost interest and is now looking at her phone.*)

CHRISTINE: Lisa wants me to get her some silk saris. I need you to go with me.

ASHOK: Why?

CHRISTINE: Cos you speak Indian, Ashok.

ASHOK: You mean Hindi.

CHRISTINE: Exactly. You'll get us a good bargain.

ASHOK: Fine, we'll go tomorrow after my brunch with the Home Affairs Minister.

CHRISTINE: What's that about?

ASHOK: He wants me to invest in some failed Belt and Road project up north.

CHRISTINE: Good luck with that.

(*The sound of someone knocking on the door. CHRISTINE checks her watch.*)

CHRISTINE: I'm not done with my makeup!

(*CHRISTINE exits to go into the bathroom. ASHOK strides to the door of the suite. He looks out through the peephole, curses under his breath, and does not open the door. Another knock on the door.*)

CHRISTINE: (Off, from the bathroom.) Get that please, honey!

(*ASHOK opens the door slightly. We see BENJY through the crack.*)

ASHOK: (*Whispering.*) This is not a good time.

BENJY: Then when? You've been avoiding me ever since you got here.

ASHOK: (*Whispering.*) Tomorrow afternoon, the dosa place at Mangaldas market.

(*CHRISTINE reenters the suite. ASHOK hurriedly shuts the door.*)

ASHOK: We don't need that tonight, thank you!

CHRISTINE: Bellboy?

(*ASHOK nods.*)

SCENE 2

The cacophonous sounds of the busy streets of Mumbai. A roadside dosa restaurant. ASHOK and BENJY are seated across from each other.

BENJY: So you got your big award last night.

(*ASHOK nods.*)

BENJY: How does it feel?

ASHOK: (*Shrugs.*) It's the culmination of years of hard work.

BENJY: You know what Mom got for her years of hard work?

(*ASHOK stands up to leave.*)

BENJY: Fine, walk away, it's what you've always done anyway.

ASHOK: What do you want from me, Benjy?

BENJY: Why didn't you ever bring us over to New York?

> *(A tense silence washes over them.*
> *ASHOK slowly sits back down.)*

ASHOK: (*Sighs.*) It was . . . complicated. My business failed, I was in a lot of debt . . . I . . .

BENJY: When I was little, I used to walk with Mom to the post office on Fridays to send you the letter she had spent all week writing. Then when I was nine, we stopped. When I asked her why, she simply said, "Baba's moved on." That's the last she ever spoke of you. She doesn't even know you're here in Mumbai or that I'm meeting you. (*Pause.*) She's dying, you know? The doctors say she has less than six months.

ASHOK: (*Stunned.*) But how? Why?

BENJY: The clothes factory she worked at is right by the coal plant—she's been breathing in those fumes for years.

ASHOK: (*Under his breath.*) Fuck.

BENJY: So those carbon reductions you're parading to your politician friends? Mean nothing to Mom and everyone else who worked in that factory.

> *(A silence washes over them again.)*

ASHOK: Benjy . . . son, you have to believe me, there was nothing I could've—

BENJY: I'm not here to listen to some excuse for why you did what you did. (*Shrugs.*) I just wanted you to know the cost of what you've done.

> *(BENJY stands up to leave. ASHOK takes out his wallet and pulls all the notes out of it. He rushes to put them into BENJY's hand.)*

ASHOK: For her. For you.

> *(BENJY looks down at the money in his hand. A moment. CHRISTINE walks towards ASHOK and BENJY, carrying bulging shopping bags.)*

CHRISTINE: Ashok? There you are! I've been looking all over for you!

(BENJY looks at ASHOK one last time as CHRISTINE approaches them.)

CHRISTINE: I got a good price for the saris, no thanks to you!

(BENJY walks away from them. ASHOK watches him walk away.)

CHRISTINE: Who's that, Ashok? . . . Ashok?

(ASHOK does not reply and continues watching BENJY with an odd look on his face. The cacophonous sounds of Mumbai take over.)

END OF PLAY

SMALL BUT MIGHTY

Mwendie Mbugua

Mwendie Mbugua is a communication practitioner, author, and Sundance Theatre Lab artist-in-residence. She has always had a passion for theatre and has been involved in staging several Easter and Christmas musicals in her hometown of Nairobi, Kenya. In 2016, her dream of becoming an author was realized, and she launched her first children's book, *Don't turn off the lights!* She currently lives in California with her husband and two children.

Playwright's Statement

> It's the little things citizens do. That's what will make the difference.
>
> —Wangari Maathai

This short story was inspired by my father-in-law, a passionate environmentalist whose mission is to green Kenya and Africa, and to increase food sustainability. His love for bees opened the door to this story. My passion is writing for children, so this monologue is written for children ages 4–7 years old. The hope is to introduce them to alternative views on industrial agriculture.

Setting

Open on a simple stage decorated to look like a garden. It could be a screen, or you can use live plants around the stage. If possible, sounds of a gentle brook and garden are heard in the background. We enter the world of the bees.

• • •

TAMU, an animated man or woman dressed as a bee, is strolling, deeply smelling flowers and taking a long drink from the brook. Satisfied, they then take a seat on a stool, close their eyes, and enjoy the sounds of the garden. They open their eyes, peer out. Ah! Company has arrived . . .

TAMU: Jambo! Hello boys and girls! Bees and drones! Welcome to the garden! As you take a break before your next stop, I'd like to share with you a short tale about a hero bee called Asali. A bee so brave that she saved her entire hive from extinction.

This garden right here—wasn't always as beautiful as this.

It all began when Bwana Farmer moved in. At first, he was harmless; the creatures paid him no heed. The plants continued to bloom, and insects would play in the wind.

Then came a day that none of us would ever forget. Bwana Farmer brought a large container we had never seen before and that evening, he sprayed the flowers and the plants. Little did we know, the next day would tell a different story.

Every bee was up and early out in the fields, pollinating—carrying pollen from flower to flower and enjoying the feel of the golden sun on their delicate wings—when suddenly, we noticed one bee after the other falling . . . dying. They had been poisoned by the spray. It was a very tragic day.

Asali and her friends survived and managed to do so for a while. But Bwana Farmer kept spraying. He believed this would help his fruits and vegetables grow better. That this, in turn, would allow him to sell more produce at the local market and he would eventually buy a bigger truck. He did not realize what this was doing to the life in the garden.

One day, Asali had had enough! She sought wise counsel from Mama Nyuki—the oldest and wisest bee in the colony. Mama Nyuki listened to Asali's cries and concerns and though she had no answers for her, she reminded Asali that even though she was small, she was mighty! And she could make a difference. That was all Asali needed to hear.

That night, she could not sleep. Buzzing to the left and buzzing to the right. Even the sounds of the gentle bubbling brook did not calm her down. A plan was formulating . . . Early the next morning, she shared it with her hive. It was very simple, with just one step.

(*Tamu puts on a voice, imitating Asali.*) "Friends!" she said. "Bwana Farmer has been poisoning us for some time now and we have lost many because of it. Before he came, the garden was alive and home to many of us. We need to return to our peaceful days. This is what we shall do . . ." All the bees gathered round to listen.

"Tomorrow," she shared, "we don't go to work!"

(*Tamu changes their voice to represent the other bees.*) "Hmmmm? No work?"

"Yes. No work tomorrow, and the day after, and the day after that, and the day after that one."

"What difference will that make? How will we spend our days?" some of the bees protested.

"We shall rest and do no pollinating. Just wait and see. If we do this together, we will make a big difference."

Asali won the hive over. The next morning, they did not go to work. The garden was silent. Day 2—silent. Day 3, 7, 10, 19, 26, 32—all silent!

Bwana Farmer grew concerned. There was no singing, no dancing, and no buzzing. Just a very quiet garden. And you can imagine his shock when a few days later, he went to pluck strawberries and found no fruit there. Tomato vines—nothing there either. Cucumbers and carrots—empty stalks too! Oh my! What would he sell? What would he do?

Deeply concerned, he called for a meeting with Asali, Mama Nyuki, and the leaders. They explained to Bwana Farmer that they had downed their tools because the poison was killing them. (*Tamu changes their voice to sound like Bwana Farmer.*) "I am truly sorry," he said. Together they reached an agreement that he would stop spraying and let the bees thrive.

After a few days, the garden began to flourish again. Soon, everyone at the local market made a beeline for Bwana Farmer's delicious berries and golden honey. On seeing this, the other farmers in the area started doing the same.

And that's how this garden became as lovely as you see it today. All because of one small single bee who believed she could make a big, big difference. I believe, boys and girls—bees and drones—that you can too!

(*TAMU rises and continues to enjoy the garden.*)

END OF PLAY

MAKE IT MAKE SENSE

Margaret Namulyanga

Margaret Namulyanga is a Ganda native from Masaka, Uganda. She currently lives in Poughkeepsie, New York.

Playwright's Statement

Downtown Kampala is where one finds self-starting Ugandans going on about their business. These people are affected by international proclamations and policies, but no one cares to seek their input when it comes to solving global crises. It's their resilience and colorful existence that inspired this drama.

Characters

CR, City Council Representative.
A, a young man, food hawker on the go.
MALIZA, a heavy woman in her late thirties.
ABDU, in his fifties, wearing a thobe and kufi.

Notes

/ interruption
. . . continuation
| in quick succession

Pronunciation

Wanji (WAN-JEE), akin to "WTF are you talking about?"
Anha (Like U-HUH), like "go on."
Aaaha (U-HUH stretched like NOPE), skeptical.
Gayaza (GUH-YER-ZER), a neighborhood in Kampala.

Kalerwe (CAR-RAIL-WAY), a market.
Ssebo (SAY-BOW, bow is silent), Sir.

• • •

Downtown Kampala. Open air meeting in progress. Murmurs.

CR: Good people. First listen /

A: No, no, no, no, no. You listen /

MALIZA: Do you know how many septic tanks we have in this arcade?

ALL: Six! Six septic tanks.

CR: I know . . . which is why the city council chose this arcade. With it being the most densely populated . . . it produces a good amount of waste . . . *our* engineers would like to capitalize on that.

A: But from what you are saying, you are not talking about emptying these things and leaving everything alone. You are talking about overhauling everything.

CR: Yes. You see, these people are going to install equipment that will work with the necessary technology . . . okay? We are talking about breaking down organic matter, conditioning, scrubbing, and cleaning gas . . . it's a different set up altogether.

MALIZA: For how long?

CR: About three months.

A: Three months while the arcade is covered in a world of stink!

ABDU: Wait a minute, wait a minute. While you carry on with the digging and emptying and . . . everything you just said, you know the stomach is a funny fellow. Before one finishes the last lunch morsel, the stomach is wondering . . . "what's for dinner?" I guess my question is . . . when you are doing all the digging . . . you see where I am going?

A: Ssebo, say what you want to say before my customer's food cools off.

ABDU: We still have to go, you know.

   (Murmuring.)

CR: Friends. Friends! Ladies, gentlemen /

MALIZA: (*Tense, aside to Abdu.*) *Anha!* Thank you for asking that question. I wanted to ask but I wondered how to put it diplomatically. For you, your shop is on the fifth floor. I am on the first floor . . . what if I am in there while their people are down there carrying on | carrying on, then boom, the whole thing falls through . . . hooo!

CR: You don't have to worry about that.

A: Not to worry, she says.

CR: You'll be using the ones in your homes.

MALIZA: (*Alarmed.*) *Wangi.*

ABDU: Are we to spend our working hours on the road going back and forth | back and forth?

MALIZA: (*Askance.*) Make it make sense?

A: That or fasting.

MALIZA: *Aaaah*, me, I am not fasting, I have stomach ulcers. I am in enough pain already.

CR: You'll stay at home and you'll be compensated.

   (*Silence.*)

A: Compensated. By whom?

CR: The city council.

MALIZA: With what?

CR: With money.

A: Money | from where?

ABDU: No wonder they have been introducing *funny* | *funny* taxes and all sorts of fines. So you are going to return to us some of the money you take from us and *then what?* We say thank you very much | thank you very much. (*Clapping.*)

   (*CR tries to jump in.*)

MALIZA: Tell you what? As soon as they get a chance, they will introduce new taxes to offset this compensation. The nerve of these people. I guess when you look at us it is jackfruits you see sitting where our heads should be.

CR: Please allow me to finish. It's not your money. The people who are funding the project will take care of that. (*Sticks it to them, argumentative.*) By the way, the taxes we collect from you don't even cover a quarter of the budget for this project, I'm telling you. If you see the size of the budget . . . thousands of pages . . . rest assured . . . the project is well funded . . . All we need is for you to stay at home so that the work gets done as soon as possible. In the meantime, we need evidence pertaining to your monthly expenditures, incomes /

A: These people have bank loans while we are on the subject.

CR: All that. And how much you pay for your household bill /

ABDU: Like bring receipts?

A: For onions?

MALIZA: Madam, this is downtown Kampala. Or have you forgotten and you think you are talking to those uptown people who buy things from supermarkets and get receipts?

CR: Maliza, Maliza, come on! We both stay in Gayaza. You and I buy our groceries from Kalerwe market. I'm on your side, people. (*Pause.*) We only need justifiable rough estimates. Our accountants and planners will work with what you give us. Okay?

A: Ah, well.

CR: Questions?

(*Silence. CR sorts through her paperwork and files.*)

ABDU: (*Aside to A and MALIZA.*) The way I see it, these people have a lot of money.

A: No doubt.

MALIZA: But do you trust them?

ABDU: Only if the compensation is delivered pronto.

MALIZA: That's what I am also thinking. We need to see cash first. Otherwise, the powerful can be a nuisance when they owe the common person money!

(Silence.)

ABDU: *(Stunned.)* We are going to be using our *what?!* To cook our food!

MALIZA: Stop. Stop. Stop. I don't want to think about it.

A: As long as the brand name is not reckless . . . they are in business . . . otherwise . . . / someone comes selling poop gas, I'm sending them back to wherever they came from.

ABDU: What do you know? In the end if they gave you a can of our usual gas and gas made from our *stuff* . . . you wouldn't know the difference. Science is—*(Gesture | amazed.)* eh!

A: We are here . . . but I tell you, someone out there is going to say no. *(Laughs.)* As if . . . as if . . .

ABDU: *(Quietly.)* . . . no, as if they can put it on a plate . . . *and*

MALIZA: *(Laughing.)* Alright, alright, stop it. Stop it.

(Laughter stops.)

CR: If you can tell me the language you are most comfortable in, I'll be sure to furnish you with the right paperwork.

ABDU: Luganda.

CR: Okay . . . how about you, *ssebo?*

A: Whichever. I need to get this food to my customers while it's still warm.

CR: Here you go. And you, Hajji.

(ABDU holds paper close to his face, tries to read.)

CR: For now, we only need your names and shop numbers. After our people have created your profiles, they will visit your stalls to get the rest of the details into computers. That's why we didn't want to waste too much paper.

MALIZA: *(Friendly.)* After all, you are in the business of saving trees, the planet, and whatnot.

CR: There you go.

   (Exits.)

ABDU: Maliza, I need help with mine. The font is too small.

   (Silence as MALIZA fills out her paperwork haltingly.)

MALIZA: We need to ask her if we shall be getting a discount . . . you know.

ABDU: You and discounts.

MALIZA: It's only fair, my friend. (*Silence.*) Also, going forward the city council needs to scrap the toilet service fee! We are now stakeholders in this business of saving the planet . . . given we are contributing capital in this project.

ABDU: (*Jolly good.*) Maliza!

MALIZA: Eeh. Why should we pay to use the toilet when we go in there to make electricity? No, no, no no, payments should stop immediately. (*Pause.*) Here. Give me yours.

   (Silence.)

END OF PLAY

RANGER

Yvette Nolan

Yvette Nolan is an Algonquin playwright, director, and dramaturg. Her works include the play *The Unplugging*, the dance-opera *Bearing*, the libretto *Shawnadithit*, and *Breathing Space* for Climate Change Theatre Action. She co-created, with Joel Bernbaum and Lancelot Knight, the verbatim play *Reasonable Doubt*, about relations between Indigenous and non-Indigenous communities in Saskatchewan. From 2003–2011, she served as artistic director of Native Earth Performing Arts. Her book, *Medicine Shows*, about Indigenous performance in Canada, was published by Playwrights Canada Press in 2015.

Playwright's Statement

I have always had a fantasy about turning huge swaths of this country we agree to call Canada into national parks. As climate change accelerates, and as "the lungs of the earth"—the Amazon—is destroyed, my vision for Canada has evolved into a global one. In 2016, I did a piece in Boca Del Lupo's Symposium from 150 years in the future, in which all of Canada was a global park. This piece looks at a moment along the road of how we might get there.

Setting
A border.

. . .

A series of goodbyes. Partners parting, children waving goodbye to parents, good friends hugging, then letting go. They are not violent goodbyes, though there is sadness, wistfulness, pride, resignation.

NIALL: please, Brook

BROOK: please yourself, Niall

NIALL: please come with me

BROOK: I can't
I am needed here

NIALL: I need you

BROOK: then stay

NIALL: and do what?

BROOK: do what the rest of us are doing

NIALL: park ranger?

BROOK: (*Laughs.*) yeah

NIALL: well, that's what it is, isn't it?
A glorified—
No, not even glorified
Just a park ranger
Less than a park ranger
A gardener

BROOK: oh, not a gardener
If they only wanted gardeners
I would be shit out of luck
You know I am all black thumbs

NIALL: you're going to get bored

BROOK: I don't think so

NIALL: babysitting a park?

BROOK: you are so— so—

NIALL: so what?

BROOK: so condescending

NIALL: Brook, you are a city creature
You love cities
New York, Vancouver, Florence
How are you going to survive in a luddite society?

BROOK: just because we don't use fossil fuels does not mean we are a luddite society

NIALL: no vehicles

BROOK: we have cart
And wagons

NIALL: you're afraid of horses

BROOK: Niall
I am staying
You are going
They're going to close the border soon
Is this how you want to say goodbye?

NIALL: what about your mother?
She's not getting any younger

BROOK: I'm doing this for my mother
For all my relations
So people can breathe again

NIALL: why do they have to close it permanently?
Why can't we visit?
Why can't you come out?

BROOK: you know why
We need to give the land a chance to work
We need to give the lungs a chance to grow
We can't have traffic moving through
Everyone who is staying is committed to caring for the park
For four years
In four years
If this works
Then maybe we will open it up to the public
And people can come and visit
And hike or ride into the park
And see what we have created

NIALL: an overgrown bush

BROOK: by then the animals will be back
By then the water will be clean

NIALL: you hope

BROOK: I do hope
It is the only reason I signed on
To be a glorified park ranger
No
Not the only reason
This is my land
This is where I grew up
I could've moved east with the rest of you
But to never see this land again

NIALL: you are risking your life, Brook
You don't know how this experiment will turn out
No power

BROOK: clean power

NIALL: what happens when people get sick
Get injured
Get attacked by the bear
Who suddenly does not have to contend with traffic
Or hunters

BROOK: we have doctors, Niall
We have biologists
We have all the skills we need

NIALL: you did not exactly train for this

BROOK: my skills are transferable
I was getting bored with money and paper anyway
I am an organizer
What bigger challenge than to organize
A million people in 5 million square kilometers of land
It's a monumental task

NIALL: it's a fool's errand

BROOK: and that is why you are going, Niall
To the crowded, choking city
And I am staying to be a part of creating a global park

NIALL: Brook

BROOK: you gotta go, Niall
They're plowing the roads in after you go
You gotta go now

(A RANGER appears.)

RANGER: sir?
I will escort you to your vehicle now

NIALL: I'm going
I'm going
Can I just—?

(The RANGER steps back but not away.
BROOK goes to hug NIALL. They hug, then part.
The RANGER moves in to herd NIALL away.
BROOK waves and walks away, and does not look back.)

END OF PLAY

GREEN NEW STEAL

Corey Payette

Corey Payette is proud of his Oji-Cree heritage from Northern Ontario and has worked as a playwright, actor, composer, and director across Canada. He is the artistic director of Urban Ink (Vancouver), past artist-in-residence with the National Arts Centre English Theatre, and founder of Raven Theatre. His musicals *Children of God* (Urban Ink, National Arts Centre, The Cultch, Citadel Theatre, Western Canada Theatre, Segal Centre), *Les Filles du Roi* (Urban Ink/Fugue/Raven), *Sedna* (Urban Ink/Caravan Farm) have toured across Canada. www.coreypayette.com

Notes

Performed as a vlog.
/ indicate cuts.

• • •

KARA is 16 years old. Rich, but doesn't know it because all her friends have more money than her. Privileged, but doesn't know it because one time she didn't get chosen for the travel soccer team and that sort of "oppression" really left a mark on her life. She is a daily vlogger, and is a passionate advocate for climate change and sun chips. She's holding her cell phone in front of her and is scrolling through questions.

KARA: Hey guys, welcome back to my channel. Sorry that I forgot to post the Sunday Gossip but I had dry mouth and could hardly speak. / Anyway. Here I am. / On today's Wednesday Wake Up, I'm going to be breaking down the Green New Deal. / You've heard about it and I'm here to answer your questions, but I'm no expert—I'm just like you. So last week I asked you to submit questions via the socials and I'm going to try to make my way through as many as I can but I'm making no promises. / So anyways, / here's the first question: What kind of lip gloss do you wear? You guys, this is supposed to be a video explaining the Green New Deal . . . Monday is our Q & Slay and I can answer all your questions about my daily beauty regime then. But the answer is Bubble Betty lip balm—link in the description down below. / Ok, back to questions . . . let's see. Why do they say global warming when last year our winter was still super cold? That's a great question—and I totally agree, it was super cold. I remember when I was a kid, like a couple years ago, and the snow used to melt by end of March and this last year it stayed until April so . . . not sure what's going on there? Ummm, you guys are mostly asking about if I have a boyfriend and my cute outfits here in the questions. I'll get to that during our next Friday Fashion Haul. This was to dispel the rumors of the Green New Deal. / Oh, hold on, here's one: Why don't we stop transporting food all over the world and riding in planes and grow our own food and stop driving cars and ride horses instead? You're all being brainwashed by this Green New Steal . . . / Ok, well, thanks for your question, that wasn't really a question but a message from a hater. But that's ok. / That's a pretty common statement though . . . and it isn't about that, it is about needing to acknowledge that there's a problem and work on ways to fix it. It's not like we're saying we're going to stop shipping food, but it is better for the planet to buy local food or for people to grow food in their own garden. / These things are good things to do on a small scale, and then the Green New Deal is a larger vision for what needs to be done on a larger scale all around the world. Moving away from the oil and gas and trying to find more green solutions. / I would love to ride horses to get around though. / That wouldn't be so bad. / Today's sponsor is Yum Yum Go Off, the only eco friendly meal delivery service that provides you with tasty meals from around the globe for a low, low price delivered right to your doorstep, use the code Kara at checkout for 10% off. Link below in the description. / Well, that's all for today's Wednesday Wake Up, leave your questions below for next week's episode when I'll be covering the Syrian conflict. / Tomorrow I'll be back with my day-in-the-life video, taking you along with me from the moment I wake up until the time I close my eyes. / Like, subscribe. And I'll see you tomorrow. Byeeeeee.

(Credits play with a cheerful image bouncing across the screen.)

END OF PLAY

PAYING FOR IT

Thomas Peterson

Thomas Peterson is a writer and director whose work focuses on the climate crisis. He also works as a shareholder advocate, pushing the world's largest corporations to eliminate deforestation in their supply chains and commit to substantive emissions reductions. He is the artistic associate with The Arctic Cycle, with whom he has co-organized Climate Change Theatre Action. He has written about theatre and locality, climate propaganda, and the aesthetic of the sublime in climate theatre.

Playwright's Statement
This is a play about paying for climate action or paying for climate inaction; a play about who pays, and how.

Note
/ indicates an overlap

• • •

SOMEONE: Who is going to pay for it?

SOMEONE ELSE: You'll pay for this.

SOMEONE: Are you threatening me?

SOMEONE ELSE: No.

SOMEONE: You told me I'd pay for this.

SOMEONE ELSE: Yes.

SOMEONE: That's a . . .
I mean.
Usually. That's a threat.

SOMEONE ELSE: What.

SOMEONE: "You'll pay for this" is . . .
famously a threat.

SOMEONE ELSE: . . . but you asked me who was going to pay for it.

SOMEONE: That doesn't give you the right to threaten me, it's a reasonable
question!

SOMEONE ELSE: I didn't threaten you, I answered you.

SOMEONE: How?

SOMEONE ELSE: You asked me: who is going to pay for it?

SOMEONE: And?

SOMEONE ELSE: I said you'll pay for this.

SOMEONE: There you go again. Intimidation!

SOMEONE ELSE: . . . I just want you to pay a lot of money. In the right way.

SOMEONE: We can't afford that.

SOMEONE ELSE: No, we can.
You can, especially.

SOMEONE: . . .

SOMEONE ELSE: Clean air clean water good food good care good job safe
home that's good, actually.

SOMEONE: We can't . . . invent money for this.

SOMEONE ELSE: You invent money all the time.

SOMEONE: For valuable things!
Valuable!
Hot coal fast gas telephone tablet airplane Bitcoin large truck large home big
lawn big law big oil palm oil big meat concrete. Valuable! People pay for
that! You pay for that.

SOMEONE ELSE: I think taking a deep breath that is so clean . . .
I think that is valuable.

SOMEONE: That's nice but unfortunately the market tends to disagree.

SOMEONE ELSE: . . . and a day that is the right amount of hot
. . . the air hugs you a little bit
but not too hot.

SOMEONE: That's nice but unfortunately the market tends / to disagree.

SOMEONE ELSE: Being wet sometimes, but not all the time. And when a
doctor is nice . . .
And also
free?

SOMEONE: These are nice but / unfortunately the market—

SOMEONE ELSE: And beauty—

SOMEONE: . . . I don't even need to say it.

SOMEONE ELSE: We'll pay for it.

SOMEONE: You're threatening me again.

SOMEONE ELSE: I said we'll pay for it.

SOMEONE: So now you're also threatening you.

SOMEONE ELSE: I mean . . .
If we keep on like this, we're threatening us.
In fact, if we put aside words
and look at, well, deeds,
you're threatening me so much more than I am threatening you.

SOMEONE: Let me remind you that you said "you'll pay for this."
A threat.

SOMEONE ELSE: And I . . .
The thing I said about words and deeds?

SOMEONE: I didn't hear that.

SOMEONE ELSE: All signs point towards
all of us paying for it. One way or another. Some more dearly than others.
But I think . . .

I think it would
 ... be nice
to pay for it by paying people to care as much as they can.
And to keep caring.

END OF PLAY

I SAW YOU WELL

Nicole Pschetz

Nicole Pschetz is a Brazilian theatre-maker and performer based in Paris. She has created shows in Brazil, the United Kingdom, Italy, Portugal, and France. Her first company, Energinmotion Physical Theatre (2010–2013), was co-directed with Mexican performer Antonio Blanco in England. Since 2015, she has been the artistic director of Poulpe Électrique, a physical theatre and multimedia company that focuses on contemporary themes through a critical and poetic dialogue between physical expression and the digital arts.

Playwright's Statement

My inspiration comes from the wonderful book by Simon Lewis and Mark Maslin, *The Human Planet: How We Created the Anthropocene*.* It is here that I read for the first time about the Half-Earth Project, a proposition by biologist E. O. Wilson where half of our planet's surface would be protected for the benefit of other species. This would help sustain biodiversity, as well as allow Native people to continue living in harmony with these ecosystems. The Brazilian *Cerrado*, featured in this play, is the second largest biome in South America, the most biodiverse savannah in the world, and the birthplace of several rivers. Its conservation is important not only for the survival of its unique fauna and flora but also for the survival of the human species. In recent times, its devastation has been accelerating. In my ideal future, Half-Earth and rewilding could be solutions to stop mass extinction in this area.

Characters

GUIDE, a local person dressed in plain clothes, wearing leather sandals and a straw hat.
MAN, a foreign person, dressed in trekking clothes.

---

* S. L. Lewis and M. A. Maslin, *The Human Planet: How We Created the Anthropocene* (London: Penguin Random House, 2018).

BIRD, a *bem-te-vi* (*Pitangus sulphuratus*), a bird found all over Brazil. It can be a puppet or an actor wearing a mask and/or a huge costume.

Setting

A place in the Brazilian *Cerrado*, a savannah.

Note

There are many sound recordings of this bird available on the web. This play could also be adapted to another biome under threat. In that case, it would be interesting to try and find a bird with a similar call that is known and shared in popular culture.

• • •

Two people walk in. They look tired. They've been walking for hours, and have arrived at their destination.

GUIDE: That's it.

MAN: It's amazing . . . Who would have thought it would work out this way?

GUIDE: Time can heal.

MAN: Can't we go further?

GUIDE: It's forbidden. We've reached the fence.

MAN: But there's nobody around . . .

GUIDE: Look better.

MAN: I don't see anyone.

(*A BIRD sings: Bem-te-viiiii. Bem-te-viiii.*)

GUIDE: He saw you.

MAN: That's a bird.

GUIDE: Exactly, and he saw you.

MAN: He's just doing his bird thing.

GUIDE: He said: bem-te-vi! In our language, that means: "I saw you well."

MAN: Well, that's popular culture. He could as well have said: "come and see!"

(The BIRD sings again: Bem-te-viiii. Bem-te-viiii.)

GUIDE: What you call popular culture isn't as ignorant as you may think. This bird doesn't want us around.

MAN: Are you scared of a bird?

GUIDE: I'm respectful. That's his place. And he's sending us a gentle reminder.

MAN: These birds are everywhere. I'm going in.

(He jumps over the fence, but the guide stays immobile.)

GUIDE: You are breaking our agreement.

(The MAN walks away and disappears. We hear a scream. Black out. Lights come up and he's lying unconscious on the ground. We hear the BIRD singing and approaching: Bem-te-viiii! Bem-te-viiii! Te-viiii! The MAN wakes up with the sound and sees the bird right in front of him.)

MAN: Argh!

BIRD: Did I scare you?

MAN: What?!?!

(The MAN moves away from the BIRD with difficulty. He has hurt his leg but he tries to hide it.)

BIRD: Did I scare you?

MAN: Do you speak?

BIRD: Don't you?

(The MAN doesn't reply.)

BIRD: What are you doing here?

MAN: I thought I could . . .

BIRD: *(Cutting.)* Have a peek?

MAN: Yes.

BIRD: You know you shouldn't.

MAN: But why?

BIRD: Here it comes again. "What's the matter? I was just curious. Anyway, I wasn't going to take anything . . ."

MAN: (*Cutting.*) I didn't take anything.

BIRD: So what's that in your pocket?

(*The MAN searches both pockets and finds a pebble, small branches, etc.*)

MAN: How did these end up in here?

BIRD: I see.

MAN: I'm so sorry . . .

(*The MAN places all objects on the floor. The BIRD looks at him very carefully, as if trying to read his mind.*)

BIRD: When this part of the *Cerrado* was closed, many were against it. There were even protests. But I thought it was all over now. Is it why you are here? To protest?

(*The MAN doesn't reply.*)

BIRD: I thought those of your kind had changed.

MAN: It's a shame all this has to be kept away from us.

BIRD: Maybe I was mistaken.

MAN: We are not all the same.

BIRD: I see.

(*The BIRD stares at the man, examines him.*)

BIRD: Are you hurt?

MAN: Yes, I fell.

(*The BIRD stares at him again, then looks away.*)

BIRD: Years ago, tourists used to swim in that river. They would bring food and share it with us. We got used to it even if it was like poison. They were mostly nice, often very loud, sometimes aggressive. They were everywhere with their tents, families, and pets. Many of us died in the mouths of their dogs and cats. Other animals also got hurt and died from their wounds. It was a relief when they finally disappeared. But then, we understood things were getting worse. The mining companies arrived with a "magnificent" project of a pipeline. That gluttonous snake was made to carry metal from the mountains to the ocean, using the water from that same river. We were in distress. Some would leave their nests for a few hours and when they were back, the trees were gone. Many mountains started to disappear. We no longer knew where it was safe. It became so dry, there were huge fires. Death was everywhere. (*Pause.*) But suddenly . . . it all stopped. They packed and left! Other people arrived. They spent a long time studying the area and discussing with locals. Together, they started planting trees. They took care of the river so we could drink from it again. Little by little, other birds, mammals, reptiles, insects, started joining us. Those humans built up that fence and for a while, they were surveilling it so nobody would come in. Finally, they also left. Now from time to time, locals cross this area. They live peacefully on the other side. Others like you approach the fence and take a picture. But I've heard those of your kind are busy working in other places. I have no details because those of my own migrate less nowadays. We don't need to. The *Cerrado* is so rich. Anyway, everybody knows our story. It seems like there has been a world revolution!

MAN: Yes, a revolution on how we see other species. Humanity has changed its relationship with the planet. We realized our ways of living didn't allow a dignified life for everyone because only a few were profiting from the destruction of the Earth. And that was leading all of us to extinction. In the beginning, it was difficult. But when we started seeing the transformations, we understood it was worth it.

BIRD: It seems to be working well for all of us now. (*Pause.*) So why are you here?

MAN: I thought that in a respectful manner, we could start entering these spaces again.

BIRD: Sharing this planet means you don't have the right to take over the whole of it. This is our place. Being respectful is also recognizing that.

MAN: It's not easy.

BIRD: You've said you're not all the same. I understand now. I thought it was all over but it seems we still need to remind you from time to time about the past.

MAN: I'm sorry.

BIRD: You should go back now.

MAN: What about my leg?

BIRD: What about it?

(The MAN realizes his leg is back to normal. Black out. Lights come up and he's back at the fence. He jumps over it. The guide is there, resting in the shade.)

GUIDE: You made it!

MAN: That bird . . .

GUIDE: You're lucky. The last person who tried that didn't come back.

MAN: What happened?

(We hear the sound of a puma. As lights fade out the BIRD sings again: Bem-te-viiii. Bem-te-viiii. Te-viiii. Te-viiii.)

END OF PLAY

SAMMIE & GRAN

Mark Rigney

Mark Rigney's plays have been produced in twenty-two states plus Australia, Canada, Hong Kong, and Nepal. In New York, his work has played off-Broadway at 59e59. He is a member of the Dramatists Guild and has won multiple national playwriting contests, including the John Gassner Award, the Panowski Playwriting Award, and the Maxim Mazumdar New Play Competition. His published work is available from Playscripts, Inc., and Smith & Kraus's *The Best Ten-Minute Plays*. www.markrigney.net

Playwright's Statement

I have a long-running feud with unused parking lots. They trap heat and give nothing back. If we're visioning for the future, let's reimagine how we use our supposedly lost-cause spaces. As for theater, well. In five minutes? Better make it fun!

Characters

SAMMIE, a very precocious child of eight (most likely played by an adult).
GRAN, Sammie's grandparent (definitely played by an adult).

Setting

A place with a comfy chair for reading.

Time

This morning.

• • •

Lights up on a very comfy chair where a loving grandparent might read to a child. Nearby, a selection of children's picture books. SAMMIE is skipping rope and chanting.

SAMMIE: Miss Lucy had a turtle
She named him Tiny Tim
She put him in the bathtub
To see if he could swim.

(GRAN enters as SAMMIE stops skipping.)

SAMMIE: Except, I don't get it. I mean, even an exclusively terrestrial turtle, if it had to—in an emergency—it could swim, right?

GRAN: Sammie, there are no emergencies around here. Now. (*As she selects a book.*) It's story time. Are we ready?

SAMMIE: How come you always get to choose?

GRAN: "Once upon a time, there was a magical kingdom where everyone was inordinately happy."

SAMMIE: Objection.

GRAN: Honey, are we reading, or not?

SAMMIE: Can I say my objections first?

GRAN: How many do you have?

SAMMIE: Three. So far.

GRAN: All right. But then we read.

SAMMIE: Okay, first, magic doesn't exist, so this place you're talking about can't be true, and second, what's magic about putting some random rich guy in charge of everything and calling him king, and third, who the heck uses "inordinately" in a kids' book?

GRAN: Are we done?

SAMMIE: Yes.

GRAN: Page two. "The reason this kingdom was magical is that most of the people who lived there had everything they wanted, or at least had the possibility of someday getting everything they wanted, which explains why all the people who mattered were happy very nearly all the time."

(SAMMIE bleats like a sheep. Loudly.)

GRAN: Sammie, it's not polite to interrupt, plus I have no idea what you're doing.

SAMMIE: I'm being a sheep. Because the people in this story, they're sheep, and because you are always and forever telling me not to blindly follow others!

GRAN: Yes, and I tell you this because you're my grandchild, and I love you, but the fact is, when you grow up and do grown-up things like taking psychotropic drugs and shopping for three-pound bags of Idaho potatoes, you run out of time to research and fact-check what's really going on in the world. So, you pick a name or a faction or a party, and you just—you go with it. Now. Page three. "The happy people in the magical kingdom were kept distracted by all manner of fabulous entertainments, including—"

SAMMIE: No, no, no. Stop. This book—I mean, first, there's no plot, and second, it's trying to deny that we live in a dynamic world.

GRAN: Trust me, hon, nobody sane wants to live in a dynamic world.

SAMMIE: Okay, but you know Cousin Eddie? The one with the farm pond? Everybody thinks all he does is cast for bluegill and spit nasty plugs of tobacco into his triple-nasty Tennessee Titans solo cup. But you know what he's really been doing all these years?

GRAN: Hand to God, I have no idea.

SAMMIE: Dreaming up a better mousetrap, which in this case means a brand-new business model.

GRAN: Are we talking about the same Cousin Eddie?

SAMMIE: When he's not reciting Wendell Berry or communing with nature, Eddie is a seriously talented contractor. Hard to believe, I know, so, to explain, lemme lay down some bars.

(Sammie grabs her jump rope and proceeds to rap out a skipping chant. If there's a handy post, perhaps Gran can be the one rotating the rope, controlling the meter by default.)

SAMMIE: Now Eddie had a notion
'Bout the rising of the oceans.
So, he took in all the facts

Didn't listen to the rumors
(If you fall for all the rumors
That's a cancer, that's a tumor).
Now, people say he's lazy
Kinda hazy, kinda crazy
But he kept on with his fishing
Making chains of endless daisies
While he dreamed his plan of action
Made sure it had some traction
And now I'm out of breath
Just breathe and breathe and go!
So. Eddie called his buddies
Said, "This idea is muddy,
But it's also kinda money."
Then they drove to the mall
On a hot summer's day
And they sat in Eddie's car
—No AC, no shade—
And Eddie says, "Guys, what
We're feeling is the future.
This heat is like a suture.
I'm a newborn climate booster,
And parking lots are trouble.
The heat, it's like a bubble,
So, let's turn it into rubble,
'Cos there's money to be made
With a pond, or a glade,
Or planting trees for shade.
Then the heat-sink is gone
And our temps go down
And we'll still have parking lots
All over town,
But they can be smaller,
An appropriate size,
As we plan better cities
Get smart, get wise
As our Green New Deal
Keeps our eyes on the prize."

GRAN: Hon, you're not making any sense.

SAMMIE: The way it all works

Is a buy-back plan
Where Eddie does the labor
And the feds cut a check
(It's kinda low-tech)
We the People get the perks
We the People stay cool
As Eddie puts to work
What we shoulda learned in school.
And that's a hop, skip, and a jump! Ta-da!

(Possibly, SAMMIE takes a bow.)

GRAN: Child, the government doesn't pay people to rip up perfectly good parking lots.

SAMMIE: The government has lots of buy-back programs. Refrigerants, for one. Freon.

GRAN: We need parking lots!

SAMMIE: Gran. Even at the holidays, Christmas, they're half-empty.

GRAN: You are getting too big for your eight-year-old britches.

SAMMIE: No, but I'll tell you one thing this future voter is done with: stories where the world never changes.

GRAN: But this book, this is my favorite! Ever since I was a girl, younger than you!

SAMMIE: Gran, I love you, and I get it that for your entire generation, this was the book, but at this point, now, today? I just helped Eddie get a meeting with our congressional rep, so things are happening, right? And you can either lead, follow, or get out of the way.

(A moment. GRAN makes her choice.)

GRAN: All I know for sure is that right now, it's story time. But this time, you get to pick.

(SAMMIE hands GRAN the rope and selects a book.)

SAMMIE: This one. *(Reading as if this, too, is a jump rope rhyme—which it is, of course.)*
"Once upon tomorrow

Around the world did roll.
It's hard to bend the future,
But it's good to have a goal."

> (*GRAN summons up her courage and tries a single skip with the rope. Success. SAMMIE turns the page. Blackout.*)

END OF PLAY

AT WHAT COST

Kiki Rivera

Kiki Rivera (she, we, they) is the child of Andra Rivera Souza and Puipui Fuamatu. Kiki was born and raised on the island of Oʻahu in the district of Waiʻanae and the smaller (yet largest ahupuaʻa) district of Lualualei. They identify as a theatre artist who comes from a line of island warriors, healers, artisans, and storytellers who have traversed the Pacific ocean and call it home.

Playwright's Statement

At What Cost is inspired by Hawaiʻi's Aloha ʻĀina warriors who continue to protect Hawaiʻi, its natural resources, and fight for its sovereignty. I imagine that a Green New Deal in Hawaiʻi would look like a sovereign nation restored and dependence on tourism, military occupation, and American capitalistic approaches abolished.

Characters

TŪTŪ PONI/PURPLE LADY
KUʻULEI/PROTECTOR 1
ANA/PROTECTOR 2
NĀMAKA/PROTECTOR 3
POLICE VOICEOVER

Characters can be double-cast for the flashback.

Setting

The play takes place in Waiʻanae, Oʻahu, Hawaiʻi in the year 2071. Fifty years have passed since the Green New Deal has been put into action. Hawaiʻi is now independent and sustainable.

Note

See below for a pronunciation guide for Hawaiian words.* I can also provide a voice recording if that's helpful. English translation appears in (parentheses).

TŪTŪ PONI	too-too poh-nee
KUʻULEI	koo-oo leh-ee
ANA	ah-nah
NAMAKA	nah-mah-kah
TŪTŪ PELE	too-too peh-leh
PAU	pah-oo
AKUA	ah-koo-ah
PAʻI	pah-ee
MOʻO	moh-oh
KŪPUNA	koo-poo-nah
PIʻILANIWAHINE	pee-ee-lah-nee-vah-hee-ney
KIAʻI	kee-ah-ee
KAHUKU	kah-hoo-koo
WAIʻANAE	wa-ee-ah-na-eh
AMELIKA	ah-meh-li-kah
KULA	koo-lah
KALAELOA	kah-la-eh-low-ah
NĀ PUA MAKANI	nah poo-ah mah-kah-nee
OʻAHU	o-ah-hoo
PAPAHĀNAUMOKU	pah-pah-haa-now-moh-koo
PAPATUANUKU	pah-pah-too-ah-noo-koo
WĀKEA	wah-keh-ah
RANGINUI	rah-gee-noo-ee
E OLA	eh oh-la
LŌLŌ	loh-loh
ALOHA WAU IĀ ʻOE	ah-loh-ha vao ya oh-eh

• • •

The stage is dark. A rumbling sound is heard for a few beats, then screams from the girls. It's an earthquake. Lights fade up to all three girls frightened and huddling around TŪTŪ PONI.

KUʻULEI: What is that *tūtū*?!

---

* See also www.wehewehe.org.

TŪTŪ PONI: Nothing to worry about. It's just *Tūtū Pele* going to work, probably moving the earth to make room for new lands.

NAMAKA: She not *pau* (done) yet?!

ANA: I wish mommy and daddy were here.

TŪTŪ PONI: The earth rumbling is nothing to be afraid of. Think of it as the *akua* (god) speaking to us.

KU'ULEI: Why is it so scary then?

TŪTŪ PONI: Well, when the *akua* have something to say, they like to make it a big announcement.

NAMAKA: Please *Tūtū Pele*! Don't destroy us!?

TŪTŪ PONI: Nonsense. Would I destroy you? I'm your *tūtū*.

KU'ULEI: No.

NAMAKA: You would *pa'i* (spank) us!

ANA: When we no listen.

TŪTŪ PONI: Correct, but I would never take the life of my *mo'o* (grandchildren) and neither would *Tūtū Pele*. But there was a time when man, when humans, made a lot of scary noise. Some noise good and some noise not so good. Those days were much more worrisome than now.

KU'ULEI: Tell us, *tūtū*!

TŪTŪ PONI: Ok, well, this is a story of one of your *kūpuna* (ancestor), *Tūtū Alice Pi'ilaniwahine*. She was a fearless *kia'i* (guardian, protector) who also had the power to channel the ancestors.

NAMAKA: *Tūtū*, this better not be one scary story!

TŪTŪ PONI: It's not. I promise. This story takes place during a time the *kia'i* of Kahuku and Wa'ianae came together to protect the people, birds, and bats that live in Kahuku from giant turbines being built by American businessmen.

NAMAKA: What is a turbine?

KU'ULEI: Just listen to the story, Namaka! Go, *tūtū*.

TŪTŪ PONI: Long ago, Hawaiʻi was a very different place. It was occupied by America still and not independent like we are today.

ANA: But ʻAmelika still here.

TŪTŪ PONI: ʻAe, they protect us like old friends. They just not our boss anymore. Anyway, there were these American businessmen who made a deal to sell clean energy that they would get through a wind farm to the electric company, except this clean energy came at the cost of making the people of Kahuku sick.

KUʻULEI: Oh, we learned all about clean energy at the *kula* (school), *tūtū*.

TŪTŪ PONI: But in this case, the wind farm was too giant and Oʻahu is too small to house that kind of power. The turbines caused a sound one could not hear, but would sneak into the body making people sick. Some people even had to move away from their homes because they had seizures that worsened by the turbines.

So *Tūtū Alice* and about one hundred *kiaʻi* marched to Kalaeloa, where the giant turbines were being held, and blocked the entrance so the trucks couldn't leave with the turbine parts.

> (*Flashback. Lights transition and the memory comes to life. The girls become PROTECTORS and TŪTŪ PONI plays TŪTŪ ALICE.*)

ALL PROTECTORS: (*Singing.*) "*E Hawaiʻi e kuʻu one hānau e Kuʻu home kulaīwi nei . . .*"*

POLICE VOICEOVER: You have one minute to clear the entrance or you will all be arrested.
Please move to the side.

ALL PROTECTORS: (*Singing.*) "ʻOli nō au i nā *pono lani ou E Hawaiʻi, aloha ē . . .*"

TŪTŪ ALICE: Can you feel the heat?
Not yet, but I feel the clock and see the fires.
I feel the fires. What does the clock feel like?
It feels like thumping, like a heart racing, running from approaching disaster.

---

* "Hawaiʻi Aloha," lyrics by Rev. Lorenzo Lyons, music by James McGranahan, https://youtu.be/rFEZeJrPmLo.

POLICE VOICEOVER: I repeat: You have one minute to clear the entrance or you will be arrested.

PROTECTOR 1: Do what you have to. We will not move.

PROTECTOR 2: Stop the wind turbines from being built! AES is lying! This green energy is not green if it means the displacement of Indigenous life and endangering native birds and bats!

PROTECTOR 3: The infrasound causes migraines, anxiety, depression, cardiovascular problems, and sleep disorders! My son has epilepsy and the shadows can trigger more seizures!

ALL PROTECTORS: (*Singing.*) "*E hauʻoli nā ʻōpio o Hawaiʻi nei ʻOli ē! ʻOli ē! . . .*"

TŪTŪ ALICE: Hot and getting hotter. Loud and getting louder. A roaring. A roaring of new gods eating the land, eating life, eating away at hope.

It's the ticking of a clock. It's the old gods crying. Crying? Or laughing?

Laughing they are. We wanted our independence, they gave it to us. Now it's up to us to solve our own problems or burn up and drown. A Green New Deal. Green New Deal. Deal. It's a deal. We have it!

PROTECTOR 1: *Nā Pua Makani* failed to disclose significant public health risks associated with the turbines!

TŪTŪ ALICE: You're late, Fake State! Your leadership has failed! Your dependence on tourism and protection of foreign investments and the price of progress has accelerated us into our demise! (*Dancing.*) Climate change is here! Climate change is here! Bring in the deal, abolish the system, climate change is here!

POLICE VOICEOVER: You have one minute to disperse or you will be arrested. Clear the area immediately.

(*TŪTŪ ALICE walks to the middle of the circle and is free dancing.*

Sound of sirens plays over the singing and the crowd. Light change. Song stops. Police officers in bikes surround the PROTECTORS. This action is indicated by TŪTŪ ALICE and the PROTECTORS huddling in stage center. They link arms and sit on the ground.)

TŪTŪ ALICE: Embarrassing. You are the best and worst of us incarnated. In ancient times, in your youth I should say, you always listened, always relied on us gods. We were spoken to frequently, communicated with, consulted with, worshiped, respected. We were called by our many names— *Papahānaumoku, Papatuanuku, Wākea, Ranginui*, Earth Mother, Sky Father . . . We are the earth, soil, winds, the great seas, the fresh waters.
As you've grown, you've taken from us, from the land, made spectacular creations of your own, turning yourselves into gods. Our relationship is broken.

POLICE VOICEOVER: You have the right to remain silent. Anything you say can and will be used against you in a court of law. You have the right to an attorney. If you cannot afford an attorney, one will be provided for you.

(TŪTŪ ALICE and PROTECTORS stand together with hands behind their backs indicating they are being taken into police custody.)

TŪTŪ ALICE: A Green New Deal—another name for justice, a name for balance. Another name for what was once lost. A renewed vision. Your children are speaking. They are remembering and envisioning the principles of your ancient past, your collective beginnings—balance and a deep love of restorative relationships with all life. Long live the earth and its protectors! *E ola! E ola! E ola!* (Live! Live! Live!)

(TŪTŪ ALICE faints taking the group down.

PROTECTORS separate themselves from TŪTŪ ALICE, leaving her limp and lying on the ground. They encircle TŪTŪ ALICE and lift her up.

Black out. Transition back to 2071.)

NAMAKA: Was *Tūtū Alice lōlō* (feeble minded, crazy)?

ANA: Namaka!

NAMAKA: I just asking.

TŪTŪ PONI: Your *Tūtū Alice* was very different. That's what happens when you allow the *kūpuna* to take over your body.

ANA: *Tūtū Poni,* are the turbines still in Kahuku?

TŪTŪ PONI: Yes. You may have seen them. When Hawai'i became independent, they were shut down. Now they just sit like trees with no life.

KU'ULEI: Is that called pollution?

NAMAKA: No. It's called ugly. (*Laughs at her own joke.*)

TŪTŪ PONI: It sounds like my work here is done. Off to bed now.

ALL GIRLS: *Mahalo* (Thank you) *tūtū*!

TŪTŪ PONI: Oh, *mahalo* to you for listening. Now off you go. *Aloha wau iā 'oe.* (I love you.)

END OF PLAY

WHAT WE GIVE BACK

Madeline Sayet

Madeline Sayet (she/her) is a citizen of the Mohegan Tribe and executive director of the Yale Indigenous Performing Arts Program. For her work as a theater-maker, she has been honored as a Forbes 30Under30, TED Fellow, and recipient of the White House Champion of Change Award from President Obama. www.madelinesayet.com

Playwright's Statement

This piece was inspired by the idea that even a Green New Deal still operates out of a commodity economy as opposed to a gift economy principle, and if we are truly to heal our planet, we must go further to remember the Earth's natural principles of exchange in relation and reciprocity, or we will never give her what is owed.

Note

This piece may be spoken by one or many voices.

• • •

Do you need a deal
A plan
An offer
A man with charts
to assure you
that killing your mother
is wrong?

A points system
that awards cute perks
if we can all agree
killing our mother is wrong?

Well, is it?

Can you admit it without incentive?

Or would you destroy what creates you?
Would you murder your Mother
Earth?

Have you forgotten that particular relation?

Has penny pinching politics
got you hooked on the belief
that survival is supposed to be expensive?

That existence is not a right
but a luxury
bought by the abuse and extraction of our mother?

Our Mother
I'm talking about our mother
Our abuse of our mother
Can you really accept that?

What are you thinking?

Silence the noise for a moment
The should dos and will bes
The
Next time
The
I
She
Separation
Of understandings
Cut it all out

And remember this
Remember:

To get to the future
we have to go all the way back

Yes
We

Together
We

Have to go back

To the most important economic principle
The economy of Our Mother Earth

Whose rules of exchange
are the rhythms
of an ecosystem
in harmony

Each gift given
A bond
forged
A union
built
between relatives
A Partnership
of Reciprocity

Increase aids increase
Life creates life

Her business is the constant flow between beings
that nurtures a bountiful planet
I am responsible for her because she is responsible for me

But when you break that cycle
When you stop returning the favor
Snatch and steal with no accountability
Give nothing back
We destroy ourselves

After all, how could
plunging and pillaging
the veins of your own mother
bring anything but harm?

Were you hoping there's a discount for that?

Some way to avoid
curses
for the generations to come?

As long as they do come

But if we continue down this path
they will not come for long

You see we are bound

As human beings
we are bound
to care for the Earth
Bound by the care we've received
and the knowledge that our lives
are all in her hands
Have always been

Moment to moment
Pulse to pulse
There is no way out
That's what it means to be in relation
Our molecules
Blood
Bone
Water
belong to her as well
There is no way out

So, why are we looking for one?

Do you think Mars will ever hold you the same way?

Offer you love and kindness the way she has?
Show you a soft springtime
or a bountiful autumn?

Home is what we are made of
We cannot attach ourselves to any rock

I am bound
Bound to tell you that

Money
Deals
Commerce

These are the poisons of a world
whose foundation has been laid
Stolen
brick by brick
in the trespass against nature

By owning what could never be yours

A world built on taking
without reciprocity

A world manufactured by the corrupt desires
of mortal men
Drilling deeper and deeper
Clawing higher and higher
Shattering every spirit in their way

How much poison can she take?

Sometimes now

I see her
Our mother
reaching out

Toward this world of greed

As if to say:

Wait
My children
Wait
Where are you going?
Where do you think you are going?
Running so fast
Away from everything that holds you together
So fast
You can't see yourselves falling apart

Why have you forced my arms away?
Battered, cut, abused, forgotten

What is it you are after
on this mission of harm?

And what would we say?

What would we say
to our poisoned relation?

To the mother we choked, kicked, and disregarded
when all she did was offer us love

That our destiny is beyond her now?
That our eyes are on the stars?
That we will fix it later?

Mother, one day, we will clean up our rooms
You will see, after this, someday after

But no, she will not hear it
We are running out of time
You see global unity is no longer an option
It is the only possible way

She knows now
We have shown her
who we are
We've shown her
we are not to be trusted
Our lack of responsibility
is apparent

And she is stronger than you think

When she next turns to us
It may be in love no longer

Her eyes are getting colder
Her tempers hotter
less easy to bear
Her moods more
what we have deserved

She gave us gifts
but we were meant to give them back
She knows now
who we are

If we cannot do better
She will take them away
She will take them all away

We are responsible for the land
The land was responsible for us

But this Earth lives in relation
In rules of exchange
Reciprocity

We have polluted and poisoned
Carved, drilled, mined, and extracted, stolen and snared.

And she is angry

If we can't prove our responsibility back

We may not be welcome home anymore.

END OF PLAY

HUMMM

Donna-Michelle St. Bernard

Donna-Michelle St. Bernard a.k.a. Belladonna the Blest is an emcee, agitator, playwright, and librettist; Bequia born, Grenadian by nature, based in Canada on Dish With One Spoon territory.

Playwright's Statement

I was reading about noise pollution, about the detritus of radio signals, the unknown accumulation of all the things we emanate. I was rinsing out nesting white plastics to recycle while listening to people with the power to effect significant action refuse to do so. My computer decided to shut down and I thought about leaving it off, about shutting down other things; then it got real quiet.

Characters

TIIG
WAYO
GOOB
MALIT

• • •

As many instruments as possible should be shut off in the theatre, ambient noises silenced. Utilize natural lighting or none if none is available. Any number of people may be incorporated into the hummm chorus. Specific references may be changed for regionality.
Wild bird call, distant.

MALIT: Shhhh . . . Whippoorwill.

GOOB: Emu.

WAYO: Emu? Here?

GOOB: I dunno what it's called. The one that goes (*perfect impression of bird call*).

TIIG: Wow. Okay, you're not wrong. It is that one.

(*Quiet.*)

WAYO: We didn't have to go first.

TIIG: Well, we did go first, though.

MALIT: Technically we didn't. If you count folx who never had.

WAYO: I do count them.

GOOB: Me, too.

TIIG: Anyways everyone has to go sometime.

TIIG: And somebody has to go first.

WAYO: Doesn't have to be us.

TIIG: Well, it is us, though.

GOOB: Isn't.

(*Quiet.*)

MALIT: (*Computer hummm.*)

TIIG: What are you doing?

MALIT: Working.

WAYO: In the dark?

MALIT: No, in the blue screenlight.

MALIT: (*Hummm.*)

GOOB: What's that noise?

TIIG: CPU!

WAYO: Mine don't sound like that. Y'all keep your fans dirty.

(*Laughter.*)

GOOB: I'm cold. (*Heater hummm.*)

WAYO: Ugh, now I'm too warm. (*Fan hummm.*)

GOOB: Stop moving.

WAYO: I'm oscillating.

> (*All of the different hums commence simultaneously. Others may be added, with specificity.*)

TIIG: Okay, everybody. Power down so the kids can sleep.

> (*All power down.*
> *Whisper.*
> *Giggle.*
> *Laughter. Sigh. Comfortable silence.*)

MALIT: Shhh. Hear veins, varicose, creaking. Cracking crust and sludge shifting. We each do the least and in stillness hear echo of what's already done. Creaking. Can't extract but down pressing crushing those pipes flat, squeeze out space to see salmon fat.

TIIG: I think I hear Winnipeg.

MALIT: How can you tell?

TIIG: They've got a great philharmonic.

WAYO: I don't see why we had to switch off at all. Drastic as hell, is all.

GOOB: Cuz you don't know nothing.

WAYO: I know stuff.

TIIG: So, answer this without thinking. What one thing will you want, when you get your first thing back?

WAYO: Switch.

TIIG: Goob! What one thing would you like to have?

GOOB: Kettle. Forever to boil, the other way.

TIIG: See?

WAYO: So how's Goob's answer better than mine?

TIIG: Cuz Goob lived rough for a decade before. Goob knows need. You still have to find out.

WAYO: Yeah, but we could . . .

MALIT: We could go live on the moon. We could build more stuff and burn more fuel to find another place to go, where we can build more stuff and burn more fuel until we need to find another . . .

TIIG: We don't go, then Italy doesn't, then why should Japan? We don't go, it's all down to Tonga.

MALIT: New roots and moves and ways. Rougher routes and roles and soles . . .

WAYO: Winnipeg sounds alright.

MALIT: You got good shoes? Start now you'll get there just in time for their turn.

TIIG: You should. Arrive there as good as Goob started out. Watch it shut down.

WAYO: I should.

MALIT: You won't.

WAYO: Three years.

GOOB: You all think it passes faster if you never stop talking about it?

WAYO: You still cold?

GOOB: A little.

WAYO: (*Heater hummm.*)

   (*Quiet. Bird call.*)

WAYO: Loon!

GOOB: (*Perfect impression of bird call.*)

END OF PLAY

LOVE OUT OF THE RUINS

Zoë Svendsen

Zoë Svendsen directs the UK-based performing arts company METIS, making participatory performances exploring contemporary political subjects, and working with a wide range of collaborators. Zoë is an associate artist at the Donmar Warehouse, London (as "Climate Dramaturg"), and Cambridge Junction, and has worked as dramaturg of several productions at The Globe, the Young Vic, the National Theatre, and the Royal Shakespeare Company. Zoë lectures on dramaturgy at the University of Cambridge. Zoë's roots are migratory: Welsh, Danish, Australian, and Italian. www.metisarts.co.uk

Playwright's Statement

This play has emerged from multiple conversations with multiple collaborators—about the culture we in the United Kingdom live in, that we have come to call "high carbon culture" (extractive, transactive, individualist, colonizing, fossil-fuel addicted). It has emerged from the sense that there is no single one-size-fits-all utopia but many overlapping potentialities, complementary and conflicting—an ecosystem of utopias.

It is interested in the idea that the crucial work now is to create, imagine, build, and make—in full knowledge that we don't, can't, and won't know "what works" before we start, or even as we are making this attempt. In this, there is jeopardy, and there is little time. Any transformation will be living with climate unpredictability—the time for a "savior" mentality is past. The act of imagining alternative futures might usher into reality possibilities that previously had been excluded. But at the very least, I hope you will find, as we have, that imagining otherwise can offer a refuge from the ruins of the present—bearing witness to the fact it doesn't have to be like this.

Note

This is an invitation to an act of cowriting across time, the seas, and difference. All of the invitations to name specifics in the text are shown in brackets [name . . .]. These need to be prepared in advance, in conversation between all those participating. It is recommended that you select a place you know, and can visit, to imagine the transformations in concrete terms. If you cannot agree on a place, you could include two places (this will extend your imagining beyond five minutes!). The point is, it is never either/or, but always and/both. Do what makes sense for your context and the people involved—including adapting more of the text than indicated here, to render words familiar, specific. What matters is the spirit, not the letter.

The words are my responsibility, but they emerge out of an epic project of imagining otherwise, through a multiplicity of conversations, in particular with Andrea Ling, Anna-Maria Nabirye, Arturo Tovar, Cecilie Sachs Olsen, Charlie Folorunsho, Elisabet Topp, Jess Mabel Jones, Mariama Ndure, Heiki Riipinen, Mona Grenne, Nicky Childs, Rob Awosusi, Shôn Dale-Jones, Stefanie Mueller, Tom Ross-Williams, Renata Tyszczuk, and Lucy Wray.

For between one and five performers—of a range of ages, genders, backgrounds, and lived experiences, with the text split between voices any way you decide (the actor possibly should not match the playing age(s) of who they are voicing). Once you've added in your specifics, the piece should run about five minutes.

Although there are no stage directions, attention to sonic, spatial, and visual design, including the positioning of all bodies involved and the orientation of their attention, will shape how you take care of your audience, and enable their imagining.

Although the time jumps, "you" and your location remain.

• • •

You were born this year. You live in

[name a place you know].

It is late

[name a season].

It is early morning.
It is now

[warmer, colder, wetter, drier, or ?]

this time of year than it used to be.

• • •

You are EIGHT years old & you are running down your street, slaloming between bikes and
elders sitting out and newly planted

[name a type of tree, resilient to the future—consider its purpose—fruit? shade?]

trees, you're late for school which today is at the

[name an unlikely but brilliant site other than a classroom for teaching kids by example—for example: a library for literacy (or even a publishing house) / a bank for maths (or a grocery store) / a fashion house for drawing / a farm for biology/ecology—anywhere that, supported by teachers, workers might share their specialism in an educationally relevant way]

where you are learning about

[name the subject—maths, literature, biology, chemistry, or something else, a new subject perhaps].

• • •

You are TWENTY-TWO years old & preoccupied, you turn the corner onto

[name a relevant residential street/road],

nearly tripping over the

[name a nationality that has recently settled in your area in the future]

tech team reengineering peoples' individual

[name wind/solar/biomass/air source heat pump]

systems, to create a street-length cooperative.
Energy will cost less now, which is just as well as you see at the crossroads
that another

[name another kind of tree appropriate to your locality]

tree is down, meaning more co-shouldering of storm costs . . . You ponder where its branches, now embracing scattered bikes and a mobility vehicle, will end up—

[name some possibilities for the future use of uprooted trees in your locality—for example: Pulped to paper? Honed into a park bench?]

Roused by the chatter of

[name three languages that might be spoken in your area in the future]

as the bio-repair team arrive, your thoughts return to calculating the level of support your basic income will provide when you

[name something that at the moment might be very difficult to do due to lack of financial autonomy coupled with cultural disapproval—for example: move in with your same-sex partner / keep the baby growing inside you / start studying / leave an abusive cohabiting relationship / start up a (name a business)].

• • •

You are THIRTY-EIGHT & with your friend's four-year-old,

[give the child a name],

you take the slow walk through your local climate corridor:

[name the climate corridor—designed to provide continuous connection between areas to allow the movement of wildlife without the hindrance of roads/buildings—with the name of an endangered bird in 2021, that is now plentiful in your area, for example: "Nightingale Way"].

Ahead of you someone collapses. In shock, you realize it's your neighbor and friend,

[give your friend, who is 30 years older than you, a name].

You and the other strollers stop and offer what you can, as

[your friend's name]

draws their last breath, encircled by foliage, friends, and strangers. You're mindful of the child's presence, yet not shielding them, not shying away. Since the Hope Act of [name a likely date for the Act],

you are never far from a

[think up a name for a local health facility, free at the point of access, dependent on what you think such a place would most usefully do and what the values of healthcare—in its broadest sense—should be],

so you know that a health specialist will soon be on the scene.

[name of your four-year-old child companion]

asks you what happens next, and you explain how after death the body returns to life. You point out a decaying

[name a plant or animal living in the climate corridor]

and a thriving

[name another plant likely to grow in the climate corridor],

to explain how all living creatures are part of a life cycle.
Still, on the way home you drop into your [name of health facility, as above].
While

[name of child]

has a

[name of locally produced drink]

you book a well-body-scan—as usual, you opt-in to contribute all your data to the citizen well-being project. You feel you can trust it, since

[name a policy/law/other mechanism for the protection of citizen data and ensuring it is generated in an unbiased way, and put to use for public good—for example: "since it became illegal to mine data for profit"].

It takes you back to your participation in scrutinizing the policies, when you were seconded to the Parliament of Values in your late twenties.

• • •

You are FIFTY-NINE & starting a new role tomorrow, as a

[name a job of the future that contributes to the common good].

You feel energized, after your year's paid sabbatical, where you *[name something you educated yourself in/course you took that's relevant to a transformed 2090, but not "career" relevant].*

You also took the chance to travel, more or less for the first time. You took a

[name a carbon neutral, low impact, egalitarian form of transport]

to visit your roots, a land devastated by

[name a likely climate disaster rendering a home uninhabitable, whether in your country, or another country].

You activated the "climate migration integration allowance" to extend your residency rights to those with whom you have ancestral connection. Once you'd made contact, it felt odd not to do what most people round here do—and share living space. Your home is now lit by laughter and energy and determination. The climate grief therapy that the

[name of the health facility on your street]

provides, has helped.
A shout rouses you from your daydream. It's your good friend

[give your friend a name]

from your Care Union, looking smart—not surprising given they earn more in their role
as a

[name a job role of the kind that clean, clear, take care of, repair, deliver, one that is undervalued and underpaid in 2021, but is key to becoming less wasteful of resources, for example: used-materials-collector/ community cook/caretaker]

than your mate who is a

[name a role that is currently very highly paid but benefits no one but the company/individual/shareholders].

[Name of your friend]

tells you they've done your allotment hour for you today AGAIN, and that your

[name a vegetable that will adapt and still thrive according to the likely rise in temperature in your area in 59 years' time, and are appropriate for the season]

are doing well. By way of apology you put an hour in

[name a locally plausible structure for swapping time / volunteering—for example: a "time bank" or "community volunteer network"].

• • •

You are EIGHTY-NINE & you have lived through a near century, lived past 2100.

In 2021 they said that by 2100 the globe would be warmer by 3.2 degrees, the sea levels would have risen by

[name the data for your part of the world]

meters, that

[name the nearest large city that will be impacted—this may be your actual location, of course]

would no longer be fully habitable—and that was if the Global Paris Climate Agreement held. As we know, it got off to a rocky start, with the

[name some challenges of the present].

But having survived the first pandemic, the Agreement was strengthened by the spreading conviction that reparation, restoration, and a global rebalancing were the way forward. As you ponder, you wonder if the shadowy shapes in the sky could be

[name another currently endangered bird species, living in your area (or who used to live in your area), who is around at the time of year/time of day you've selected]

. . . back in droves, these days.
And it all went faster than the predictions—
Oh yes [or alternative exclamation particular to you, your area, your people, that expresses joy and conviction]
You were glad to have been alive in this particular century
To watch—and to take part in—the turnaround
You like yourself better now than people did then
You sit down to eat with

[name your fellows—family? friends? colleagues?]

Your local

[name a place for growing/farming food, appropriate to your area, that can sequester carbon]

is celebrating 25 years of being a carbon sink & has donated

[name a food—that is consumed a lot less these days, but which can be produced locally, without pesticides and other chemical interference]

to the weekly street cook-up.

[Name the type of food—for example: meat or fish or dairy]

is a rarity now that it's rationed.
You lead the thanks.

Let us thank the earth that bore fruit
Any animal that died so we could eat
The people who planted, farmed, and harvested our food
Let us thank those who transported it, packed it, and sold it to us
Those who shopped for it
& those who chopped, combined, cooked, and placed it here before us on our plates.
May you be safe.
May you be healthy.
May you be at ease.
May you be glad.

END OF PLAY

NOT BECAUSE WE'RE GOOD

Chris Thorpe

Chris Thorpe is a writer and performer from Manchester, United Kingdom. He works mainly as a playwright, and occasionally for radio and TV. Currently he is collaborating with China Plate, Rachel Chavkin, Javaad Alipoor, Yusra Warsama, Lekan Lawal, Hannah Jane Walker, the Royal Court Theatre, Staatstheater Mainz, Nationaltheater Mannheim and the Royal Exchange. His new piece, *Always Maybe The Last Time*, written at the Royal Court/Methuen Climate Commission, opens in 2022.

Playwright's Statement

I've been thinking a lot recently about how change happens, and how we think change happens, and what the difference is. How—particularly for a more materially comfortable society, or section of a society—change doesn't necessarily stem from inspiration or desire for the majority of people. It's something that happens due to the dedication and work of others, is implemented, and then just gone along with, because most of us in that situation find it the easiest path to take. This bit of writing tries to imagine—if the problems facing us got solved—what that part of us would say about our role in that solution.

Note

A text for as many people as there are—divide it up whichever way works for you.

• • •

We did this thing
Not because we're good
Not because we're virtuous, or even because we cared

We did it because deep down, we know we're selfish
And we know we're lazy
And we know how susceptible we are to lies

Yeah, there were evangelists, we even knew some of their names
There were righteous fighters
The people who were all in from the very start

But they were the minority, mostly
The rest of us just stood there
With a vague desire to keep the lights on

It's because it was made easy that we went along
Which isn't to say there weren't sacrifices
But we realized making them was easier than the alternative

And yeah, it wasn't til the last possible moment
That most of us signed on
We only made the changes when we had to

If anything, we did it, in the end, we did it
Because remembering is hard
And we realized how much of it we'd have to do

We didn't want to remember our bones in the desert
We didn't want to remember panic
We didn't want to remember what happened when the lights went out

We didn't want to remember setting out with just one bag
We didn't want to remember leaving our pets behind
We didn't want to remember walking from our houses for the final time

We didn't want to remember guns pointed at the sea
We remembered the boats capsizing—that happened
But in the end, we didn't want to remember when it was us in them

Even then, the desire to somehow keep ourselves together
Didn't unleash an all-consuming wave of action
It was more a theoretical preference for life over death

There was a time, way back among the decades
When there was still faith in us
If we could only be told in the right way, we'd believe, they said

If there was a magic form of words, in the perfect tone, the right image
Of a terrible consequence or a shining future
How could it fail to make us more than ordinary

If you want to hear we were good, in the end
Then I'll say it, that we chose this
That we all became believers and this was why it happened

That when the deal was made, and the laws were signed
We went out onto the streets in joy
Because we were good, and unselfish, and we cared

But most of us weren't any of those things
We just wanted to live our lives
And only changed them because change was made easy

Most of us weren't any of those things
We didn't want to remake the world—
We let others change it round us, and then lived in it

Of course, some of us have been persuaded
But most of us are quietly drifting
Most of us are on the path of least resistance

The effect is the same, though, the thing was done
Some people got to be heroes
Most of us didn't, and we're so fine with that, we didn't notice

We went along with it, because in the end most kinds of living
Are better than most kinds of dying
When the dying we're talking about is ours

END OF PLAY

MENTORING SESSION #4

Peterson Toscano

Peterson Toscano is a US-born performance artist, Bible scholar, and queer rights activist. He currently lives in Pretoria, South Africa, with his husband Glen Retief. Peterson produces multiple podcasts, including *Citizens Climate Radio* and *Bubble&Squeak*. His one-person online performances include *OK Zoomer!* and *A Queer Response to Climate Change: What Would Walt Whitman Do?* His film, *Transfigurations: Transgressing Gender in the Bible*, explores the stories of gender nonconforming Bible characters.

Playwright's Statement

With climate change I find myself doing a lot of time travel, seeking wisdom from the past as I imagine a better future ahead. The TV series *Firefly* and the anime *Cowboy Bebop* inspire me to see a future that is both different and very familiar. The reality is, wherever humans go in time and in space, we bring our weaknesses, we develop new prejudices, and we can be surprisingly resilient and empathetic. My research for this play came from multiple sources, including the Slate podcast, *Lexicon Valley*, "The Other F Word."*

Characters

ELDER, thirty years older than Younger. Elder is scripted as male.
YOUNGER, can be someone of any gender.

---

* Mike Vuolo, "The Other F-Word," *Lexicon Valley* (podcast), "Episode No. 2: A Bundle of Faggots," Slate, http://www.slate.com/articles/podcasts/lexicon_valley/2012/02/lexicon_valley_the_history_future_and_reclamation_of_the_word_faggot_.html.

Setting

The conversation is set around the year 2110. It can be either an in-person or virtual conversation.

• • •

ELDER: You sure you want to invite him?

YOUNGER: He's my age and . . . (*Trails off.*)

ELDER: (*Playfully.*) and you like him . . .

YOUNGER: (*Laughs.*) I don't even know if he's queer.

ELDER: I heard he is a faggot.

YOUNGER: A what?

ELDER: An incandescent guy.

YOUNGER: Incandescent??

ELDER: Lightbulb. It's old technology. Didn't they teach you that in ICS classes?

YOUNGER: ICS?! When were you born?

ELDER: 2062.

YOUNGER: Ah, I was born in 2090. It's not Integrated Climate Studies anymore. It's Climate Arts.

ELDER: Back in the seventies, we mostly learned climate history phases: Inaction, Action, and the Great Transition. That, and a lot of pre-Transition technology.

YOUNGER: We mostly did justice studies and cli-lit. They never taught us about that lightbulb.

ELDER: Incandescent. Ancestors used those during pre-pre-Transition times. Gassy as hell!

Needed watts of energy and got so hot you couldn't touch them. Faggots like him use those bulbs, if they can find them. He's a fag, part of the Faggot Movement.

YOUNGER: I seriously never heard of that before. Why are they called faggots?

ELDER: Didn't you take Queer Classes?

YOUNGER: Haha, they call it Ligbitygens (*Pronounced lig-bitty-jens.*) now.

ELDER: That makes sense. Faggot has a long history. In Britain in the thirteen hundreds, a faggot was a pile of sticks tied up, sometimes used to burn witches. Then it evolved into a curse slur against older women. In the nineteen hundreds, it had two meanings. In England they sometimes called a cigarette a fag.

YOUNGER: Maybe because of the original meaning? Faggot is a pile of sticks but a single stick is a fag? Why would they teach us that in Ligbitygens class?

ELDER: You grew up in such a good time. When did you come out to yourself?

YOUNGER: Nine when I came out Trans-No-Bind. We had my Coming Out Reception four years ago; I was 16. It was the last big all-together before the 2107 pandemic. Shits brutal! (*Pause.*) Well, you know . . . (*Pause.*) It's good the Center connected us. I get lots from the mentoring.

ELDER: Half the time I feel like you're mentoring me.

YOUNGER: Got to keep you up to date! (*Confused.*) So, he's a faggot because he smokes leaf weed?

ELDER: No, the word kept changing. Fag stopped referring to smoking at some point. Phobes used faggot as a curse slur against Samegending Queers like me. They said it to Trans-No-Binds like you too. When a phobe beat up someone like us, they shouted "Faggot!"

YOUNGER: Shits brutal! Ancestors were so misdirected! Slavery, petroleum, slaughterhouses.

ELDER: What do you think future gens will say about us?

YOUNGER: (*Pause, thinking.*) We don't pollute like 100 years ago, but we travel too much. I prefer walking around town, checking out new spaces and ruins. If I was always far flung, I never would have met him in the Arts Center last week.

ELDER: Your generation is much more settled. Shits my gen is always on edge, like we never survived the Great Suffering. Everyone was displaced more than once. If it wasn't a flood, it was fire, or heat. Things have finally started to quiet down.

YOUNGER: How did you even go to school?

ELDER: School went with me into every shelter, tent city, and mountain town. Whenever people got to a safe place, they had to do something with us kids, so classrooms popped up.

YOUNGER: And that is why you know so much about faggots.

ELDER: Right. Faggot changed again around 2040. By then of course Samegending Queers and Trans-No-Binds had full constitutional rights most everywhere. Being queer became celebrated like a birth or a marriage. Phobes found other targets. Faggot was no longer a curse slur. It became a meaningless insult like "zoomer" or "gassy."

YOUNGER: I never understood "zoomer."

ELDER: (*Laughs.*) First faggots. Twenty years ago a fringe movement started, mostly up North. It came out of the homesteading craze. Eco Communes fell apart by the 2080s. Some people returned to cities and never fit in; they pushed back. Now you have a few who stalker after old technology. If they could, they'd burn fossil fuels. They use Pre-Transition tech and they cook with wood. A philosopher gave them the name faggot, and it stuck.

YOUNGER: Maybe because the pile of sticks thing.

ELDER: Yes! Full circle. You always have people like this, immune to group norms. I find some can be fresh independent thinkers.

YOUNGER: So you think we should invite him?

ELDER: To Queerdo? (*Rhymes with weirdo.*) Sure, he might enjoy himself.

YOUNGER: Even if he's not queer?

ELDER: Yeh, and even if he is a faggot.

END OF PLAY

CONSULTATION

Dylan Van Den Berg

Dylan Van Den Berg is an Aboriginal Australian playwright descendent from the Palawa people of lutruwita/Tasmania. His work deals with Black/colonizer relationships through a culturally hybrid practice. For his work, Dylan has received the Griffin Award for New Australian Writing and the Victorian Premier's Award for Drama. He studied theatre at the Australian National University and the State University of New York.

Playwright's Statement

When it comes to decisions about the climate crisis, First Nations voices are often ignored or forgotten entirely, even when those decisions directly impact on them and the lands their ancestors have lived on and maintained for thousands of years. The world has so much to gain from listening to these perspectives. Any attempt at a Global Green New Deal must make space for meaningful discussion and deep listening with Indigenous peoples from all over.

Characters

A, white person. Definitely in a suit.
B, First Nations person. Definitely not in a suit.

Setting

A meeting room. Imagine there's a fire raging out of one window, and the other is straining under the weight of a steadily rising body of water.

Note

The terms "Blackfella" and "Mob" are often used by Australia's Aboriginal and Torres Strait Islander peoples to refer to themselves. The term "Country" is in reference to a Blackfella's ancestral land. B can be played by anyone of a First Nations background, and these terms can be adjusted as required.

• • •

A and B sit at a table.
There's an uneasy silence.

A: Is there anything you'd like to say?

B: That I'd . . . *like* to say?

A: Yes. Anything you . . . *want* to say.

B: I can say it myself, straight to the—
People?
Wearin' suits—
Whoever they are.

A: Yes, of course.
You can—
You can say it yourself—
In time.
But now—
It's not—

B: The time.

A: That's right.

B: And so this is . . . ?

A: A consultation.

A *process* of consultation.
With the—

B: The . . . ?

A: Original peoples.

B: Blackfellas?

A: Ummm.
Yes.
That's it.
With you.
And this is our Consultation Room.
Our nicest room.
This is a necessary and . . . important step.

B: In your . . . *process.*

A: Yes. And I'll take my findings . . . your *words* and *ideas* and—I'll take it all back. And then we'll have . . . a deal.

B: Right.

> *(Pause.)*

Where are you from?

A: That doesn't matter.

> *(Pause.)*

So, what do you want to pass on?
How would you like to see—
What would you like to *do*—
To fix it all.

> *(A gestures to the window.)*

Preferably in a few dot points.

> *(Pause.)*

B: I'd say.
I'd say that—

A: Wait—
I don't have a pen.

> *(A rummages for a pen.)*

Alright. I'm ready.

> *(Pause.)*

You were saying . . . what you would say.

B: Yeah.

Umm.

So, I'd say this is all . . .

It's all—

You're late.

Quite late.

'Cause Mob like us have been here forever tryin' to . . . talk.

Tryin' to add our two bob's worth—

Stories.

Knowledge.

We've got stories stamped on our skin, stretching up our arms and down our backs.

Everything you need to know is there, like a map of this place just waitin' to be read.

The answer's sittin' up in our brains, just waitin' to come out.

But the truth's like a whisper, ain't it? Will take more than me to cure the world's deafness, that's what I know.

(*Pause.*)

But.

I'd . . .

I'd say these things.

Your plan—

It's—

A: The biggest.

It's global.

It's *major.*

It's . . . big.

B: In all that bigness—

Don't forget the *places.*

The smallness.

Every place has its own story. The ancestors said that rivers have their own songs, you just gotta dig your feet into the dirt and listen to each of 'em.

And I'd say . . .

It's bigger than that sun gettin' hotter and the saltwater gettin' higher higher higher.

Because—

Because of *you*—

We keep dyin'.
The rivers run with Blackfella blood and the trees are home to our spirits.
We watch what you do and we're here—
But we get nothin' back.
We keep tryin'—clingin' on to somethin' we can't see—a hope or a spool of a
dream which might lead us way back to how things used to be.
And we want to share what we know.
About how to stop the bush from burnin' up.
About how to talk to Country and hear it murmur right back.
But you shoot us down and lock us up and give us *looks* when you see us
and you don't know—won't ever know—what *we* know.
And there ain't nothin' more confinin' that the prison you don't know you're
in.
And . . .
And that's it.

(*Pause.*)

A: That's a lot.
But—
Thank you.
For your—
Contribution.

(*Pause.*)

I was hoping you would sign this.

(*Blackout.*)

END OF PLAY

BEDTIME STORY FOR MY (FUTURE) DAUGHTER

Caity-Shea Violette

Caity-Shea Violette is a US-based playwright whose work explores breaking cycles and learning how to belong to yourself. She's a winner of the Jean Kennedy Smith Playwriting Award, the Clauder Competition, Samuel French OOB Festival, Gary Garrison National Ten-Minute Play Award, and Susan Glaspell Playwriting Festival National Award. Her work has been developed or presented at Portland Stage Company, Roundabout Theatre Company, the Kennedy Center, and Boston Playwrights Theatre. She holds an MFA in Playwriting from Boston University.

Playwright's Statement

This play was inspired by the idea of building a better world for the next generation. As a storyteller, I'm always fascinated by how we will explain the world we are fighting to change to the children who are just entering it. As a person who doesn't (and may never) have children, I wanted to write from a place of deep care and advocacy for future generations that extends beyond the borders of immediate family.

Characters

STORYTELLER, any ethnicity, any gender identity, age 25–35.
CHORUS, two to five performers of any ethnicity, gender identity, and age.
    They silently perform the story.

Note

Ideally, this piece is performed with a CHORUS of two to five performers but can also be a solo show by assigning all of the lines to STORYTELLER.

CHORUS members should wear neutral matching clothing to direct our attention to the story they're performing until they speak at the end. Though they should use one consistent storytelling technique, they can use shadow puppetry, simple props, or interpretive dance to physically tell the story. Any objects used should look homemade and their performance should be engaging for young audiences.

• • •

STORYTELLER enters carrying a large but simple storybook. They speak to the audience as if they were STORYTELLER's daughter, as if they were reading her a bedtime story.

STORYTELLER: Long before you were born, the earth was a place of clay and dust, water and stone, sky and stars.

> *(The CHORUS enters and acts out the story like a pop-up traveling children's theatre. It is our window into the pages of the book.)*

STORYTELLER: Life sprung from the soil and soon the whole planet was dotted with people, plants, and animals.
Though they were made of the same water and warmth, each was uniquely shaped by the soil they grew in.

The people discovered the strength of their hands and the speed of their feet.
They heard their voices and created language to connect, to celebrate, to remember.
When they grew hungry and cold, they made tools to build homes and learned how to grow their own food.

One discovery led to the next: new resources, new inventions, new values.
They built buildings so tall they could scrape the sky,
Machines stronger and faster than any living thing,
Cities that outshined the stars.

Hunger turned to ambition and the more they ate, the hungrier they became.
Food was not enough, they wanted the earth itself.
They dug and drilled and mined.
The ground became brittle, the air thickened, the water turned to rust.

Their eyes remained fixed forward, always looking ahead, until they finally forgot how to look up at the sky.
Without anyone to see them, the stars grew weak.
One by one, they fell from the sky and scattered across the earth.
They lay in the dirt and rubble, floating on the ocean—waiting to be found.

As the people dug and drilled and mined
the pieces of the broken sky glimmered in the dust,
catching the eye of one person, then another, and another,
until thousands of these fractured glowing crystals were being discovered every day across the globe.

People slipped them in pockets
and tied them on strings that they wore around their necks
and one by one they remembered the sound of their voice.

Finally able to see the world around them,
They got busy doing the work that needed to be done.

They protested and legislated and organized movements.
To protect the planet.
To fight for our home.
One day the stars disappeared from their pockets and chains.
They searched for them high and low, but found nothing.
Then they remembered how to look up and saw the night sky once again freckled with light.

> (*STORYTELLER closes the book and turns to the audience. The CHORUS follows, all speaking the same love letter.*)

STORYTELLER: My sweet girl.

CHORUS 1: You were born into crisp air and clear water.

CHORUS 2: In a hospital I wasn't afraid would bankrupt us.

CHORUS 3: We spent the first few months of your life welcoming you into the world—

CHORUS 4: —without fear of losing our jobs.

STORYTELLER: I am so lucky to bear witness to your life.

CHORUS 1: You will grow in rich soil. Fed with nutrients from a planet healing.

CHORUS 2: You will understand the history of the land you live on and fight to restore justice for the people it was taken from.

CHORUS 3: You will fall asleep in a world where the current threats to our existence—

CHORUS 4: —feel as distant to you as a bedtime story.

STORYTELLER: I don't know when I will meet you, or if you will even be my daughter when I do.

CHORUS 1: Maybe I will only know you for a second.

CHORUS 2: Passing by as you play in a tree-lined park.

CHORUS 3: Or waiting for the bullet train from New York to DC.

CHORUS 4: Maybe you will never know who I am.

STORYTELLER: I am just one of many people who must come together to fight for your future.

CHORUS 1: A future you will make brighter and better than I ever could.

CHORUS 2: A future you will use to fight for someone else's.

STORYTELLER: Whoever you may be and wherever you end up, this is my wish:

CHORUS 3: May you never forget to look up.

CHORUS 4: And may you always see stars when you do.

(Lights fade onstage as stars are illuminated above us.)

END OF PLAY

THE LAST BEE IS FLYING OVER THE SKY

Pat To Yan

Originally from Hong Kong, **Pat To Yan** is a playwright, director, and educator active in Hong Kong and German theatre. He is the artistic director of Reframe Theatre, house author of Germany's Nationaltheater Mannheim (2021–2022), and an elected representative and the chairman of the Committee of Literary Art of Hong Kong Arts Development Council. His play *A Concise History of Future China* was selected by Theatertreffen Stuckemart 2016. *Happily Ever After Nuclear Explosion* was commissioned by Munich Residenztheater. He directed a Cantonese version at Tai Kwun Theatre Season (HK), and the play was selected for CINARS Biennale Official Programme (Canada) in 2021. Some of his plays are represented by Suhrkamp Theater Verlag.

Playwright's Statement

It is reported that there is a massive decline of bees. We all know that it is causing an ecological disaster. If they disappear, we may disappear. We are vulnerable. They are vulnerable.

• • •

The last bee is flying over the sky. Two people on the earth identify it. They take out a can of honey, put a drop of honey into the lemon water, and drink it all. They say, "It's really, really good."

The last bee is flying over the sky. The last bee doesn't know it is the last bee. The last bee only feels weird that it has not met any other bee for a long, long time. No, the last bee met other bees, just some time ago. On that day, a sunny day, the last bee was looking for its fellows. From a distance far, far away, it saw them. A lot of bees. Even the last bee had never seen such a large number of its fellows. When the last bee got closer and closer, it saw that the other bees didn't appear to move. They were all still. The last bee got closer, closer. The last bee saw a mountain of dead bees. They were piled up as high as the tallest tree in the forest. The last bee landed on top of the mountain of dead bees. It didn't know why its family and friends were all dead, and left there at the edge of the world. The last bee didn't feel sad. The last bee was in a panic. Its survival would become very difficult. It didn't know how to carry on with its life without other bees. Before, they worked together to stay alive.

The last bee is capable of flying. So it keeps flying. Maybe it will come across another bee. The last bee doesn't know it is the last bee. But then it discovers that being unable to meet another bee is not the biggest problem. The last bee realizes that it has not seen any flower for a long, long time. The green forest turns to yellow. The last bee finds itself already hungry. Very hungry. There is a sense of emptiness inside its body. Inside its body, it feels like an abyss. In the abyss, the last bee can't find any pollen or nectar. It suddenly feels drained of energy. It wants to stop.

A world without flowers.

But the last bee doesn't stop. Driven by instinct, the last bee keeps flying. It tries to find something else to eat. It suddenly remembers that many, many, many years ago, it was not a vegetarian. It ate insects. All kinds of insects. One day, the bees found an insect that tasted sweet. "It's really, really good," they said. They discovered that this insect lived inside flowers, covered in pollen. They wanted to understand the life of that insect. They tried pollen. "It's even better!" they said. They were unable to be predators anymore.

Now, even the sweet, sweet insects cannot be found.

The last bee sighs. The last bee sees a lot of people walking fast and slow. They're walking in and out of caves. There are so many different kinds of caves. Tall, short, rectangular, square, circular, thin, fat. Then the last bee can't see people outside the caves anymore. "Do they all stay inside the caves?" the last bee wonders. "Will there be any flowers in the caves?" the last bee asks itself. Then fireballs are thrown into different caves, into all the caves. People on fire run out of the caves. The last bee is flying over the sky and sees that all the caves are on fire.

It is too hot. The last bee has no choice and flies higher and higher. It flies above the clouds, above different layers of clouds. The last bee finds that smoke doesn't rise above the clouds.

The last bee is flying over the clouds.

The last bee still misses flowers. It decides to go back to search for them. It doesn't see any smoke, any caves, any mountains of dead bees and human bodies. The forest turns green again.

The last bee sees a flower. A beautiful bee is resting on the flower. For the first time, the last bee is feeling shy. The last bee keeps its distance from the beautiful bee for a while, wondering how to fly toward the beautiful bee—beautifully.

END OF PLAY

SO THIS IS THE LAST APPLE PIE

Haeweon Yi

Haeweon Yi is a theatre-maker from Korea. She aims to deliver various echoes heard on the Earth through theatre. In 2015, she co-founded the participatory theatre company Blooming Ludus. The company focuses on connecting people, art, and the environment to fight for climate justice and a sustainable future. Her major works include *Power Story* (2016–2017), the *Salt & Vinegar* series (2016–2020), *How Much Space Do We Need for Living?* (2020), and *How To Become A Rock* (2020).

Playwright's Statement

What are fruits and vegetables telling us about the climate crisis? In many northern hemisphere countries, including Korea and India, apple farming areas have been moving north over the last few decades due to climate change. While only a few consumers care about where their apples come from, our communities' lives have been rapidly changing and there is a high possibility of losing most of the land for growing apples within 50 years.

Characters

SIA

HANA

Note

The play is set in a near future. It shows three different generations dealing with the climate crisis. Nana doesn't appear on stage. The story is originally set in Korea, but specific details in the text can be adjusted to reflect the farming region where the play is presented.

• • •

The sound of rain stops when the light comes on. There are some chairs and a dining table on stage.
SIA is sitting at the table, not taking her eyes off her phone.
HANA enters. She brings out a freshly baked apple pie from the kitchen.

HANA: (*Putting the plate on the table.*) So this is the last apple pie.

(*SIA still does not take her eyes off her phone.*)

SIA: Did she make up her mind?

HANA: Yes. That's why this is the last one. (*SIA does not answer.*) No phones at the table, remember?

SIA: Mum . . . I'm not a teenager anymore.

HANA: That's the house rule. If you don't want to follow it, get your own house.

SIA: Ouch. You can't say that.

HANA: (*In a strict voice.*) No. Phone.

SIA: Okay.

(*She puts her phone down, but soon grabs it again to look at the screen.*)

HANA: (*Loudly.*) SIA!

SIA: Okay, sorry! You know, the stock market is frantic right now because of the government's New Deal announcement today.

HANA: Wow. So you're in the stock market now?

SIA: It's the only way to get my own house with my own rules. I'm way too late compared to my friends. I might get some . . . (*Looking at her phone screen.*) Tesla stocks? Or, what was your customer's company running that smart farm thing? Their stocks will definitely benefit from the Green New Deal.

HANA: You will never get your own house rules if you jump into the market now. Well, please put your phone down and have some pie before it gets cold.

SIA: Okay. (*Finally putting the phone down.*) Do we have some ice cream left?

HANA: Nope.

SIA: Oh, okay. (*Having a bite.*) When are you leaving?

HANA: Tomorrow evening after work. I have a few projects to finish.

SIA: Can I go?

HANA: You have a job.

SIA: A temporary job. I'm honestly thinking of quitting. I can't see us beating that big old corporation. I sit in the bush all day, looking for birds that will never come back. Just to prove that the forest is "worth" protecting. Do they even care about our forest in that "New Deal"?

HANA: Which bird?

SIA: Huh?

HANA: Which bird are you waiting for?

SIA: Skylark.

HANA: That one used to fly over Nana's orchard a lot when I was young.

SIA: Really?

HANA: But I don't see them anymore.

SIA: Why?

HANA: Pesticides. Probably, pesticides.

SIA: But Nana doesn't use them, does she?

HANA: No, but many of her neighbors do. They don't seem to have a choice now.

SIA: I'm sorry that Nana is closing down her farm. Wish I could go with you to support her.

HANA: I know. She will understand.

SIA: She's had that farm forever. Is she okay?

HANA: I think so. She actually made up her mind a while ago. She was quite determined to keep running her farm her own way, but you know . . . Since she refused to use antibiotics to keep her apples "organic," she's had a hard time fighting the fireblight. The fireblight only started happening when the spring season became too hot. And then . . . the flood came. I think that flood two years ago was the last straw.

SIA: Yeah, that was . . . unexpected . . . (*Looking over to the window.*) This year doesn't seem to be any better. Can't believe it's autumn weather.

HANA: No. The loss from this year's harvest was huge, but the new National Farmer's Insurance covered her pretty well. I hope they don't change that in today's announcement. She never imagined that she would actually qualify for benefits when she signed up for the Climate Scheme. Well, who would have?

SIA: Just a few degrees . . . I really should have joined the other kids in the climate strike when I was younger . . .

HANA: No, I don't blame you, hun. I . . . shouldn't have stopped you. (*Taking a breath.*) I'm sorry.

SIA: (*Placidly.*) Don't say sorry to me. (*A long pause. Looking at the pie.*) Mum, are we too late?

HANA: Well, for apples, yes.

SIA: I wish I had learned how to make a pie before.

HANA: You will learn. (*A slight pause.*) And I believe . . . (*HANA stops.*) Let's hope that we are not too late.

    (*SIA and HANA eat the pie in silence.*)

HANA: (*Still looking at her almost empty plate.*) When she saw the leaves turning black, Nana already knew this year's apples would be her last crop. She didn't want to let you down. The apples in the pie were almost white.

SIA: (*Slightly shocked.*) The beautiful red color had always been her pride. (*Pause.*) Is there anything I can do for her?

HANA: (*Putting one more piece of pie on SIA's plate.*) Just do your best with what you are doing now.

    (*SIA sits still gazing at her phone and the pie.*
    Suddenly there's an alert sound from a phone.)

HANA: (*Teasingly.*) Is it another stock market alert?

SIA: That's your phone, mum.

HANA: Oh, sorry . . . (*Taking out her phone.*)

> (*While HANA looks at her phone, SIA slowly walks towards the window. Her movements become subtle.*)

HANA: (*Looking at her phone with a bit of excitement.*) That was your Nana. She says she's decided to sell her farm to the government. They are going to build a solar farm!

SIA: (*To HANA, slowly raising her finger to the lips.*) It came back.

> (*SIA quietly points through the window. HANA gazes at the place where SIA's finger is pointing with surprise.*
> *The lights slowly fade to black. The sound of a bird chirping.*)

END OF PLAY

SO BEAUTIFUL TODAY, SO SUNNY

Marcus Youssef with Seth Klein

Marcus Youssef's fifteen or so plays have been produced in multiple languages in more than twenty countries across North America, Asia, and Europe. Seth and Marcus are both based in Vancouver/Unceded Coast Salish Territory, and live four blocks from each other, near Commercial Drive.

Seth Klein is a public policy researcher. He was founding director of the British Columbia office of the Canadian Centre for Policy Alternatives (CCPA) and is now team lead of the Climate Emergency Unit (a project of the David Suzuki Institute).

Playwright's Statement

The inspiration for this verbatim piece is inside of the piece itself: policy analyst and climate activist Seth Klein is my neighbor. Over the last few years we've become friends, as each of us approached 50 and navigated transitions in our work lives. Part of Seth's change was leaving his full-time job to write *A Good War: Mobilizing Canada for the Climate Emergency*, a book that uses Canada's historic national mobilization for WWII as a model for responding to the climate crisis. We also collaborate through the Vancouver municipal political party OneCity, which is most visibly represented by Vancouver City Councillor Christine Boyle, a climate activist and Seth's partner.

Note

The characters are friends, consciously choosing to have this conversation, knowing that it will be made public. The actors can feel free to include the audience if, as, or when it feels right, maybe particularly when the characters seem to acknowledge that they are speaking publicly. The dance between public and private speech feels to me like a useful way to investigate this.

• • •

SETH and MARCUS speak to the audience. They are not walking.

MARCUS: I'm Marcus Youssef. I'm a 51-year-old cisgender man, mixed race Egyptian Canadian.

SETH: I'm Seth Klein. I'm 52, also a cisgender guy. And my family's Jewish. We're friends.*

MARCUS: And we are walking.

SETH: Outside, in Vancouver, British Columbia, Canada.

MARCUS: Unceded Coast Salish Territory.

SETH: On a cold day in late January, 2021, during the second wave of the COVID pandemic.

> *(They speak to each other.)*

MARCUS: Thanks so much for doing this.

SETH: You're welcome. Hey, just before we start—I just want to say—I'm sorry about your dad.

MARCUS: Oh, yeah. I appreciate that.

SETH: You were close.

MARCUS: Yeah. I guess. Yes.

SETH: You've talked to me about him.

MARCUS: It's hard. I mean, he was a very powerful figure in my life. As dads are, I guess.

SETH: Yeah.

MARCUS: Yeah. (*Changing the subject.*) I thought we could just wander towards Trout Lake because that's where I like to walk.

SETH: I'm happy with that.

MARCUS: It's so beautiful today, so sunny. So I'm just gonna dive in. Can you introduce yourself in whatever way you feel like you want to?

---

*   These first two lines are optional.

(SETH's introduction is likely to the audience.)

SETH: Ok. My name is Seth Klein. I most recently am the author of *A Good War: Mobilizing Canada for the Climate Emergency*. For 22 years before that, I was the founding director of the British Columbia chapter of Canadian Centre for Policy Alternatives.

MARCUS: And over the last few years, you've gotten laser-focused on climate change as an issue.

SETH: I am very focused on the gap between what the science says we have to do and what our politics is prepared to entertain. Figuring out how to tackle that gap.

MARCUS: Is that the Green New Deal?

SETH: I think the Green New Deal is a central and powerful model for bridging the gap.

MARCUS: What is the Green New Deal? Give us the one paragraph summary.

SETH: Ok. So, like the original New Deal, the Green New Deal takes a profound crisis and meets it with massive public investment. It's an ambitious plan to spend billions in new green infrastructure to electrify everything and create millions of jobs. Not sure that was quite a paragraph.

MARCUS: That was a very good paragraph.

SETH: Thanks. Can I add: The Green New Deal is about linking climate mobilization to tackling inequality. What I learned in my research about the effort to mobilize Canada for World War II is that it was actually hard to do with the typical propaganda. You know, go across the sea and go get Hitler. That works only to a point. To truly mobilize people, the government had to promise that the society people came back to was going to be different. Which happened. Canada saw its first major income support programs introduced in the war—unemployment insurance in 1940, the family allowance in 1944. The architecture for the entire postwar welfare state was written during the war. It was a pledge that the society people came back to was going to look different from the one they left. That's how you mobilize everybody. It's the same with the Green New Deal today.

MARCUS: What's the best argument against it?

SETH: What's the best argument against the Green New Deal?

MARCUS: If you had to choose one.

SETH: That it's not realistic, or feasible.

MARCUS: What about that argument keeps you up at night a little?

SETH: None of it.

MARCUS: Really?

SETH: Really. I talk about it in my book. We're all trapped by the legacy of 40 years of neoliberalism that has told us what is and isn't allowed or possible. The powerful thing about an emergency, whether it's the war or COVID, is that things that seemed politically or economically off-limits suddenly become possible. If you said to Canadians in 1938, "Does the government have what it takes to completely transform the economy as actually happened during the war?" I'm pretty sure most would have said no. It's going to happen with climate, too. The only question is whether or not it will happen in time. That's what keeps me up at night.

(MARCUS maybe acknowledges the audience.)

MARCUS: I'm also conscious that some people who may watch what we're constructing here are not from wealthy industrialized countries. How does that impact what you're talking about?

SETH: That's a hard one. It's a fair question. The other piece of the legacy of neoliberalism is that it has undone our sense of our ability to do grand things together. Maybe it's wishful thinking but history is full of surprises of how quickly we pivot if and when we recognize emergencies for what they are. And each society has to excavate its history for those relevant examples.

MARCUS: When I pitched this to you, I said, "This year, the theme is Envisioning a Green New Deal" and you were like, "So this time you're not going to write something so nihilistic."

SETH: Less dystopian.

MARCUS: Right. You said, "Less dystopian."

SETH: Your last piece was very dystopian.

MARCUS: It was.

SETH: There's a lot of artistic work that tackles climate, but it's almost universally dystopian.

MARCUS: What's your read on that?

SETH: It's understandable. When we think about climate, we imagine this terrifying hellscape that is likely to emerge if we fail to rise to this moment. But I'm also struck that a lot of the artistic mobilization for the Second World War was not like that, even though they were surrounded by death and destruction. It was positive. It was rallying the public.

MARCUS: I wonder if that's artists not wanting to be propagandists.

SETH: Yeah. You can't tell artists what to do. I understand that. I think the Green New Deal needs to have a big arts component, just like the original New Deal. And in World War II, artists walked this careful line. They were forthright about the gravity of the crisis and yet they still imparted hope. I grabbed hold of the Canadian World War II story because I was trying to excavate a historic reminder of what we are capable of. And everyone's got different stories to draw on, that invite us to say, in moments of existential threat or crisis, who do we want to be?

MARCUS: Totally. Everybody goes through crisis, in some way. It's part of the human experience.

SETH: Yeah.

   (*Beat.*)

SETH: Hey, I just want to say again, I am really sorry about your dad.

MARCUS: Thanks. I appreciate that.

END OF PLAY

THE ETERNITY OF DIAPERS

Carla Zúñiga Morales

Carla Zúñiga Morales is a Chilean actress, playwright, and teacher. She was invited by the British Council to participate in the Royal Court workshop held in Chile. She also was part of the Next Stage 2019 in the Dublin Theatre Festival. She has premiered more than fifteen plays, and has won several awards. She was co-founder of the company La Niña Horrible. Four of its productions have been selected for the Santiago a Mil Festival.

Playwright's Statement

A dirty diaper takes 500 years to decompose. We are going to get back all the damage we have done to the planet. There needs to be a radical change to create a new way of life.

Characters

A, the girl's mother. Approximately 50 years old.
B, the girl. 29 years old. Vegan, artist, rebel, tomboy.
C, the girl's father. Approximately 55 years old.
D, the girl's dirty diaper. Twenty-nine years old. It doesn't have a clear gender.

I imagine the character of the diaper played by an actress or an actor, who can be seen as gender neutral. I think that character is very ridiculous, so it must be interpreted with great seriousness and sensitivity, so that there is a contradiction.

• • •

A: We thought you were bringing your new boyfriend over to the house today, child.

B: Yes, I brought him.

C: What?

B: I brought him.

A: Will he come later?

B: No, here he is.

C: Where?

B: Here.

A: There's no one here but the three of us.

B: That's not entirely true.

C: Are you okay, child?

B: Yes.

A: You have a funny face.

B: I'm fine. I just want you guys to say hello to my new boyfriend. Or girlfriend. I don't know their gender.

C: What are you talking about?

B: My new partner has been sitting here on the couch all this time and you haven't even spoken to her.

A: What is that?

C: There's something on the couch. I hadn't seen it . . .

B: She is my new partner.

C: Is that . . .

A: Is it a . . . dirty . . . baby diaper?

B: Yes.

C: Is that dirty diaper your new boyfriend?

B: Yes.

A: Are you high?

B: No.

C: Is it a joke?

B: No.

A: I don't understand.

C: Me neither.

B: This dirty diaper is my new partner. We met a few days ago when I went swimming in the Mapocho river.

A: Why did you go swimming in the Mapocho river, child?

C: That river has nothing but poop in it.

A: And corpses. People constantly jump into that river to commit suicide. Why did you do that?

B: Because I wanted to bathe in the sea, but since I'm not going to be able to go to the beach this year because of COVID, and there's no sea in this horrendous shitty city, I thought that bathing in that river would be the closest thing. And I don't regret it. If I hadn't bathed in that river, I wouldn't have met my new partner.

C: What kind of joke is this? It's not funny.

D: It's not a joke.

(A and C scream.)

A: Fuck! Shit! That diaper spoke!

C: How did you do that??

B: I did nothing.

D: Good afternoon.

A: Why is he talking?

D: I have been living on this earth for almost thirty years. And from so much floating in different things—sewage, stagnant water, garbage, oil, industrial waste—I ended up genetically mutating until I got a higher consciousness.

C: Where is the microphone?

B: He's not wearing a microphone.

C: Do you need money, child? Is that why you are doing all this?

A: You have to eat meat again, child, the lack of iron is driving you crazy.

B: Stop talking for a moment! Hear what he has to say!

A: Why do you do this to us? You've always hated us! You've always wanted to attract attention!

B: I'm not attracting attention! This is true!

C: I'm calling the cops.

(*The diaper opens violently, leaving everyone paralyzed, full of poop.*)

D: I'm here tonight because I have something to tell you. That shit that you have now running down your faces is from your daughter. You guys threw me in the trash twenty-nine years ago. You could have used a cloth diaper, however, you used thousands, millions of diapers that, to this day, continue to float on the earth. This is my message to you: the world is changing and the shit you threw away is going to be returned to you. You're all asleep and there's going to be an explosion of poop that's going to wake you up.

A: What is that sound?

C: The pipes, they're breaking!

D: The poop will run through the streets and the grass will bloom. You humans are ashamed of your shit, but it's the best you have. And with it we're going to build a new world. A world where the powerful stop destroying the world in exchange for happiness, a world where machismo, racism, and exploitation end. A world where neither Mother Earth nor a human mother suffer the injustices of patriarchy. Look out the window, a horde of dirty diapers is going to come looking for you. You're going to meet again with your baby's diapers. You're going to meet again with what you once were. Open your mouth. Do not fear. That poop is healthier than so many other things you eat. The time of resignation is over. Outside there are people willing to change everything. A new world is possible and will be built by Indigenous communities, by children, by sexual dissidents. Buildings and corrupt governments will fall.

(*A river of poop enters through the window, and next to it, rays of sunlight that illuminate the entire house.*)

END OF PLAY